PUBLISHED BY HOZAC BO
hozacrecords.com/books

Copyright © Paul Collins 2020

Design & Layout by Todd Novak
Technical Direction by Brett Cross
Additional Editing by John Santucci

Cover photo courtesy of Paul Collins Archive

All rights reserved. No part of this publication may be reproduced, stored in a retrieval system, or transmitted in any form or any means electronic, mechanical, photocopying, recording or otherwise without the prior permission of the publisher.

ISBN: 978-0-9963319-9-9

HZB-009
Third edition 2023
Printed in South Central, IL. USA

HoZac Books

I DON'T FIT IN:

My Wild Ride Through the Punk and Power Pop Trenches with The NERVES and The BEAT

PAUL COLLINS
with CHUCK NOLAN

HZB-009

HoZac Books

Dedicated to my fans.

all photographs & ephemera contained within this book are from the Paul Collins Archives, unless otherwise noted.

"I am a big fan of this book.

Man... we have heard the 'rags to riches, come from nothing, and now I'm the icon' fucking story so many times — it's a sleeping pill. That's what makes this book important, because it represents whatever most people's experience of trying to be a rock star turns out to be. It's just ad nauseam; it's such a trope, the 'come-from-nothing dude' and then he becomes the king of the world; star of the world, and then he turns into a prick, or whatever which way we want to spin that.

But what you don't hear is what most people's experience of it is. They had a dream and it didn't turn out the way they fucking thought it was going to. That's unique, and we don't hear that story enough. That's what most people's experience of the I want to be a rock star bullshit dream is.

And your (Paul Collins' book) represents that in the same way as *Moby Dick*. It's about obsession."

- Jack Lee, phone call to Chuck Nolan (November 2022)

CONTENTS

Foreword by RIC MENCK   8

Prologue   11

PART 1: Early Years
Chapter 1: Long Island To Saigon   15
Chapter 2: Athens To Greenwich Village   23
Chapter 3: Manhasset To Leonia   31
Chapter 4: Hells Kitchen To California   39

PART 2: The NERVES
Chapter 5: Hanging On The Telephone   45
Chapter 6: San Francisco   65
Chapter 7: Los Angeles   79
Chapter 8: One Way Ticket   99
Chapter 9: Breaking Away   129

PART 3: The BEAT
Chapter 10: The Dawn Of The BEAT   139
Chapter 11: Goin' All Across The USA   157
Chapter 12: Europe   175
Chapter 13: Will You Listen?   185

PART 4: Paul Collins Solo
Chapter 14: To BEAT Or Not To BEAT   201
Chapter 15: Madrid Me Mata   213
Chapter 16: Work-A-Day World   229
Chapter 17: The Nerves Movie   239
Chapter 18: King Of Power Pop   249
Chapter 19: You Can't Go Back   259

PAUL COLLINS Discography 1976 - 2020   270

Acknowledgments   273

FOREWORD

In the earliest days of the punk and new wave era, you could count the number of independently-released records on both hands. In no time at all there would be a glut of independent vinyl, but in the beginning, it seemed only to occur to a few forward-thinking upstarts that pressing your own record was the way to go. Back then, the accepted route to fame and fortune was a record deal with a major label, which in turn, would catapult you into the public eye. But for some groups this obviously wasn't going to happen. So they had to do it themselves. One of the first bands I became aware of to release their own vinyl was a rock 'n' roll trio called The Nerves. The reason I knew about their record was because I saw it advertised in the back of *Rolling Stone* magazine.

This, in itself, was very auspicious. I mean, who would think to take out an ad in *Rolling Stone*? I was smart enough to send away for a copy, and it quickly became the most-played record in my collection. The fact that it was sent to me directly by the band made it even more special. I don't think very many people must have sent away for it, because the Nerves hardly became a household name. The only people who seemed to know about them were a handful of fanzine writers. Shortly after receiving the record, I noticed The Nerves would be making an appearance at club a few miles from my house in the suburbs of Chicago. At first I couldn't believe this was really happening. How could a band based in Los Angeles have a gig in Illinois? Here again, the Nerves were way ahead of the curve.

They actually had the bright idea to book their own tour, independent of any help from a record label or booking agency. When the band hit town, they made a preemptive strike at WXFM, a tiny radio station that was the first to play punk records in Chicago. It was announced you could call in and talk to them on air, which I proceeded to do. I may as well have been talking to the Beatles, that's how excited I was to be on the phone with Jack Lee, Peter Case, and Paul Collins.

Later, they played at a club called B'ginning's in Schaumburg, and despite the fact that I was too young to get in, I stood in the back behind the stage door. A bouncer was kind enough to crack it open so I could listen to them play. I can't tell you how exciting it was to hear, for the first time, a set of songs that seemed to instantly imprint themselves into my memory. This is really a testament to how great the Nerves songs are. Hear them once and they stick in your mind forever.

At the end of the night, as they were loading their minimal gear into an old, beat-up station wagon I tried to get up the nerve to approach the band. But I couldn't do it. They were just too cool, so I stood and gawked from afar. And that's kind of how it's been ever since.

From then until now, I still consider the Nerves to be one of the great rock 'n' roll bands of the late '70s, but I've never really known very much about them. I never actually saw them play, but I knew from listening that they were writing songs with the caliber of Buddy Holly, Bobby Fuller, or the Everly Brothers, and that those songs were constructed in such a way, as to sound absolutely eternal. No amount of time would diminish their luster.

As it turns out, the Nerves imploded not long after their cross-country trek, burned out physically, and demoralized emotionally. But that certainly wouldn't be the end of the band members' story. Paul Collins was the drummer in the Nerves, but as it turns out, he was also a guitarist, and when the band split, he immediately made plans to form another group. First, he and Nerves bassist Peter Case had a short-lived combo called the Breakaways. And then, with the encouragement of his friend Eddie Money, he formed his own group called The Beat.

Unlike the Nerves, who couldn't catch a break if their lives depended on it, big-buck management and a major label record deal fell into place overnight for The Beat. Of course, this didn't mean they had it made. Despite recording what many consider to be a flawless debut album, and touring relentlessly to promote it, The Beat fell prey to a series of misfortunes that precluded them from achieving the level of infamy they obviously deserved. It's an age-old story, but one that seems to repeat itself endlessly throughout time. Sometimes the greatest bands and the greatest records fall by the wayside. But of course, this doesn't diminish their importance. In some cases, it actually *enhances it*. That is certainly the case with The Nerves, and with The Beat.

In the pages of this no-holds-barred memoir, Paul Collins lays out for you the story of his life, in rock 'n' roll and beyond. There are moments of triumph, but just as many moments of abject failure. A lesser man would have given up when the going got tough, but Collins doesn't know how to quit. He is the definition of a survivor. He still might not be a household name, but to a legion of rock & roll fans, he is a shining example of what it means to dedicate your life to something you love, and make it work despite all odds.

- Ric Menck, 2020.

PROLOGUE

Should I dress up, or should I dress down?
Should I talk, or should I just frown?
I don't fit in...

(Paul Collins - 1977)

I was born in 1956, a great year for cars, rock 'n' roll, and the American dream. Now in the 21st century, cars suck, rock 'n' roll is practically non-existent, and the American dream is only being realized by a few. It's a sad state of affairs you might say, but in the words of David Byrne, *"same as it ever was."*

I've always wanted to be famous, ever since I was a boy standing in my neighbor's backyard – in Greece of all places. I watched my friend's sister, a gorgeous sixteen-year old blonde, as she screamed, holding her head with tears streaming down her face, looking up at the clear blue sky.

"What?" I said.

"It's them!" she said.

"Who?" I asked.

"It's *them!*"

Looking up, all I could see was a plane flying overhead.

"It's *The Beatles!*" she screamed.

That's when I knew I wanted to be a rock 'n' roll star.

This is what has driven me for over a quarter of a century. It has caused me to waste innumerable hours and years of my life, consuming god knows how many drugs, watching way too much TV, and trying to screw every girl I've come in contact with. Not a bad beginning, if you think about it. Everything is a process.

In the past, I tried to write a book, and then a movie about my first professional group The Nerves. It got very bogged down with threats of lawsuits from the real-life characters, so I decided to say "fuck it" and do it on my own. I made a side deal with myself that under no circumstances would I sue myself, no matter how bad it got. This gave me the freedom to present myself in all my glory, as the flaming asshole that I am; which is what they will call you every time you try to do something on your own, *against the grain*.

I know Freud came up with the word egotist, but I didn't know what he meant. I know people have turned it and twisted it until it just leaves a bad taste in your mouth. But, *how the fuck can you do anything if you're not an egotist?* I *am* an egotist, and it has gotten me into trouble on more than one occasion. It cost me two wives, and most recently it got me beaten up by some ex-bandmates, in a small town in the north of Spain. Yet, still I persist.

Ego is a good thing. The trick is not to let people know you have it, especially those weak, simpering, untalented leeches who want to make everyone they know pay for it.

Don't let me give you the impression that I'm down on people, even though I hate most of the people I meet. That's not true, not true at all. I've had the good fortune to meet a whole shitload of really cool people, and I was smart enough to learn from them. To what end I am still not sure. I'm just beginning to get an idea of what all these experiences may or may not lead to. Depending on the day, it could be a good thing, or it could be a complete waste of time.

My mentor was Jack Lee of The Nerves, our legendary underground group from San Francisco of the late seventies. It was my first real band, and the band that turned me into what I am today. Jack told me that everything I wanted was right in front of me, all around me, and all I had to do was see it.

He told me I'd have everything I wanted, and that I'd make it as long as I stayed true to the course. I gladly nodded in agreement, neglecting to say that I didn't know what the course was.

Yes it's true. I've been driven by blind ambition all these years. I envy the fuckers who drive the expensive cars, screw all the girls, and blow money out their asses, driven by that same blind ambition. But hey, I have had a rich life, too.

OK, let's slow down. My life is what I can tell you about, because after all, that's what I know better than anything. Regarding content, Jack always said, 'don't make a laundry list. No one wants a laundry list. Select the facts to tell your story, but don't be a slave to the facts.' I agree, and it gets confusing. As usual, I'm lost - but you can be lost and still know what you're doing.

Look at me, I'm writing a book.

Don't ever lose your ego.

PART 1:
Early Years

PAUL COLLINS IN CRIB, 1959.
courtesy of Paul Collins' Archives

CHAPTER ONE:
LONG ISLAND To SAIGON

I come from a broken home. In 1962, living in Douglaston, Long Island, was so bad, my mother ran away to Saigon with her four kids and my father's best friend. My parents had separated, not that I could understand this. I just knew that my father would only come home on the weekends. He drove a beautiful light blue Simca with a real wood dashboard.

My world in Long Island consisted of riding my little red scooter, chasing the Good Humor Man, and pulling fire alarms every chance I got. I was also into stealing. Every time my mother took me to the supermarket, I would steal a pocketknife and invariably cut myself when I tried to open it.

Since my mother was on her own with four kids, we went through a series of maids. One day my father showed up with a big brown dog, and the first maid said, "Mr. Collins, either that dog goes or I go!" Then there was the German woman who, on her last day, locked herself into our bedroom and wouldn't come out. She was convinced that my mother was trying to kill her.

We lived in a beautiful little Tudor Stucco house. My mother was against us watching television, so she sat me in front of the washing machine. She told me to sit tight, and that as soon as the commercial was over, my favorite cartoon show would come on. I sat there for what seemed like hours, believing her, watching the suds wash up against the little round window. It was kind of cool, but after a while, I caught on.

My mother told me not to play with the hose, so I flooded the garage. She told me not to play with my red Texaco truck in the driveway, so I did until she ran over it with our Ford Fairlane station wagon. The next door neighbor told me to stay off his property, so I stuffed mud in his mailbox every chance I could. My sister told me to stop being such a bad boy, but I wouldn't, so she called the police. They told me I'd better behave or I was going to jail. That scared me, for a while.

My first real trauma was when my mother told me that I had to go to day camp. Why did she want me to leave our happy home? I sat under a big wooden wagon at the daycare camp and cried all day long. No one seemed to care, and I felt like my mother had abandoned me without reason.

Then, my mother said we were going to take a trip, very far away. So at age six I went from scooters and mud in mailboxes, to blistering 103 degree heat, peacocks and parrots in my front yard, small men pulling rickshaws, people with holes where their noses and ears should be, and war.

When we boarded that Pan Am flight from John F. Kennedy Airport in New York, I don't think my mother knew what she was getting into. For the thirty-six plus hour flight, she kept warning us that it would be hot in Saigon. She said she didn't want to hear one word about it. Then, as she stood on the gangway with her four kids, looking down at my new dad who was holding a dozen wilted roses, all she could say was "God, it's hot!" But it was great. My new dad was cool, and I never looked back.

That first night in Saigon, as I lay in bed with my two sisters, I knew things were going to be different. The air, sounds, and smells were all different. I was whacked out from the jet lag, and the extreme 12 hour time change, so I started to fight with my sisters. My new dad came in and gave us our first spanking. What a night.

French school was in the morning, with English school in the afternoon. Big trays of peanut butter and jelly on sliced French bread, with fresh cut pineapple, were served for a snack.

There was a period of adjustment. We couldn't drink the tap water because snake tails might pop out of the faucet. At night we slept with mosquito nets over our beds, that kept out the biggest bugs I'd ever seen.

For me, the worst thing was not being allowed to take off your shoes in school; and like most things, I learned this the hard way. I'd be sitting there, minding my own business, sweating like a pig from the heat, when it would occur to me that I might be a bit cooler if I took off my shoes. Local kids, god knows who, worked in cahoots with the teachers. These little bastards would strike, crawling like mice on the floor, stealing your shoes, and bringing them to the teacher. I thought everything was cool when the teacher would call me up to her desk, and I'd panic looking for my shoes. How the fuck could my shoes disappear?

With sweat dripping down my back into my underwear, I realized at a tender young age that once again, I was fucked.

My life has been a series of events like this, when reason and the collective knowledge of the life experience – would utterly fail me. I have given up on reason and trying to figure out why people do the things they do. I should have learned back then, when little brats were stealing my shoes from underneath me, that it's just not possible.

It's something I should have learned from Jack Lee. I spent years as his gullible assistant, while he concocted an ever elaborate plan to control events and their outcome, to no avail. His logic was infallible, success was inevitable, but reality always seemed to be diabolical. The impression Jack made on me was so deep, that more than twenty years later, I would go back to find him... and walk right into the same situation.

I wonder if there really is a learning curve, and if I went completely around it. I think I've finally gotten it out of my system.

SAIGON, EARLY 1960S.
courtesy of Paul Collins' Archives

My mother told me that when I was a kid, I had a school-administered IQ test. The principal wouldn't say what my score was, but it was very high, so high that he wished he had it. Was I bright, or was my principal stupid?

I spent an idyllic year and a half in Saigon while my mother started her career in art. She would do paintings of our life: empty alleyways, a dog lying on a mat, or a palm tree. They were quite beautiful.

My mother was my first piece of good luck. She always loved me, treated me with respect and encouraged me in whatever I wanted to do. I'm happy to say that we're still very close and she still loves me, although she would be happier if I made more money. It must be hard for her to have four children whose combined income couldn't pay her yearly rent. Our only defense is that she taught us to love art and not business.

Our first house in Saigon was like a palace. The front was all glass, with a courtyard filled with small fruit trees and a flock of peacocks. One wall of the courtyard was lined with small canary cages, and we had four live-in maids. We used to play horses and chariots for hours at a time, going around and around the courtyard. My sisters knew the score and would always be in the chariot, and I'd always have to be the horse.

Our school in Downtown Saigon had one classroom, three grades, one set of books, and one teacher. She would stand holding the one book in front of my oldest sister, who had become the "teacher's pet." The rest of the twenty-odd students would be straining to see. I don't think I ever turned in a single homework assignment. I would always say I had left it at home. Most of the other kids were either French or Vietnamese, so we pretty much kept to ourselves.

The classroom had its own bathroom, but for some reason, the kids were afraid to ask to use it. They'd just go in their pants, sitting there with pee dripping down their legs onto the floor. One time the teacher burst into the bathroom and caught a boy and a girl in the bathroom together, buck naked. The teacher had a fit, but I was just as surprised.

After school we'd come home and have our peanut butter and jelly sandwiches while the maids would sit around having their favorite snack: fried cockroaches washed down with a cold glass of chicken blood.

We moved, and our second house had a full size trampoline in the front courtyard. Everything in Saigon had a wall around it with shards of glass or barbed wire on top. For extra protection, we also had columns of red ants that would march around the top of the wall, three deep, twenty-four hours a day. Red ants are vicious and they bite you. I would take a black ant, drop it into the swarm of red ants, and watch as it got sucked dry within seconds, as it tried to escape.

Our house had a working well, and one time my sisters told me they'd thrown all my toys down it. Without checking, I threw their toys down the well, only to find out that they'd only been teasing me. Of course I got my ass beaten by my new dad, and I was learning how girls could get away with almost anything.

The food in Vietnam was great. Before the Americans, France had occupied the country for many years. As a result, Vietnamese cuisine was a mix of the two countries. Red wild rice, tender meat dishes, and exotic fruits were always fresh and good. There wasn't a hamburger in sight.

We belonged to the Le Cercle Sportif club in downtown Saigon. We'd be poolside, sipping on lemonade and watching columns of American tanks rolling down the avenue, on the way to the front. It wasn't unusual to hear a hand grenade go off and I'd rush to see people running for cover. Small, slim, Vietnamese women continued to walk stoically, balancing huge loads on their heads, or on the end of slim black poles.

We would go to market in rickshaws, and I'd hold my mom's hand, gaping at deformed people with no identifiable features. They had black holes where their ears and nose should be, and their necks were all twisted, with blotchy yellow and white skin. My mother would pull my arm to go. What the fuck happened to these people? How did they get like that? No one ever told me, but it had to be Agent Orange, napalm, and leprosy.

Everything was mixed up. There was a war raging to the north, my mother was painting street scenes, and kids at school were pissing in their pants. I was listening to "Big Girls Don't Cry" in a Vietnamese taxi cab, in the pouring rain with the windshield wipers keeping time. This became the foundation for how I would perceive life. I knew right then and there, that it was possible for anything to go down ...*anything*.

The charm of Southeast Asia was wearing off and the war was getting nasty. My parents decided that we needed to get out of town for some rest and relaxation. They hired a chauffeur and took the whole family to Cape Saint Jacques, an old French seaside resort on the South Vietnamese coast. The car had a big red flag on the front fender to let people know we were tourists on holiday. We went through several check points along the way, manned by Vietnamese soldiers. We were gliding through no man's land, oblivious to everything, having a ball in the dense green war-infested forest of South Vietnam.

Deborah, Adrienne and Paul Collins in Saigon, early 1963.
courtesy of Paul Collins' Archives

We were damn lucky we didn't get killed. When we got back, friends of my parents said they had to be out of their minds, as civilians were strictly forbidden to travel out of town. Soon after that, the bicycle bombs started going off, and all travel was completely restricted. Saigon became more and more violent and out of control. We left shortly before a monk burned himself alive on a busy street. I was seven years old. It was the summer of 1963.

Collins Family in Athens, Greece, 1963.
(l to r): Deborah, Adrienne, Paul, and Patrick
courtesy of Paul Collins' Archives

CHAPTER TWO:
ATHENS To GREENWICH VILLAGE

Still not ready to face my father and life in America, we went to Athens, Greece, where life was good. In the '60s, people still loved Americans, the dollar was worth its weight in gold, and we lived like kings. Our clothes were all tailor-made, even our pajamas. If there was ever a moment of glory for my family, this was it. Underneath the Aegean sun we blossomed, and saw that it was possible to live in a completely different way than we'd ever known. Even going to the Acropolis was free on Sundays.

There was nothing to be afraid of. Everything we saw was beautiful, from the sunsets at Sounion to the Amphitheatre at Delphi. From Mykonos to Piraeus, we were in paradise. My mother and my new dad looked like gods in their sunglasses, standing with four impeccably-dressed kids. My sister even had a pet lamb, who one night came to a tragic end when a wild wolf got to it. She cried and cried, but there was no consoling her.

Life by the Aegean Sea was slow and easy. Greece was even better than Vietnam, and there was no war. On Sundays, the neighbors would roast an entire lamb over an open fire, rotisserie style. They would always invite us over to help them eat it, head, eyeballs, brains, tongue, and all. My sisters would play with their dolls while my brother and I fought. Our backyard was filled with beautiful poppies, swaying in the breeze, bright red in the sunshine.

Shelly, our American neighbor, would come over to play chess with my new dad. After dinner, Shelly and my parents would sit around drinking ouzo and wine. By the end of the night they would be dancing on the table and throwing plates in the air.

Living overseas, you immediately became friends with any families from back home who lived near you. One of the families had a daughter about my age, and we were hot for each other. This was my first real experience with the opposite sex.

I was at her house and her parents were going out shopping. No sooner than the door closed behind them, we jumped into her bed and took off all our clothes. It was great rolling around naked with her, but her father, a military man, tricked me. He seemed to have sensed my intentions, and this delightful first experience was cut short with a 'bang.' Her father stormed into the room like a paratrooper, screaming his head off. I've never put on my clothes so fast!

I was marched home to my parents, and they looked terrified as he told them of my terrible deed. I was prepared for the beating of my life, but this was one of the times when I began to realize how cool my folks were. They just smiled and said that I should be more careful next time, but there was no next time. I was banned from ever seeing her again.

We had a blue Volkswagen camper with a white top, a kitchen, a bathroom, and enough room for all six members of my family. One morning, parked by some river in Europe, we woke up in the camper. My new dad was trying to light his cigarette, striking the match over and over, but it wouldn't light. There wasn't any air left in the camper! After that we would always sleep with the windows cracked a bit.

Sometimes we closed our eyes in protest, and refused to look at some castle or monument that my mom tried to show us. We were tough, but she was tougher. She would lock us in the camper, go out and have a nice romantic dinner with my new dad, leaving us to fight it out. In retrospect I can't really blame her. Who would steal a Volkswagen camper with four kids in it back in Copenhagen circa 1965? No one, but today it's a different story.

I took a little side trip with my mother and my stepdad, just the three of us. We drove into the mainland until we got to a rock mountain that jutted way up into the sky. On top of it there was a monastery. It took hours to get up there, where we met three tough-looking Greek guys. They took us to an empty apartment to look at some ancient statues.

They offered my parents some coffee, and my mother answered them in Greek. She was always trying to show off, and this time it almost got us killed! The men suddenly got very serious, suspiciously pulling down the shades and turning up the radio. My parents started to look very uneasy. What was going on? My mother started to laugh nervously, explaining that she had been studying Greek, and that she took any chance she could get to practice. Later, I found out these men were really gangsters, who sold illegally obtained statues to American tourists in order to get cash to buy guns. The Greek Secret Service had asked my stepfather to have us pose as tourists so they could catch these guys.

COLLINS FAMILY (PAUL AT TOP) AT ACROPOLIS, ATHENS, GREECE, 1963.
courtesy of Paul Collins' Archives

My stepdad made a deal with the gangsters. He would meet them back in Athens at an abandoned house, with a briefcase full of cash. The cue was when my stepdad lit his cigarette. The cops would come charging in to arrest these guys! I never even got a medal.

After all that fun I decided, with the infinite wisdom of a ten year old, to spend a year in New York with my father and his new wife. My mother, in her infinite wisdom, let me go. We both realized too late that we were wrong. Talk about culture shock, going from the fairy-tale life of an American family in Europe, to the streets of Greenwich Village.

Half of what I know today, I probably learned on my first day of school at PS 42 on 11th St. and 6th Ave. Certainly, I learned most of the swear words I know on that day. I thought I knew the facts of life, but they were rammed home when some kid told

PAUL COLLINS AT NEW YORK METROPOLITAN MUSEUM, CIRCA 1968.
courtesy of Paul Collins' Archives

me the reason I existed was because my father fucked my mother. I never wanted to think of it that way, but there it was, and life would never be the same. New York kids are tough.

I learned how to turn stupid things to my advantage. Once, I accidentally gave myself a black eye with a seesaw. I told some chicks an older kid had punched me out, and it worked great. I loved the sympathy it got me, until the older kid found out and actually did beat the shit out of me. Everything has a price tag.

Even back then, New York was an expensive town, and I was always in need of extra pocket change. On the way to school, I'd pass a phone booth in front of the Women's Penitentiary on 6th Avenue. This became my unlimited source of spending money. It was a very simple yet effective routine: I'd unscrew the phone's mouthpiece and remove the internal voice piece from the handset. Throughout the day, people would insert coins into the phone, and wonder why the person they called couldn't hear them. They were unable to get their money back. Later, I'd replace the voice piece, hit the coin return and change would come spilling out, filling my pockets. All the while I'd watch women in the penitentiary windows, screaming at their boyfriends and husbands to come bail them out.

My father was a good guy, but life had gotten the better of him, making him a hard man. His parents were a pair of fine Irish drunks, who fought day and night. At age eighteen, fresh out of the Marines, he ran away to Oregon with my seventeen-year-old mother. He became a lumberjack. I loved the stories my mother would tell me of their life there. In their small cabin, she'd anxiously await my father while he was out cutting down trees. At night they'd lay in bed singing songs together, and that image always seemed so beautiful to me, of two people so in love.

I wish I could say I've known that kind of love, but I haven't – at least not yet. I've been insanely in love, but it's always been with the wrong girl, for the wrong reasons, or both.

My father never mentioned my mother's name again after she left him for his best friend. This didn't happen out of the blue. My father was a control freak and my mother was, and still is, a very strong and free-spirited person. According to her, this was because she lost her mother when she was three years old, her father remarried, and her new stepmother hated her. It forced my mother to fend for herself. To me, she always seemed to know what to do, and was never on the wrong end of a situation. Above all, she always enjoyed herself. Under no circumstances did she seem to have any regrets or guilt. I don't know why this didn't rub off on me.

That year in New York impacted me greatly. My father was very domineering and if you didn't submit to his will, he'd hit you, usually in the face. Since I hated being hit, I did what he said. I loved my father, but I was afraid of him. He was the opposite of my mother and I think somehow the switch caused me to become slightly schizophrenic. I had to completely change my way of being to suit my father. Since I wasn't always sure about how he wanted things, I became so nervous that I started to wet my bed. I was so afraid of what would happen if my father found out, I'd dry my sheets in the middle of the night on the bathroom heater.

My father was a snappy dresser and he gave me the "pleasure" of shining his shoes. Actually, I didn't mind doing it. I just hated it because I *had* to do it. It made me feel like I was his boy, even though I was his boy! He ran his import-export business out of my grandfather's warehouse way uptown in Harlem on 125th Street. I loved to go with him and roam around the warehouse filled with all kinds of stuff from years ago. My favorite was an old mint condition black Cadillac that looked straight out of some old gangster movie.

His wife Lida, my Czechoslovakian stepmother, was very kind to me and I grew to love her very much. She had escaped Hitler's Germany underneath a pile of rags, in the back of a horse-drawn wagon. She was very elegant and I loved the perfume she wore. Tall, thin, with chestnut brown hair pulled back and her big black sunglasses, she was a star. Unfortunately her star faded with cancer, and she withered away for over a year in a New York City hospital in the winter of 1969.

Years later, after my father died in the late '80s, my aunt told me that he'd never really loved Lida. This made me very sad. After she passed away, I once thought I saw her on the streets of New York. I thought that maybe she hadn't died, but had run away from my father. I still miss her.

When the year was up, I was ready to go back to my fun-filled life with my family in Europe, but it wasn't to be. My father wasn't going to let me go. This could have been a real disaster for me, but fortunately my mother packed up the family and moved us back to the States. Manhasset, Long Island to be exact. This ended the glory years for my family.

PAUL COLLINS AT NEW YORK METROPOLITAN MUSEUM, CIRCA 1968.
courtesy of Paul Collins' Archives

PAUL COLLINS, EARLY 1970S.
courtesy of Paul Collins' Archives

CHAPTER THREE:
MANHASSET to LEONIA

The sixties were practically over, and my family and I were right back where we started in Long Island. That's where my life in music really began. I didn't have a stereo yet, so I spent every night falling asleep to WABC Radio, with all the great disc jockeys like Harry Harrison, Cousin Brucie, et al. There was something magical in the sound of their voices, and with a touch of reverb, they sounded like gods to me. The music they played was the tops. It was truly a golden age for rock 'n' roll, with Elvis, Motown, and the British Invasion. You had the Detroit, West Coast, East Coast, Memphis, and Nashville sounds all being rolled up into one big hit single after another.

> *This was what I wanted to do. I didn't know how, but rock 'n' roll is what really turned me on. It has been the one constant thread that has stayed with me throughout my entire life.*

Since I had no formal training I decided to play the drums. It seemed easy enough; all you had to do was bang away. With a Remo snare I got for Christmas and a foot operated garbage can, I had the makings of my first drum kit.

Thank god for America and all the cars we built. Without them we would have never had the garage: birthplace of all the great music created in my lifetime. This was my refuge. Over the next four or five years I'd spend countless hours banging away, dreaming of the day The Beatles would happen by, hear me, and ask me to join the band.

Back in Douglaston, Queens, I'd been a small time thief. But in Manhasset, I became a full-fledged kleptomaniac. I'm not sure why, but you name it, and I'd steal it: clothes, lighters, food, and once even a sun lamp, just for the hell of it. I gave it to my mom as a present, but when my new dad came home from work, he made me bring it back to the store. He knew what I was up to!

One time, my friends and I had cut school and were hanging out by the railroad tracks. We got picked up by the cops, who found a stolen bottle of Gillette hair tonic in my pocket. They were convinced that I was sniffing it to get high. When the cops brought me home, neither my parents nor I had any idea what they were talking about. We had been out of the country too long.

I got my first paper route, delivering a paper that no one really wanted. Once I realized this, I would just dump them down a sewer. Eventually I got caught by my supervisor. He came to my house and told my parents that this "serious offense" could be reported to the FBI. It would be on my record for life. My parents must have thought this guy was out of his fucking mind, but they sat there nodding and looking very concerned.

My stepdad was an engineer. He had to leave us in Manhasset to go build an airport in Saudi Arabia. We were all set to follow, when my brother came down with tuberculosis. We had to cancel our trip, boy was I mad! Now my mother was alone trying to raise four kids. She was an artist, and making plastic sculptures out of polyurethane. She would disappear for hours at a time in the basement. Who knew about ventilation? My mother was getting stoned out of her mind. Once she even lost her voice for three days.

My brother and I were out out of control. My mother would ask our uncle to come smack us around a bit so we'd remember who was boss. This wasn't like being hit by my real father. We knew he didn't mean it, and he was just trying to help his sister out. Intent is everything.

Finally, my mother told my new dad to get his ass back home, and to get us the hell out of Long Island. We moved to Leonia, New Jersey, the most intellectual square mile in the United States, according to the *Encyclopedia Britannica*. Look it up. Because of its close proximity to New York, a lot of lawyers, professors, actors, and writers lived there. Not that I noticed, because I've always tended to be impervious to these kinds of things.

I could only see the girls.

Ah, youth, and the wonderful world of girls. As girls became more beautiful, so did my desire for rock stardom. I was convinced this was how I could get girls morning, noon, and night. When girls turn fifteen, sixteen and seventeen, they bloom like flowers and become goddesses. They also become smart and won't let you near them. God, I was aching to get laid. It was all I could think about. I was always ready to go, in my super tight pants. There was a sexual revolution going on in America but it was completely avoiding me!

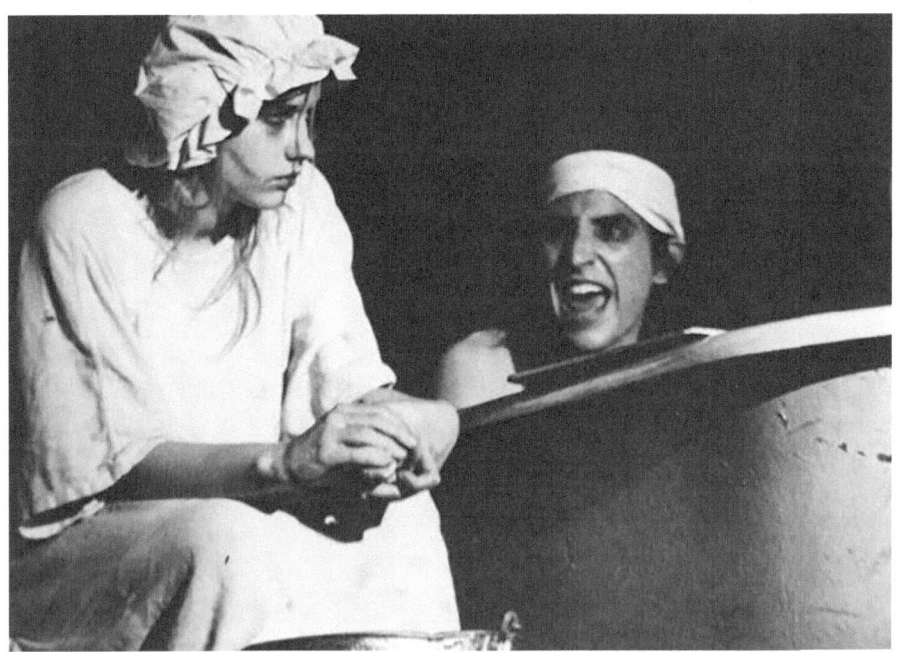

PAUL COLLINS (RIGHT), WITH PEGGY GABOR IN *MARAT SADE* LEONIA SCHOOL PLAY, CIRCA 1973. *photo courtesy of Dave Marx*

The first girl I had sex with was three years older than me. The whole thing was over in twenty seconds, and I couldn't get out of there fast enough. This paradox of wanting something so bad, getting it, and becoming repulsed has stumped me for a long time. I know it's some kind of character defect. I do not know why or where it comes from.

When I was seventeen, I met my girlfriend's thirty year-old roommate. Sometimes dreams can come true! We started to get it on. We'd fuck, fuck, and fuck until we were both too sore to go on. What a great feeling. It was lust and not love, but at the time I didn't mind. Unfortunately, you start to feel like a real shit, just trying to get your rocks off. I didn't know what real love was.

> *Life is full of so many maybes. Maybe you can't have an ego and be in love? Maybe what you need is to meet someone who won't be torn apart by the rough and tumble of life? Life is tough, and it weeds out the assholes and the weaklings. It makes me wonder if I'm not one of them. I feel like this on a bad day, then I bounce right back with my usual gusto and bravado. Life never gets me down for too long.*

Sometimes it's a blessing to not get too deep. Maybe it's time to check back in with my mentor, Jack Lee. He has always warned me not to preach: "Never preach to the audience. Do not rob them of the joy of discovery." Well, I don't think I am preaching. I'm just saying what happened to me and what I've thought about it.

My education was practically complete. I'd had sex and I still wanted to be a rock star, so it was time for me to leave. In keeping with its intellectual status, Leonia set up one of the first 'alternative schools' in America. *The School Without Walls* took advantage of all the very creative and successful professionals in town who would give classes in their homes. I was lucky enough to be in the first class, of their first year. It was amazing. I knew there was no way I was going to make two more years of high school. I was too anxious to get out on my own, but I really didn't want to start life as a dropout. I doubled up on English and Math and graduated a year early at the age of 17. It was 1973.

The Vietnam War was at its height, there were protests all over America, and I went to the ones in my area. Since I had actually lived in Vietnam, my outlook was different from most kids. I knew it was no picnic for the young men who were going over there to fight, and I felt bad when my friends would call them 'baby killers' and 'hawks.' When my schoolmates' brothers started coming home in pine boxes, it made me sick to hear people saying stuff like that. Young soldiers had no idea what they were getting into. They were dying far away in a very strange place, defending their country.

I read in the *NY Times* that the draft was being cancelled, so I missed it by a matter of months. I was off the hook! There was no way I'd have gone back to Vietnam. I don't know what I would have done; enlisted in the Army Core band? The war was ripping the country in two. I'd feel a twinge in my stomach as I'd watch news reports about how devastating the war was in Vietnam, my former home.

The war wasn't the only thing killing kids at school; drugs were starting to take their toll. A lot of kids were starting to experiment with acid and heroin, trying to emulate their idols in the rock world. 'If it's good enough for Jimi Hendrix, then it's good enough for me.' Unfortunately, like Hendrix, Morrison, Brian Jones, et al., some of them died.

I pretty much escaped unharmed from experimenting with drugs, mainly acid. *Double Barrel Sunshine* – you were only supposed to take half a tab. I was always so impatient to get off, I'd wind up taking the whole thing and getting royally fucked up. "Why is your face turning green, man?" I'd take that shit and go to school, or worse, drive. I once sat in the car for about an hour holding the emergency brake with all my might, thinking the car was 'moving.'

I'd hang out every single day with two of my best high school friends, Phil and Bobby. We were always listening to music, trying to scare up a joint, and making big plans for the future. We were very, very tight. I'd imagine everyone has that special moment when they're coming of age. They have friends who they spend a lot of time with, and share whatever their passions may be. In the late '60's, the three of us shared our passion for music. Bobby knew how to wail on his red Gibson SG guitar, and we'd spend hours listening to him play.

Bobby was different, but he wasn't crazy. Actually, I think he was extremely intelligent, but like most kids, he just didn't get along with his parents. He was the first kid I ever heard tell his mother to "Shut up." I couldn't believe it. If I'd said something like that to my mother, I'd have gotten my ass kicked.

We were experimenting with marijuana and acid. I remember Bobby saying stuff like, "Feed your head, feed your head," from the Jefferson Airplane song. At the time, I knew the difference. It was just a song, not an instruction to go out and fry your brain, but somehow Bobby took it to heart. Most of us had parents who were aware spiritually and politically, but Bobby's parents didn't get it. They wanted something for their kids that no one understood.

When he turned seventeen, Bobby's relationship with his parents severely deteriorated. Then one day, Bobby's mother told me he wasn't home and wouldn't be coming home for quite a while. They'd sent him to a mental institution somewhere in Connecticut. We found out where he was, drove up to see him, and were shocked. He came into the visiting room completely doped up on Thorazine like a zombie. A few days later, he jumped out of a window and killed himself. I couldn't understand it, so I blocked it out of my mind until many years later.

I had another good friend in Leonia: Artie. My folks called him 'The Artful Dodger' since we were always up to no good. We both loved rock 'n' roll, so one night we snuck out and saw the MC5 at Ungano's, a small club on the upper west side of New York City. By the time the MC5 hit the stage, Artie was sound asleep with his head on Wayne Kramer's amp! Wayne came out, saw Artie, and gave him a good kick in the head.

As a fellow artist, my mother didn't want to discourage me musically, but drums are noisy. So when we moved to Leonia, she took me to folk guitar lessons. This gave me the foundation for my guitar style today. It's all basic folk, with open chord positions. I had a songbook with "Savoy Truffle" by the Beatles in it, and I played it over and over. I loved that song.

My family always had a piano, so I took some lessons in Leonia. I never really excelled at it, but I learned the basics. I also played French horn and flute, which I picked up on my own.

During that time, I joined my first band. It was called Homegrown. One day my bandmates showed up with ARP synthesizers, a drum set, amps, a PA, and a Sony 2-track recorder. How they got all this brand new equipment was questionable, but suddenly I had a full-blown sound studio in my basement.

This was when my mother and I collaborated on a project called *The Elements*. Her art had become very abstract, and she began oil painting directly on to transparent slides. When projected, they were stunning. I made a tape of experimental music to go along with the slide presentation. I spent hours experimenting with different sounds and tape speeds.

The Elements was the first time my mom and I worked together as artists. All of a sudden she wasn't my mother and I wasn't her kid. We were two artists working on a project. I still have the tape. It's about thirty minutes long, and kind of bizarre. I should have kept it up, but I wanted to be a rock star.

My mom lives for her art and she was really excited about how it all came out. We showed *The Elements* at a whole bunch of places, even at my school. It was very impressive and people really liked it. For years, the very large posters my mom made for the show were hanging around her studio, as a reminder of what we had done. It was great, and we were both very proud of it.

One morning my mother walked into the kitchen while I was having breakfast. She said, "Get dressed! I'm driving you into New York to audition for The Juilliard School of Music."

"Mom, you're nuts. I don't even know how to read music!"

"I don't care, take that tape you made in the basement and get dressed! Today is the last day for auditions."

Juilliard is one of the most prestigious music schools in the world. Kids would audition and wait an entire year to find out if they were accepted. I was accepted the very same day. The way I got in was by going to admissions, filling out an application as a composition major, and listing myself as a composer. The only person able to determine if I could compose (or not) was the head of the composition department.

They sent me over to his house, I played him my basement tape of avant-garde music, and he was impressed. He called admissions, said he'd take me on as a student, and that was it. I was in! Juilliard was the best school of music in the whole fucking world, and I couldn't write a note of music.

No one in Leonia could believe it.

"Collins got into Juilliard? Un-fucking-believable!"

The smart things I've done without knowing it could fill a book.

I hope it's this one.

Paul Collins & Cindy, in Leonia 1972-73.
courtesy of Paul Collins' Archives

CHAPTER FOUR:
Hell's Kitchen To California

I left home, or rather my home left me. My sisters were safely off to college, and my mother was fed up with my new dad. She decided to move to Yugoslavia with my 13-year-old brother. When I got accepted to Juilliard, I never asked my mother if leaving me was part of her plan. But apparently everything had all been worked out for me. I'd move to New York City and share an apartment with the daughter of friends of the family. She was a skinny and bony dance major who reminded me of a chicken.

We packed all my belongings into my first girlfriend Cindy's VW bug, and drove to my new pad. It was late, so we decided to unpack in the morning. This should give you an idea of how naïve we were. At about four in the morning, there was a loud knock at the door.

"Who is it?"

"The police. Someone broke into your car and all your stuff was in the street."

"You're kidding!"

"Don't worry. We picked it all up and put it back in your car, but there might be a few things missing."

They had found a picture of me in the street, and I can't imagine how they tracked me down since it was only my first night there. I only remember losing a camera. This squelched any fear I had about living in New York. New York City cops are truly amazing, and to this day, are still a special breed.

While going to Juilliard, I got a job selling stereos around the corner. It was funny how I was two minutes from work, yet always late. Everything was great. You couldn't ask for anything better than selling stereos. Come on! We'd sit around inhaling nitrous oxide, listening to *Dark Side Of The Moon*, and blowing up thousand-dollar speakers.

Nitrous is a weird drug. You'd take a big hit, slip into a state of semi-consciousness, think you'd discovered the answer to the entire universe, and forget it as soon as you'd come to. Frustrated, you'd take another hit trying to remember. It was fun in hindsight, but a big waste of time.

One of the big fringe benefits of my new job was "installation." You'd sell a stereo to some college girl who needed help, so of course you'd offer to come over and help 'plug it in.' You can guess the rest. It happened to me once, but it was an awkward and unmemorable experience. To top it off, she returned the stereo.

At first I was really impressed with our new manager. He looked like the perfect dude: great hair, a cool dresser, confident, and chicks loved him. He was everything I aspired to be. I don't know why, but this guy slowly began to undermine my confidence. It got to the point where he'd walk into the room and I'd turn to mush, unable to function. The more I built him up in my mind, the worse it got. In the end, he fired me and I was devastated. Even if you hate the job, there's something about being fired that makes you feel horrible and worthless. It's like being jilted by a lover.

I went to the unemployment office and got a big kick explaining to my social worker that I was a stereo demonstrator. She asked why I couldn't look for other kinds of work, like manual labor. I told her I was a piano player and I had to be careful with my hands. She bought it, or at least acted like she did. It was great. Unemployment checks were like mad money to me. To top it off, I met an out-of-work secretary who took me home and screwed me. All I needed now was fame, and I'd be a happy little piker.

Back at the apartment things weren't going so well. After a few months, I couldn't stand my roommate. I couldn't even watch her eat. The smell of her food made me want to puke, but in the end, *it was the piano that did me in*. One night, I was trying to impress another girl by playing a song from my very limited repertoire. Suddenly our neighbor, a demented priest, was pounding at the door, ranting and raving about how 'I was the devil, playing devil music' and that I would burn in hell. After he left, my roommate made it clear that she was on his side. The very same night, I moved out at midnight.

I learned a very valuable lesson: always travel light. I had two vanloads of shit, and nowhere to go. My mother was unreachable in Yugoslavia, and my new dad had gone AWOL. I was jobless and homeless, but I was getting an education in life.

I began the 'crashing' phase of my life, which sucks. You have to eat, smoke dope, go to sleep, and do everything at the same time as the people you are staying with. You're on a couch with dirty sheets, or worse yet, the floor. I started at my friend's house in Jersey, but when the smell of PCP and the commute to New York got to be too much, I moved out.

A young student from school let me crash at her pad on 83rd and West End

Avenue. She was a dancer: short and sweet, with long black frizzy hair, like a little gnome. Her place was huge and was built for one of those pre-war middle-class families who no longer existed in New York. She was sharing it with two other girls and a Jamaican ping-pong star. Day and night, he smoked those king-sized Jamaican joints. He had a full-sized ping-pong table, and an absolutely beautiful girlfriend.

One night I wound up in bed with my friend, *and then something important happened*. Don't forget, I was a middle-class kid with a fairly privileged background. I started whining about my woes, so she grabbed me by the shoulders, pushed me away, looked me squarely in the eye and said, *"Stop feeling sorry for yourself!"* That moment has stayed with me till this day, and I remember it every time self-pity sets in. I moved out the next day and started looking for my own place.

So what does Jack have to say about all this? Nothing. He says "You're doing fine. Keep up the good work. Don't worry. I'm always right around the corner, ready to rip it all to shreds."

I was a skinny little white boy with shoulder-length hair, living on the streets of New York City. Doing this kind of shit when you're seventeen is fun, no matter how bad you think it is. I had no place to go, and snow fell as I shuffled along the downtown streets, freezing my little white ass off.

I saw a guy squatting over a sewer grate on the sidewalk, wearing only a t-shirt, shorts, and a piece of plastic over his shoulders. I asked him if he was freezing and he motioned me to sit beside him. I discovered the grate was actually a vent blowing hot air, so I spent the night next to him, toasty as could be. He told me aliens had captured his mind, and that the CIA was desperately trying to find him. He had been to college, and once had a good job, something sophisticated like a researcher or a biochemist.

I asked how he wound up on the street. He said there were a lot of guys like him who had 'checked out, unable to hack it in the real world, with no plans of returning.' People walked by giving us unsolicited change, but he dropped it down the grate. What can you say to a guy like that? I was just happy to be warm.

The next night, a guy playing a tambourine downtown said I could stay with him. When we got there, it became clear he wanted to screw me. Something about his roommate not feeling well so we could sleep together on the couch. "Come on, man. It's freezing out. I ain't got no place to stay, and there's no way in hell I'm going to let you screw me." Thank god he wasn't aggressive, so I spent the night on the couch guarding my ass. I was out of there at dawn, deciding to get the fuck out of downtown.

Midnight, in an empty Baskin Robbins on 72nd St. was where my luck changed. A guy killing time asked if I wanted an ice cream and I told him I needed a place to stay. It turned out there was a vacancy on 45th Street, and I moved in the next day. Rent was a hundred bucks a month, and after I cleaned out all the used rubbers and needles, it was home. Girls I knew were afraid to visit me, but I didn't care. Whores, pimps, drugs dealers, and thieves never do anything in their own neighborhoods, so I was perfectly safe. I was really living: my own pad in the middle of Hell's Kitchen.

My pad was a cool railroad flat on the fifth floor, with a bathtub, a gas burner for heat, loft bed, and no TV. The back room was my junk room where I set up my drums. I had a real set now, and I used to practice and drive the old German couple downstairs nuts. They'd retaliate by blasting authentic recordings of Hitler's speeches to The Third Reich.

This was a good time for me. I was alone, away from my family and everyone else I had ever known. I had picked up a trumpet somewhere along the way, so I would sit by the window sill for hours, playing call and response riffs to the car horns floating up from the street below.

The neighborhood was an oasis of nuts. No one was judging anyone, so I fit right in. I met George, a typical Greek stud unsuccessfully pursuing an acting career. Our conversations covered the broad spectrum of life, and would go into the wee hours of the night. George would be primping himself in the mirror. The hard-working Puerto Rican family living next door would get drunk on a couple of sixers, and play their one Salsa record over and over. They laughed, sang, and carried on. I didn't have the heart to complain.

My building was next to a park, between 45th and 46th St., that Paul Simon would eventually write a flop Broadway musical about. It was called *The Capeman*. I would listen to all the wisdom and truths that bums, hustlers, and street people would give me back then. I had no idea that one day someone would make a big deal out of this park.

My landlord Mr. Jay was short, fat, Jewish, and always wore a suit with a pork-pie hat. He collected the rent personally. Every time I'd put $100 in his hand, he'd always say:

"That's right. You're a good kid. I said to myself the first time I saw you, this here's a good kid."

He was nice, but I got worried when he tried to check a gas leak with a match.

"Don't worry Mr. Jay, I'll fix it myself!"

When I moved into 45th Street, I started to take drum lessons from Sam Ulano, a crusty old guy and a great jazz drummer. He was an insomniac who lived over on 55th street off of 8th Avenue. I loved going over to his small basement apartment for my lessons, crammed with all kinds of drum stuff. He would always ask me:

"What's a beat?"

Then he would say, "A beat is the same sound over and over again! Don't you forget that!"

Being a drummer in New York was the pits. You would lug your drums up five flights of stairs, for a short audition with weirdos, playing music you'd never heard of. Most memorable was Colonel Dak: four guys in space suits who said, "We don't play music. We construct notes from outer space."

I only played with one band during this time: Tiffany, a lesbian singer's 'revue' playing at the emerging gay clubs around the city. It was my first brush with real showbiz theatrics, and Tiffany loved medleys. Her favorite was "Piece Of My Heart" by Janis Joplin, into "Lola" by The Kinks. She'd change outfits, from woman to man, and vice-versa. Off and on, she'd stay with me, and sleep in my bed. We didn't have sex, but she'd let me watch her using her vibrator. I'm pretty sure she won't sue me.

My year at Juilliard was up. I was getting nowhere, not getting laid, and my unemployment was running out. In the end, Juilliard was a big disappointment. Everyone knew everything there was to know about music, except how to play it. I'd try to get a jam going with students who could sight-read Scriabin. Believe me, that's difficult. These guys would look at me, not knowing what to play without sheet music. On the few occasions I managed to get a blues jam going, they'd look at me dumbfounded.

The hall monitor would storm in screaming, *"This is not music!"* Oh yeah? Well fuck you, too. Sometimes it's enough to know what you don't want to do – *and I knew I didn't want to do this.*

When I told my drum teacher Sam Ulano about all the crazy auditions I was going to, he told me repeatedly: "If you want to make it in rock 'n' roll, you need to go to California. The West Coast is where it's happening, kid!"

A girl from high school fueled my quest for stardom, saying the only time she ever had an orgasm was when listening to the Grateful Dead. She asked if I wanted to drive to California with her. It was time to leave NY, so I packed a few things, sublet my apartment, and headed out. *Go West, young man.*

The ride was pleasant enough until we decided to cross through Canada into Sault Ste. Marie, Michigan. We had an ounce of pot, and thought the best place to travel would be a lonely old border. Some old geezer cop on duty told us to pull over for an inspection. He tore the car apart and found what he was looking for: a marijuana seed in the carburetor. We were just kids, and we were scared. We didn't know they were just shaking us down for the two hundred dollars in bail money we'd never get back. Now we were broke, but at least we were free.

I tried to screw my friend a whole bunch of times, but nothing ever happened. I was starting to learn about chemistry, and I'm still learning. I left her in Lake Tahoe, hitchhiked to Berkeley, and by the time I got to San Francisco, I had eighty bucks in my pocket.

PART 2:
THE NERVES

The NERVES emerge, original lineup early 1975, (L to R):
Peter Case, Paul Collins, Jack Lee, and Pat Stangl.
courtesy of Paul Collins' Archives

CHAPTER FIVE:
Hanging On The Telephone

In November of 1974, I was in San Francisco. I was eighteen, and I guess you could say it was the first day of my adult life. Everyone was saying; 'Have a nice day' and I was hoping it would be. I had one phone number, of a woman named Patricia I had known back in Connecticut. She said I could crash at her place, but only for a few days. Not what I wanted to hear, but beggars can't be choosers. She was studying theology, living with a bunch of people in an enormous house on Russian Hill, and dating a car salesman. *A car salesman?* Give me a break.

On my third day, everyone in the house was going away for a while, and they asked if I'd mind taking care of the place. No problem. I was in this huge house alone, and now I had to find a band, since that was the real reason I was in California.

I asked around where the cool music stores were, and I was directed to Don Wehr's Music City. I pushed open their door, with the motto 'When You're Ready' emblazoned in gold on it. I was ready. But for what? I'm not sure. I was hit with a symphony of discombobulated sound: musicians trying out gear all at the same time. It reminded me of Colonel Dak. I waded through hippies in flowered shirts and bell-bottoms. I scanned the bulletin board and found the 3" x 5" index card that would change my life forever.

WANTED: DRUMMER FOR ALL ORIGINAL BAND

A LA THE BEATLES AND STONES…

CALL JACK

I ripped it down and stuck it in my back pocket. No one else was going to see this one, it was all mine. I ran immediately across the street to the pay phone and called

Jack Lee, who told me to come on over. I liked that. When you want to be a rock star, you don't have a moment to waste. I knocked on the grey dingy door, it opened, and I was face to face with a set of pale blue eyes that seemed to look right through me.

"Jack?"

"Come on in."

Jack is really cool. I mean, he is the shit. I have never met anyone like him, before or since. I looked around the disheveled room, and there was stuff piled up everywhere. Jack sat down on his unmade bed, where it looked like he had been all morning. There was a red cherry sunburst guitar lying next to him, and he began playing his amazing songs. I whipped out my drumsticks, grabbed a phone book that was lying around, and started playing along. I felt like I'd played these songs a million times before and knew them inside and out. I was really digging it, and so was Jack.

"I made a record," said Jack.

Until that moment, I'd never met anyone who had made a record. I was getting goosebumps as Jack pulled out a shiny black 45 out of a plain white paper sleeve: an acetate with one song on it, "Hanging On The Telephone." He laid it carefully down on the turntable.

"I'm in the phone booth - it's the one across the hall!"

Gone! My head was reeling. It was lovely the way he recorded it in the studio. He had a bird chirping, a telephone ringing, Jack's wife Connie saying hello, and then the song starts. This was exactly what I'd been looking for. It was the same effect as when I heard "Big Girls Don't Cry" on Saigon radio for the first time – the thrill of music; an adrenaline rush like no other. I looked at Jack, who seemed like a god to me. He made this? He had done what I'd only dreamed of.

"There's more where that came from," he said.

I asked Jack where the rest of the band was.

"Oh… them? Forget about them. We are going to start a new band!"

Jack said we needed one more guy, and he knew who it was: *Peter Case.* Jack had made several unsuccessful attempts to start a band with Peter, so he said we needed to "play our cards right, and come from sideways with Peter, kind of like the way you'd fuck a grizzly." I wasn't sure what that meant, but I went along anyway.

Jack was sure we'd find Peter down at the wharf in the Marina district, and he was right. I was knocked out by Peter and his friend Danny playing to a crowd of tourists, singing songs from the '60s. They were nailing all the licks, and most importantly, the harmonies. Peter was a great singer, as well as an original songwriter.

As they worked the crowd for tips, another street musician who called himself 'The Human Jukebox,' started inching toward them. He was playing the trumpet very loudly and very badly. His gimmick was wearing a jukebox costume made out of a refrigerator box. When it got impossible to hear, Danny walked over and popped him one. The Human Jukebox fell over in his box and went rolling down a grassy hill.

Danny said, "How many times do I have to tell you? Stay out of our spot!"

We walked up to Peter, who was drinking a beer out of a paper bag, as was his habit practically the whole time I knew him. I ignored Jack's advice and blurted right out, "You wanna start a band with me and Jack?" Jack cringed and Peter was taken aback.

"I don't know man. I've got a lot going on. I'm thinking about starting a band myself."

I said, "Not like this one! This one is going be great."

Peter's response was: "Yeah, that's what they all say."

I walked away completely discouraged, knowing there couldn't be too many guys like Peter around. Jack wasn't worried, and said he was certain Peter had 'a real hair up his ass' to see what we were up to. Peter did come around, and when he did, it was pure magic. He even switched from guitar to bass to do it. I thought he looked like 'the shit,' wearing those Buddy Holly-style glasses and a beat-up varsity jacket.

The three of us sat in Jack's rundown room. I played drums on a phone book. Jack was on the bed with his cherry red Rickenbacker guitar. Peter sat on the window sill playing his light brown Hofner bass. We spent hours and days on end as Jack taught us the songs he had written: "Stand Back and Take A Good Look," "Give Me Some Time," "Are You Famous," "Letter To G," "Come Back and Stay," and of course, "Hanging on The Telephone." We played those songs over and over, and they sounded wonderful stripped down like that. When Jack and Peter harmonized, it was even better.

I started singing in the band right from the get go. I didn't have the best pitch, and Jack and Peter would take the time to help me. They showed me how to find the right note, and sing in key. Jack said he had been working on a name for years, and was convinced it would be the key to our success: *The Nerves*. At first I didn't like it, but in a short amount of time, I grew to love it.

In 1975, a fourth original member ended up joining The Nerves: Pat Stangl.

He was Jack's best friend from Sitka, Alaska where they were both from. Pat played on Jack's original "Hanging On The Telephone" acetate, along with an unknown drummer. Pat was a gifted and accomplished guitarist.

I first met Pat when Jack decided to move our rehearsals from the bedroom, to his flophouse basement. Unknown to me, Pat Stangl was living down there. In fact, we showed up and Pat was all plugged in, and ready to rehearse. I think Jack planned it this way all along, waiting to introduce Pat after Peter and I learned the songs. I found out there was a history between Jack, Peter, and Pat - some good, and some not so good. Nothing had ever happened for them.

In January of 1975, Jack asked me to move into his basement on Pine St. and Gough. Our rehearsals were just insane. There was no such thing as tempo, and everything had to be played fast as possible. Sometimes, my hands would be covered in blood from playing so hard. Jack was an absolute Nazi about the music, and sometimes it took hours just to get through one song.

The neighbors from across the street, inspired by our music, wrote us a letter and stuck it in the window.

"WE HAVE NEVER HEARD SUCH BAD MUSIC, BUT AT ALL COST PLEASE FIRE YOUR DRUMMER AS HE IS THE WORST WE HAVE EVER HEARD!"

There's nothing like some fan mail to encourage a young group.

My mother began worrying about her little boy's living situation. I wouldn't go out for days. The owner of the flophouse lived onsite, and his wife was whacked out, sexually-starved, and on serious medication. She would come down screaming about calling the cops, pounding, and smashing plates on the door. For some reason there was an endless supply of plates. Jack and Pat would ignore her, Peter would just laugh, and I would sit there and cringe.

Pat Rush was a friend of Jack's, and one of two junkies living next door. He'd frequently burst into our rehearsal room in his underwear, throwing a huge bowie knife at the wall with all his might. It didn't seem to matter to him if it landed right above your head. He'd leave as quickly as he came in. Pat Rush would get into terrific fights with his skanky girlfriend. It was common to see huge welts on their faces and arms. One night he burst in sobbing. "That bitch smashed me in the face with the telephone receiver while I was sleeping!" Soon after, you would see them on a Saturday night, out on the town and dressed to the nines.

To make ends meet, we would raid the supermarket Goodwill Box late at night, and sell the clothes to thrift stores. The routine was for one of us to stand guard,

THE NERVES
WITH A BEAT !

(415) 543-5280
(415) 332-9100

The NERVES original lineup, early 1975, (l to r):
Jack Lee, Peter Case, Paul Collins, and Pat Stangl.
courtesy of Paul Collins' Archives

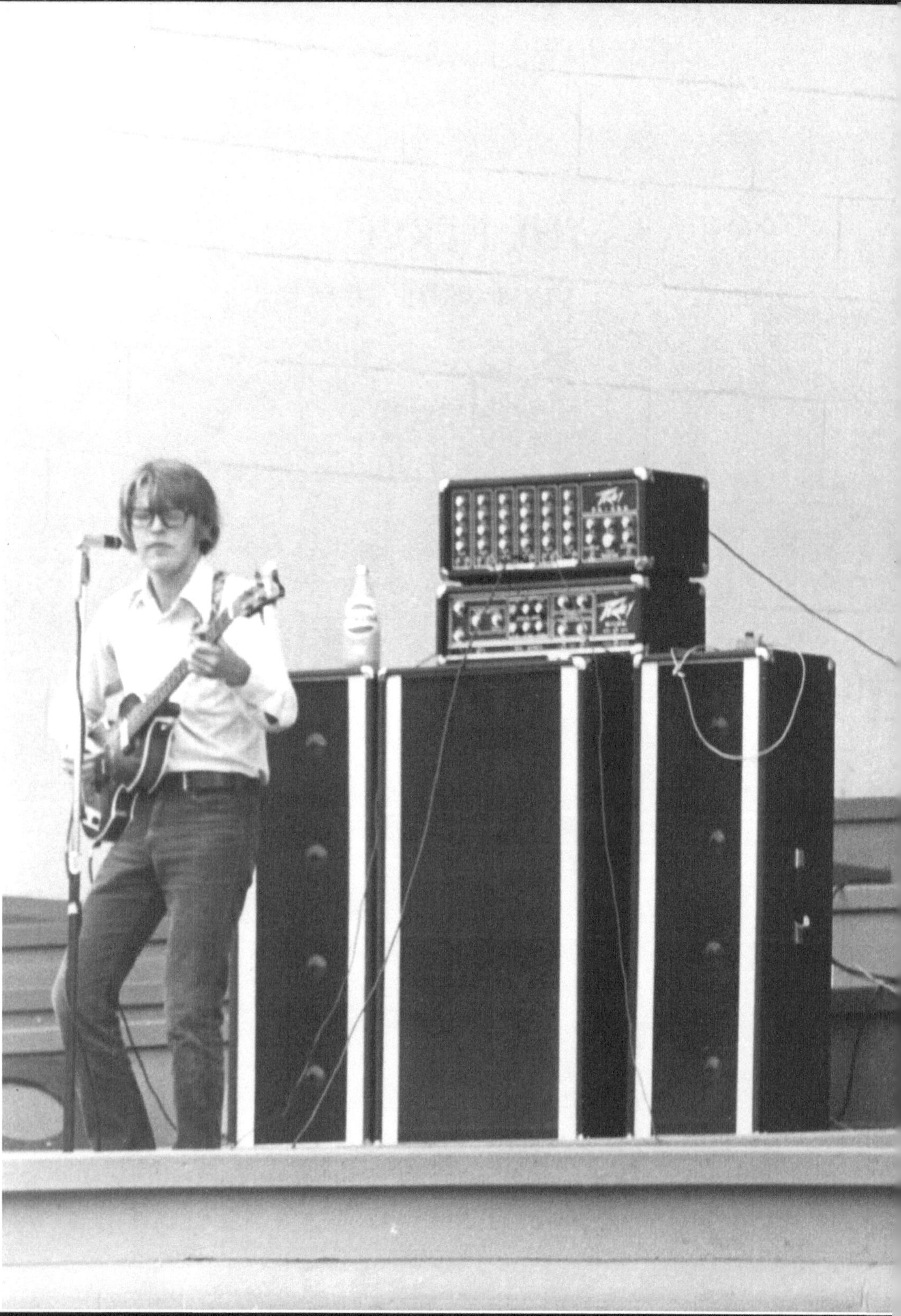

The Nerves original lineup, September 1975 at Golden Gate Park, (l to r):
Peter Case, Jack Lee, Pat Stangl, and Paul Collins.
courtesy of Paul Collins' Archives

while the other two would climb in. One foggy, chilly night, Peter and Jack climbed into the dropbox. I stood guard in my recently acquired garb, a long red velour coat, a white pimp's hat, and a big white pair of sunglasses. That was when a San Francisco Police patrol car pulled up.

"Where the fuck did you get those clothes? Let me see some I.D."

San Francisco police officers aren't known for their hospitality. I've seen them take a man down in a choke hold in the bat of an eye. I gave the officer my driver's license and he dialed my name into something I'd never seen before: a computer. Each line of information started with my name. Flashes of Big Brother ran through my veins and I was getting scared. I knew if he found the guys in the drop box, we would wind up spending the night at the precinct house.

His partner got out of the car, opened up the flap, gingerly stuck his head in the Goodwill box, and returned to the patrol car. The first cop handed back my license.

"I'd better not catch you hanging 'round here again. Next time I might have

THE NERVES ORIGINAL LINEUP CIRCA 1975, (L TO R):
PETER CASE, JACK LEE, PAUL COLLINS, AND PAT STANGL.
courtesy of Paul Collins' Archives

to get rough, and break an arm or something. Now get lost!"

I walked away slowly, but doubled back when the cops were out of sight. I gave Jack and Peter the 'all-clear' signal. They scrambled out, and we hightailed it out of there, carrying our little bundles of clothes, disappearing into the cold foggy night.

At some point, living in the basement got to be too much for me. I checked into The Baker Hotel, a real dump right down the block on 1485 Pine Street. People would break in all the time and it didn't matter whether you were there or not. I didn't have jack shit, so I wasn't worried. But it gave me my first glimpse of what happens to the aged in America. The lobby was always filled with broken down old people sitting around watching TV. I thought they were eating tuna fish, but on closer inspection I realized it was cat food.

At first, we couldn't get many real shows. In March of 1975, we played at a biker bar called The Garden Of Earthly Delights. I also got us these military gigs, playing the Fort Mason Officer's Club in the San Francisco Marina. At that time we were doing mainly covers, and they really liked us.

It's a real shame that this era was never committed to tape. We had some absolutely stellar versions of "Rescue Me" (Fontella Bass), "Nadine" (Chuck Berry), "I Saw Her Standing There" (Beatles), and "Come On Up" (Young Rascals). Peter did an amazing version of "One Night With You" (Elvis), and I did "The Letter" (Box Tops). Other songs included "Cat Scratch Fever" (Ted Nugent), "Rock The Boat" (Hues Corporation), "Rock Me Baby" (David Cassidy), and "Jet Airliner" (Steve Miller Band). We would do 10-15 minute versions of these songs, figuring if the kids loved it, why stop? We would do high school dances, playing only ten songs for over an hour, and everyone was happy.

By mid-1975, the scene at Jack's basement got too nasty for everyone. The Nerves went on a brief hiatus, and I went to New York for a visit. When I got back, Pat Stangl had moved into his own place. Jack had moved in with his wife-to-be Connie, at her parent's house in Atherton, California. I had nowhere to go, and wound up living in the back of a school bus, parked in Connie's parent's driveway. My first two songs were written there. I woke up every day with one burning desire: writing a song. I had to do what both Jack and Peter were doing.

Jack loaned me an old Harmony guitar with rusty strings, and I'd bang on it all day and into the night. Finally it happened, and I wrote "You Won't Be Happy" and "Working Too Hard." Jack was tough, but he was also very supportive. When you had something good, he would be the first to tell you. He was very generous and loved the whole idea of creating something good, no matter who did it. He would smile his big smile and say, "Now you're talking!"

> **FREE CONCERT**
>
> **THE NERVES**
>
> WITH A BEAT!
>
> FRI.-SEPT. 5TH
>
> 12 TO 3 P.M.
>
> **GOLDEN GATE PARK**
>
> MUSIC CONCOURSE

> NOW APPEARING
>
> COBB MNT. LODGE - HWY. 175
>
> **THE NERVES**
>
> WITH A BEAT!
>
> UP FROM THE CITY - FIVE NITES ONLY
>
> SUN. AUG. 10 - FRI. AUG. 15

(TOP): ORIGINAL FLYERS FOR GOLDEN GATE PARK SHOW, AND COBB MTN LODGE RESIDENCY, CIRCA 1975. (BELOW): PAUL COLLINS AT THE NERVES SHOW AT GOLDEN GATE PARK, SEPTEMBER 1975. *courtesy of Paul Collins' Archives*

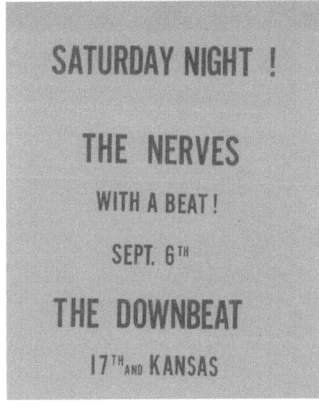

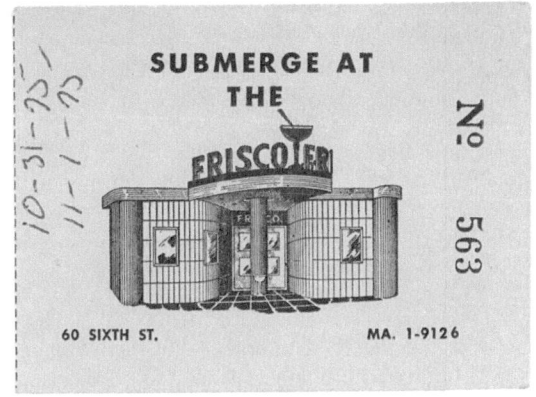

(TOP): MARCI MARKS, SAN FRANCISCO, 1975.
(LOWER LEFT): ORIGINAL FLYER FOR THE NERVES AT THE DOWNBEAT, 1975.
(LOWER RIGHT): FRISCO-DISCO TICKET STUB FROM THE NERVES LIVE RESIDENCY,
OCTOBER 1975. *courtesy of Paul Collins' Archives*

Jack, Peter, and I moved our operation to Folsom Street. We found a building with six apartments and a large basement for the extravagant sum of $600 a month. This began our foray into the world of real estate. In order to keep our rents down, we rented out three of the apartments at a slightly inflated price.

Once we were done fixing the place up, we continued rehearsing non-stop. Rehearsals became more insane. We decided to start sitting in a completely blacked-out room. We would try to keep time to the orange blinking light of a metronome set at top speed.

On Folsom, instead of a crazy lady throwing plates, we had an irate neighbor who gave me a black eye. My drumming had ruined a birthday cake his wife was making. The shit just wouldn't stop!

Folsom Street was where I met Marci Marks, a five-foot tall redhead bombshell. Marci became one of our tenants, and we began dating. She was a stripper at The Victoria Theater in the Tenderloin. It was the last real burlesque house in San Francisco, and perhaps in all of America. Marci would strut on stage in a top hat, long pink boa, a silver sparkle top, black mini skirt, and red-sparkle high heel shoes. She would proceed to strip down to her pasties and a G-string.

Marci even got me a gig playing drums in the orchestra pit, with her buddy Doug, the organist. Playing drums and looking up at girls taking their clothes off was something else. I got canned when the owner decided to use tapes instead of live music, something that was happening all over the place.

Then the Nerves got a break: a residency at The Frisco Disco. It was once a very elegant nightclub, but now it was a dive off of Market Street. You could see the remnants of its glory days in the marble entrance, with 'Frisco Disco' written out in copper inlay. The patrons consisted of drunks, sailors, lowlifes, and a few out-of-work Native Americans.

The barkeep was a spitting image of Sonny Bono, complete with matching white pants and patent leather shoes. He fancied himself a drummer, and on some nights he would sit in for me, while I would tend bar. I was surprised when I'd give the bums a break, pour double and triple shots, and they wouldn't touch the drinks. They wanted it just the way they always got it – nothing more, nothing less.

Every night, the owner of the Frisco Disco sat at one end of the bar, and his cheap blonde floozy of a girlfriend at the other end. Invariably, some poor misguided soul would try to buy her a drink and chat her up. That's when the fireworks would begin. The owner would jump up, draw the pistol he always carried, and fire a couple of shots into the ceiling, threatening to kill them both. Everyone would run for cover but the floozy, who would just sit there sipping on her drink, looking at herself in the mirror. This place was so bad, we couldn't get bums on Market Street to come in, even with free drink tickets.

The NERVES original lineup performing on the
Joe Bavaresco TV show, circa 1975.
courtesy of Paul Collins' Archives

Another place we played was The Downbeat, out in the flats on Kansas Street. It was a rough neighborhood. The owner Jimmy ran it like it was his own little kingdom. He would tell me stuff like, "Paul, your soundman is like the fourth member of your band. If you don't have a good one, you're going to sound like shit!" Or this one, which is actually pretty true:

"Just make sure you have tight beginnings and endings. Then people will love you. No one gives a shit about what happens in the middle of the song!"

The Downbeat had one rule: when a fight breaks out, the band has to keep playing. There were a lot of fights, and we played through them all. Our last night there was one of the worst. A guy came in around last call and decided to nurse a drink. The bartender told him it's time to go, and the guy said, "I paid for this drink and now I'm gonna drink it!" That's all the encouragement Jimmy needed. Before you knew it, the guy was chained to a post, and Jimmy and his two goons were beating him within an inch of his life. The guy's face was covered in blood, and I thought they were going to kill him. Jimmy was screaming at us to play, but we had already packed our shit up. We left and never came back.

In late 1975, on the way to one of our Officer's Club gigs, I remember Jack, Peter and I telling Pat Stangl that we had worked up a version of the *Batman* theme. We had changed the lyric to "Mothra," the monster from the *Godzilla* movies.

"*Mothra! Na-na-na-na-na-na-na-na... Mothra!*"

Pat looked at us and said, "You guys are fuckin' nuts." That was it. He didn't want to do it anymore. Pat was a very accomplished guitar player, but Jack said:

"It's no big deal, Pat and I have been through this many times. This is going to be great. We don't want to have guitar solos in all our songs. We want to streamline them and be more economical." And that's what happened.

The bass and drums became the real motor of The Nerves sound. Jack has a very unusual style of guitar playing. It is just so perfect, with very unusual fingerings, chord positions, and not your typical rock guitar stuff. It just sounds great. Rickenbacker single cutaways have such a beautiful full sound.

We were all set. Peter Case, Jack Lee, and Paul Collins: The Nerves (as the world knows us) were born. This was the only real band I'd ever be in. We did it all. Nothing has happened to me since, that didn't happen in The Nerves.

USO

UNITED SERVICE ORGANIZATIONS, INC.

September 7, 1975

Oakland USO Center
518 - 17th Street
Oakland, California 94612

Mr. Paul Collins
"The Nerves"
568 Folsom Street #4
San Francisco, California

Dear Paul:

On behalf of the servicemen and volunteers at the Oakland USO, I would like to thank you and the members of the band "The Nerves" for your great entertainment on Friday, September 5th. The dance was a great success due to your terrific enthusiasium and talent. Everyone I have spoken with about the dance thought the band had a great beat and hoped you would come back soon.

As a follow up to our conversation concerning paying jobs in the Bay Area I have listed below the military clubs on base that use live entertainment. You will have to contact the manager of each club and make further arrangements with him. Enclosed also is an article taken from the Carrier, a military newspaper, with the line up of club entertainment.

Many thanks again for donating your time and talents to the USO, I am sure we will be incontact with you to arrange a future playing date.

Sincerely,

Barbara Mellin

(Mrs.) Barbara Mellin
Director

Encl: 2

USO MEMBER ORGANIZATIONS
YOUNG MEN'S CHRISTIAN ASSOCIATIONS • NATIONAL CATHOLIC COMMUNITY SERVICE • NATIONAL JEWISH WELFARE BOARD
YOUNG WOMEN'S CHRISTIAN ASSOCIATION • THE SALVATION ARMY • TRAVELERS AID ASSOCIATION OF AMERICA
USO IS SUPPORTED PRIMARILY THROUGH UNITED FUNDS AND COMMUNITY CHESTS

LETTER OF APPRECIATION FROM THE USO FOR THE NERVES LIVE PERFORMANCES, SEPTEMBER, 1975.
courtesy of Paul Collins' Archives

THE NERVES ORIGINAL LINEUP (L TO R):
PAUL COLLINS, PAT STANGL, PETER CASE, AND JACK LEE, CIRCA 1975.
courtesy of Paul Collins' Archives

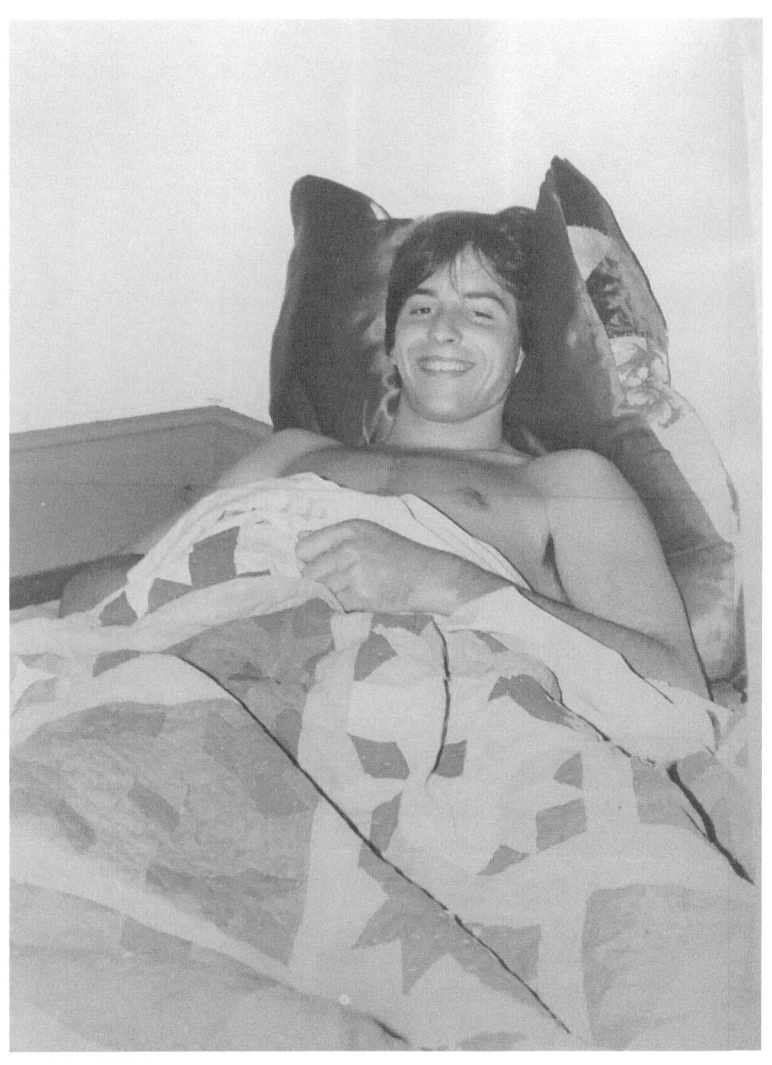

PAUL COLLINS, FOLSOM STREET, SAN FRANCISCO, CIRCA 1975.
courtesy of Paul Collins' Archives

THE NERVES ORIGINAL LINEUP (THIS PAGE L TO R):
JACK LEE, PETER CASE, PAUL COLLINS, AND PAT STANGL, CIRCA 1975.
courtesy of Paul Collins' Archives

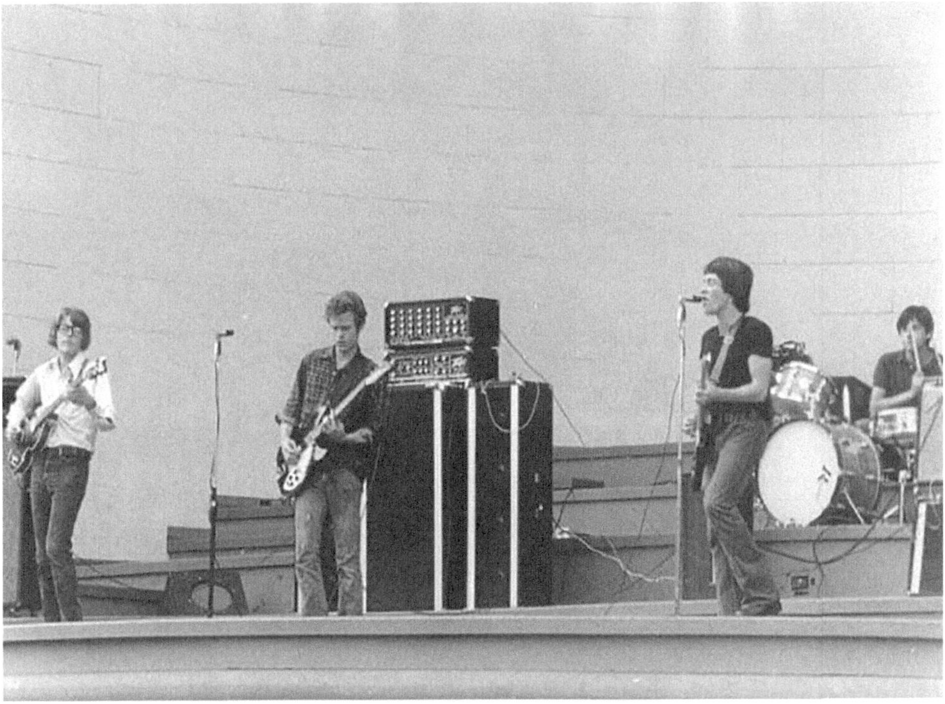

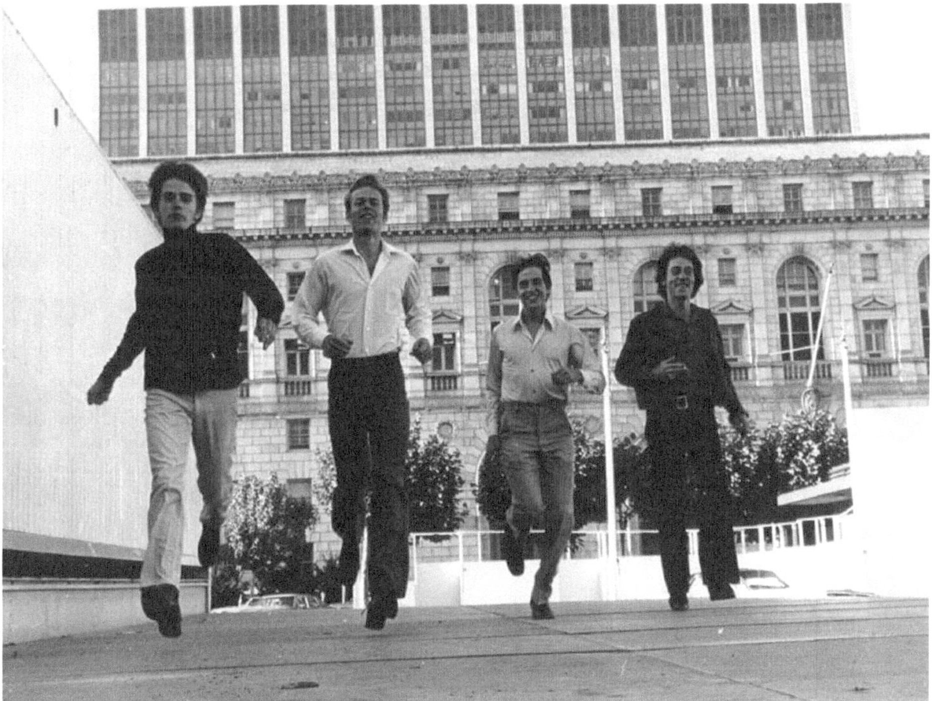

THE NERVES

THE NERVES THREE-PIECE LINEUP, (L TO R):
JACK LEE, PAUL COLLINS, AND PETER CASE, CIRCA 1976.
courtesy of Paul Collins' Archives

CHAPTER SIX:
San Francisco

In those heady days, in the barren landscape of San Francisco, we lived in a complete vacuum. We saw no one, knew no one, and became completely immersed in our fantasy world. It's safe to say we lost touch with reality.

We were so desperate to play that we loaded our gear into Peter's friend Danny's Buick Super 8 with the back seat ripped out. We drove over to The Omni Night Club in Haight-Ashbury. We'd play unannounced, certain all would be forgiven once they heard us. No one said a word as we set up in front of six drunks, and a bartender who sat there reading his paper.

We suddenly started playing Jack's song "Are You Famous?" very loudly. The drunks fell off their bar stools and ran for the door. The bartender ran to the front of the stage waving his arms.

"What the fuck do you guys think you are doing? Get the fuck out of here before I call the cops, Jesus fucking Christ!"

Even Danny was pissed off, saying "If you had told me this, I wouldn't have wasted my gas driving you guys here!"

Peter said, "That's why we didn't tell you!" I was heartbroken. We didn't even get to play one song all the way through.

In 1976, the world, and San Francisco in particular, wasn't ready for The Nerves. We were being thrown out of every place we played, but the more it happened, the more we became convinced of our greatness.

Every week, we lived for the Arts and Entertainment section (called the pink section) of the *San Francisco Chronicle*. I would read it cover to cover, and try to find places where The Nerves could play. In April of 1976, we began gigging at a club called The Longbranch, in Berkeley. In the newspaper, and on a Longbranch flyer, I kept seeing this name... *Eddie Money.*

Somehow I got Eddie's phone number. I figured I'd see if we could get a gig opening up for him. "Hey man, I've got this band The Nerves. We'd like to play with you!" Eddie said "Okay man, why don't you come on over to the house, and I'll see what we can do!"

I never really went outside of San Francisco, and he lived in Oakland. I remember it was a big deal taking the BART route and finding his house. It was scary. Eddie was maybe five or six years older than me, but he had his own place – a cool pad. He said "Come on in, man!"

When Eddie found out that we were both from New York, we just instantly bonded. He said, "You've got to be really careful out here! These guys will eat you up. It is really cutthroat, so I'm going to help you out, man... us New Yorkers will stick together!"

He had a good following, and he got us some gigs opening up for him. People were like, "You know Eddie? Who the fuck are you guys?" On May 13th, my birthday, we opened up for him at The West Dakota Club in Berkeley.

The worst gig we did with Eddie was someplace way out in the East Bay. We didn't have a vehicle yet, so we got in Eddie's equipment van, an old milk truck painted green. We arrived with the roadies, did the first set, and the owner threw us out. He was screaming at Eddie. "Where the fuck did you get these guys? They don't play music! They are fucking horrible!"

Eddie said, "No they're not, man. They're great! They've got good songs."

"I don't give a fuck. They're driving people out of the club. They can't play another set!"

This guy was so incensed by us, not only couldn't we play the second set, *he wouldn't allow us back in the club*. We were 86'd. We spent three hours in the parking lot, waiting for Eddie to finish his show, so we could get a ride home. I didn't hold it against Eddie. He was trying to help us, but people just didn't get it, so we kind of drifted apart.

We were broke, disgusted, and not going to give up, so we came up with one of our best money making ideas ever: *The Dance Machine*. If people didn't want original music, we decided to give them what they wanted. The Dance Machine was a fictitious group we created. We would just call up the local San Francisco Musicians Union, and

(NEXT PAGE TOP): FLYER FOR THE NERVES SUPPORT SLOT FOR EDDIE MONEY, 1976.
(NEXT PAGE BOTTOM): THE NERVES CIRCA 1976, (L TO R): PAUL, JACK, AND PETER.
courtesy of Paul Collins' Archives

THURS MAY 13
THE WEST DAKOTA CLUB
THURS MAY 13
EDDIE MONEY
& THE NERVES
1505 San Pablo Ave. near Cedar St
CALL: 526-0950

find the band members we needed. We would make one of them the leader, and tell them where the gig was. We didn't even need to show up!

We made about six hundred flyers, and sent them to high schools all over The Bay Area. The deal went something like this: For $600 bucks you could have a six piece band, for $500 a five piece, all the way on down to $300 for a three piece. The Dance Machine would play your favorite tunes, all *Top 40* hits. It worked like a charm. Some nights we'd have three or four bands out playing, and money started rolling in. Unfortunately, the union eventually called, and we closed the operation down in fear of legal action.

In August of 1976, we were rehearsing in the basement. Somehow, we found out that a band from New York was playing at Savoy Tivoli in San Francisco. We called the club and the doorman said "Yeah, they're doing their last song now."

"Please, please, will you hold up the phone so we can hear them? Please?"

That's when we heard The Ramones.

We crowded around the phone. Jack and Peter were freaking out.

"They're playing eighth notes! They're staying on the fucking D chord; I don't believe it!"

We had never heard anyone play like that before, and were blown away. With long hair, leather jackets, t-shirts, torn jeans, and sneakers, The Ramones defined cool with a look that was all their own. It wasn't what we were going for, but we did want an image, something clean and classic, like the sound we were going for.

Jack knew that our days in San Francisco were almost over, and we had to do something big. We were in the basement making tacos on a hot plate, when Jack laid it on us. We needed suits, and not just any suits. No way. We needed three-piece custom-tailored Yves Saint Laurent (YSL) suits.

"Where the fuck are we going to get three-piece suits?" I asked.

"Don't worry" said Jack, "I've got it all figured out." This was Jack's standard reply to everything, which meant we would argue about it for three days and then come up with a plan.

Peter's response was a flat out 'no.' There was no fucking way he was going to wear a suit. Well he did, and we all did. On October 1st 1976, we booked a promo photo session wearing our brand new suits. Unfortunately, the suits didn't make people warm up to us. In fact, it shocked the shit out of people and created a lot of controversy. The most common response was "Where the fuck did you get those suits?" It did

(ABOVE):
JACK LEE WITH THE NERVES
IN TORONTO, MAY 1977.
photo courtesy of Ralph Alfonso.

(RIGHT):
'THE DANCE MACHINE' FLYER
DISTRIBUTED TO HIGH SCHOOLS
AROUND LA, CIRCA 1976.

courtesy of Paul Collins' Archives

THE DANCE MACHINE

GET DOWN & BOOGIE   DANCE TO THE LATEST HITS
THE DANCE MACHINE   PLAYS THAT FUNKY MUSIC
BY THE OHIO PLAYERS EARTH WIND & FIRE AWB
DISCO WILD CHERRY HALL & OATES   SYLVERS
KC & THE SUNSHINE BAND   BT EXPRESS   ROCK
FRAMTON   FLEETWOOD MAC   ELTON   WINGS
BOZ SCAGGS   STARSHIP   DOOBIE BROS   ZZ TOP
BTO   CHICAGO   TOWER OF POWER   PLUS TOP40

Make your next gig a success at a price you can afford. For further info call (415) 543-7655.

Straight Bill of Lading — Short Form

O·N·C MOTOR FREIGHT SYSTEM
WASHINGTON OREGON CALIFORNIA NEVADA BRITISH COLUMBIA

Original — Not Negotiable ☐ 483 9570 Memorandum ☐
Shipping Order — must be legibly filled in, in Ink, in Indelible Pencil, or in Carbon and retained by the Agent.

Shipper's No. _____
Carrier's No. _____

SHIPPER: WAKEFIELD MFG., INC.
STREET & CITY: 1745 W. LINDEN   PHOENIX   ARIZONA   85005
DATE SHIPPED: 1-10-76

CONSIGNED TO: THE NERVES COMPANY c/o PAUL COLLINS & JACK LEE
DESTINATION STREET CITY & STATE: 568 FOLSOM STREET #4   SAN FRANCISCO   CALIFORNIA

CONSIGNEE CHECK OK _____
C.O.D. AMT. $ _____

C.O.D. Charges to be paid by Consignee ☐ Shipper ☐ remit to: _____

No. Packages	Kind of Packages, Description of Articles, Special Marks, and Exceptions	*Weight (Subject to Correction)	Class or Rate	Check Column
6	CTNS: UNBREAKABLE PHONOGRAPH RECORDS	211#		

TO BE PREPAID

WAKEFIELD MANUFACTURING, INC. CUSTOM RECORD PRESSING   P O BOX 6037 PHOENIX, ARIZONA 85005

DATE APR 20 77   **INVOICE NO.** 009267
SHIP TO: PAUL COLLINS

SOLD TO: PAUL COLLINS & JACK LEE
THE NERVES
568 FOLSOM ST #4
SAN FRANCISCO, CA 94105

OUR ORDER #	YOUR ORDER #	TERMS	DATE SHIPPED	SHIPPED VIA	PPD OR COLL
29527	PHONE	1\2 DOWN BAL COD	4-20-77	UPS	X

QUANTITY ORDERED	QUANTITY SHIPPED	SIZE-RPM	DESCRIPTION	PRICE	AMOUNT
	2		MOTHERS THE NERVES		

SUBTOTAL .00
SHIPPING & HDLG 1.68
TOTAL 1.68

THIS INVOICE 1.68
LESS COD AMT 1.68
BALANCE DUE .00

THE NERVES

(PREVIOUS PAGE): PAPERWORK FROM THE NERVES EP PRESSING.
(ABOVE): THE NERVES LANDMARK SELF-RELEASED DEBUT 7" EP, NOVEMBER 1976.
courtesy of Paul Collins' Archives

conform to the age-old adage in show business: *get the people talking about you.*

We also decided to make our own DIY (do it yourself) record. Our EP would be the same size as a 45 rpm, but instead of the customary two songs, it would have four. We estimated that all we needed to record and press two thousand copies of our EP was $2,000. We put on our three piece suits and convinced a very young banker that we needed to expand our business. He believed us, and thanks to the Dance Machine, we were able to get a loan. We even had enough money left over to buy a car – 'The Mothership,' a black 1969 Ford LTD station wagon with a 432-cubic-inch engine. It was one big gas-guzzling, money-sucking, smoke-belching tank of a car, but we loved her.

The real studios in town wouldn't let us in the door. We went to the Automatt, a major label studio in San Francisco, and met with Glen Kolotkin, who is still a big time player in the music world. We told him we wanted to make a record, and he immediately asked what label we were on. We said we wanted to do it ourselves. Kolotkin said "you can't do that. Your record won't get on the radio or get in stores, and you are basically wasting your time." It got to the point where he was basically yelling at us, and he literally threw us out of his office. I remember standing outside in our suits, telling him we had the money to do this, and that we would get back to him.

He yelled "Like hell you will! Get the fuck out of here!"

That wasn't going to stop us.

Finally, we found a small recording studio on the outskirts of Chinatown that wanted our business – Kelly Quan's, up on Union Street. I don't know if they had ever recorded rock bands before. On October 14th and 15th of 1976, we recorded The Nerves' one and only EP. It was one of the most thrilling moments of my life. I wish I could remember the name of the engineer, but I guess you could say we produced ourselves. We finally did it! I loved everything about it: the smell, the sound padding (baffles) on the walls, and the vocal booth. It was a dream come true sitting in the control room, listening to Peter cut his vocals for "When You Find Out." The engineer told Peter:

"Make love to the mic! When I say we are rolling, we are rolling!"

Jack loved "Working Too Hard," the first song I wrote for The Nerves. He wanted it to start with a distinctive sound, a ball peen hammer striking the metal base of a microphone stand. It sounded great with a touch of reverb, classic, exactly what we wanted. When we were mixing the record and listening to the final playback, the hammer was gone. We screamed "What happened, where is it?" The engineer looked at us and said "Oh, that? I thought it was just for the count off. It's over there in the garbage can." So we fished the ¼ inch piece of recording tape out of the garbage, and the engineer spliced it back on.

Oh, a side note: the bank that lent us the money to cut the record was called Yerba Buena, which means "good grass" in Spanish. Fitting, because as soon as we finished recording the EP, we celebrated by buying and smoking an entire ounce of weed, and seeing *The Exorcist* three times in a row. That was San Francisco in the '70s for you. For a dollar you could stay all day, have all the popcorn you wanted, and smoke cigarettes and pot in movie theatres.

We mastered the record at CBS studios on October 17th, and sent the recordings off for pressing. On November 11th, the Wakefield Manufacturing pressing plant from Phoenix, Arizona shipped us 2,000 copies of The Nerves debut EP. When we finally got the records, we stuffed them into the picture sleeves, and they were ready.

We placed the record on consignment in local stores, including Phonograph Records, a store with branches in Sunnyvale, and Redwood City, CA. Greg Shaw of Bomp Records (and magazine) got a hold of one, wrote us a letter praising the EP, and offered to distribute our independent release. Greg was a musicologist and knew everything that was happening on the national level. He loved this music and was a real champion in an environment where no one else was.

We heard about a radio station in town, where the all-night DJ would play your record if you stopped by. I'd never been to a radio station before. In the middle of the night, from outside the lit-up sound booth, we watched the DJ spin discs and pre-recorded cartridge tapes. His microphone was on a metal arm that he could move around as he worked. The big red 'On The Air' sign was lit and glowing. It was so exciting! At the first commercial break he came out, said 'hi,' and grabbed our new 45. I was tingling as he announced our record:

> *"Ok nightbirds, you are in for a real treat! The Nerves just stopped by to bring yours truly their new record! Hot off the presses, this is the debut performance of 'Working Too Hard' by The Nerves!"*

I knew this was our moment. The Nerves were about to jump into the big time and make rock 'n' roll history! Then something went wrong, horribly wrong. The DJ was alone in his soundproof room, playing our 45 at 33 rpm! It sounded like a dirge. We waved frantically to get his attention, but he was reading a magazine and not looking up. It was useless. We were over and done with now. He slipped the record out the door to us. We and our brush with radio fame were gone into the night. There was no consoling me. Just like that, the dream slipped out of my grasp. With The Nerves, it often felt like that. We would be so close, but so far away.

Jack had another great idea to promote the record: "*Let's take out an ad in* Rolling Stone*!*" Back then, there weren't many music magazines to speak of, and *Rolling Stone* was definitely the biggest. For $78.00, we took out a very small 1" x 1" ad with a photo of the 45.

Rock Collectors:

THE NERVES' MAXI-SINGLE everybody has been looking for.

Send M.O. for $2 + 25¢ postage to:

Records c/o Paul Collins

568 Folsom

San Francisco, CA 94105

Surprisingly, when the ad finally appeared in early 1977, we ended up getting orders from all over the country. Music people like Alan Betrock from *New York Rocker*, and Gene Scullati from Warner Brothers Records ordered copies.

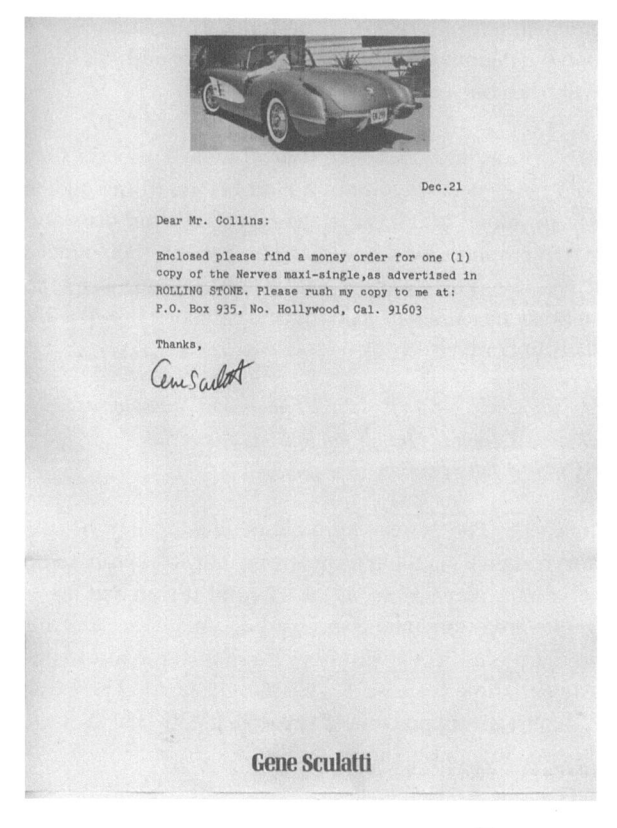

(LEFT):
DIRECT ORDER FOR THE NERVES EP FROM WARNER BROTHERS' GENE SCULATTI.
courtesy of Paul Collins' Archives

Believe it or not, people still buy and pay a lot of money for that record. Back then, no one wanted it. I don't think I ever got what that single really meant to people until much later. I eventually saw that people passionately remembered, wanted, and collected this music.

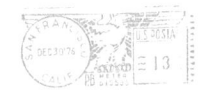

(ABOVE): THE NERVES ADVERTISEMENT FOR THEIR DEBUT EP IN ROLLING STONE MAGAZINE, DECMBER 1976.

(NEXT PAGE SPREAD): LONGBRANCH SCHEDULE, APRIL 1976.
courtesy of Paul Collins' Archives

Doors Open 8:30pm Music Begins 9:30pm Men 21 yrs. Women 18 yrs.		THE LONGBR[ANCH] 2504 SAN PAB[LO]		
SUNDAY	MONDAY	TUESDAY	WEDNESDAY	THURS[DAY]
COMING IN MAY — SPECIAL RETURN ENGAGEMENT: CLIFTON CHENIER				[with] A.S. BAN[D]
Stoneground and The Shakers [4]	Bump and Grind [5]	Carrie Nation with Back Road [6]	Nimbus / Stallion [7]	Kat M. Don[ald] and San Fra[ncisco]
Harvey Mandel with Stallion [11]	TO BE ANNOUNCED	Nerves and Frisco Nickel [13]	Spoons / razmataz [14]	Edd[ie] Mon[ey] with Mil[l] H[ill] [15]
Nick Gravenites [18]		Nerves along with Frisco Nickel [20]	Back Road and Nimbus [21]	Char[lie] Musselw[hite] and Grays[on]
The Moonlighters and Stallion [25]		Carrie Nation [27]	Little Roger and The Runners [28]	Edd[ie] Mon[ey] with Mill [H]...

ICH 848-9696
AVE., BERK.

What's goin On? Join our mailing list by sending us a card with name, address & zip.

APRIL 1976

FRIDAY

- EDDIE MONEY $ AND BACK ROAD — 2
- MILE HI AND SASSY — 9
- THE SHAKERS and Queen Ida Bon Ton Zydeco Band — 16
- $ EDDIE MONEY $ with R.S.B. BAND — 23
- THE SHAKERS and David LaFlamme — 30

SATURDAY

- Original Haze with JERRY MILLER, CORNY BUMPUS, ALEXIS — 3
- THE METERS exclusive — final bay area performance!!! — 10
- CARRIE NATION along with BACK ROAD — 17
- GRAYSON ST. AND HOT KNIVES — 24
- TICKETS AVAILABLE AT ALL BASS OUTLETS

THE NERVES, 1977.
photo courtesy of Gary Green

CHAPTER SEVEN:
Los Angeles

In late 1976, San Francisco was really starting to kill us, *and it almost did.*

All three of us were like brothers, and we did everything together, including collecting the rent. Our building was a stone's throw away from the bus terminal, so our tenants were a collection of transients and down-and-outers. One night we were in good spirits and standing in the darkened hallway. Jack was clowning around, making goofy faces, and he knocked on Mr. Wilson's door. Unbeknownst to us, Mr. Wilson was taking medication for mental problems he had dating back to World War II.

"Who's knocking at my door at this hour? You boys already collected the rent! If you want the rent, then you're going to have to take the rent!"

Mr. Wilson opened his door and stabbed Jack with a large kitchen knife. Jack fell into my arms with the knife still stuck in his chest. Blood was everywhere. Mr. Wilson pushed past us screaming, fleeing down the stairs and into the night. I was sure Jack was going to die right there. We dragged him downstairs and laid him on the hood of our station wagon. Peter ran to call the police. Since we were right by the bus terminal, undercover cops swarmed the place in seconds. Jack was whisked away by an ambulance and survived. It was a close call.

After Jack fully recovered, we packed up and left San Francisco. We decided to move to Los Angeles, and swore never to return. We rented out all the apartments, taking the first and last month deposits with us. We left the actual owner high and dry. The tenants all stood in front of the house waving goodbye. We pulled out in our station wagon loaded to the gills with everything we owned. I ran into some of these folks later at shows. No one seemed to hold a grudge.

Los Angeles was, and still is, the entertainment capital of the world. When we pulled in that first night on January 1st, 1977, we were sure this time things would be different. The Capitol Records building loomed over the exit we took to the Vine Street Lodge, where we had booked a room. Our first order of business was going to

The Starwood, one of LA's hottest night clubs.

As we drove into the parking lot, we thought we had died and gone to heaven. It had been ages since we had seen so many good looking chicks. LA was not into the hippy look at all. These babes were dressed to the nines – in miniskirts with fishnet stockings, halter tops, skin-tight jeans, and baby tees. They had high heels, low heels, leather boots, or were just plain barefoot. These girls were dressed to kill.

We got out of the car dressed in our suits. A young man approached us, wearing funny glasses and a jumpsuit. "Hi, I'm Larry Lazer, and you must be The Nerves!" He got us in for free, took us under his wing, and introduced us to all the LA royalty who hung out at The Starwood every night. This was the big time. *This was where it all happened.*

The first person he introduced us to was Rodney Bingenheimer, the king of LA punk radio. He was sitting at his booth with a bevy of beautiful babes. We stood there like farm boys, wide-eyed in amazement. Rodney said "Oh, 'Hanging On The Telephone!' I played it the other day on *Rodney On The Roq*. It sounds great! You should come by the studio sometime."

The next person we met was famed record producer, songwriter, musician, and music industry impresario Kim Fowley – a man who could get you a record deal in his sleep. That night, I actually overheard him tell some young blonde, "Come home with me baby, I invented the word *lllllove*!"

We were starved for attention, or any kind of scene that involved young people with a passion for rock 'n' roll. Why did we wait so long to move here? Back at the hotel, I laid my head down on the pillow and thought it wouldn't be long before The Nerves were famous. As W.C. Fields liked to say, "There's a sucker born every minute."

The LA scene was actually stifling. If we thought San Francisco was bad, LA was worse. San Francisco is kind of arty, so the suits were kind of cute. In LA they didn't have time for that kind of shit. We rarely got a chance to play. "Get the fuck out of here, and don't come back until you have a record deal."

We were broke and hungry, so we started donating blood, five bucks a bag. One time Peter fainted; lack of food will do that to you. The nurse got pissed off and threw us out. Now we couldn't even give blood. We would just hang around day after day with nothing to do, and nowhere to go. All the music stores knew us and wouldn't let us in. Even Tower Records on Sunset banned us from hanging around.

Thankfully, my girlfriend Marci Marks followed me to LA and got a place. I moved in with her. Compared to San Francisco, the stripping scene was sleazy and far from glamorous. Some nights, Marci would come home from work filled with hatred for all men. "You are all such fucking pigs!" We would get into a fight and she would chase me around the bed. I would let her catch me and then we would fuck.

FLYER FOR THE NERVES LOS ANGELES LIVE DEBUT AT THEIR VERY OWN DIY VENUE, THE HOLLYWOOD PUNK PALACE CIRCA MARCH 1977.
courtesy of Paul Collins' Archives

Within two to three weeks of us getting to town, we stopped by Kim Fowley's office. He was all business, and said something to the effect of, "Look, I'm going to give you a deal, a 30 to 90 day contract. Within that period I will get you a record deal, but I take 50 percent of the publishing." Whatever he wanted, Jack said, 'No fucking way,' and that was it. Obviously Jack was very smart, because Jack's publishing for "Hanging On The Telephone" subsequently turned into a multi-million dollar affair when Blondie covered it a little less than two years later.

I don't know what Fowley said to the powers that be after that meeting, but I felt like we got blacklisted. We were never able to get anywhere in LA after that. Of course, I'm not really sure, and now that Fowley's passed away, I will never be sure. Maybe Rodney could shed some light on it? There were so many things that it could have been. There were so many bands back then that couldn't get anywhere. Either way, this negative situation resulted in one of The Nerves' greatest ideas ever.

We decided to start our own club, and this was a lot easier than you'd think. All we needed to do was rent a hall for a night, and print up some handbills. It was a stroke of genius, and a forerunner to the whole "pop-up" club movement that is happening all over the world now. Our first pop-up gig was on March 25th, 1977, and we called it 'The Hollywood Punk Palace.' The lineup was The Nerves, Kid, and Zolar X, with host KROQ's Rodney Bingenheimer. It was held in a movie studio basement, on the corner of Sunset and Gower.

We did a lot of our rehearsals in a place called Skip Saylor's Studios, where we were running into another band having trouble finding a gig – punk rock legends The Weirdos. When rehearsing, they would line up in a straight line, legs apart, with guitars and no drums. They were tight and had great songs. When The Nerves heard them, I said "Man, we are about to book another show. You should just play, and fuck the fact that you don't have a drummer!"

The second pop-up event was held was on April 2nd, 1977, and we called this one the 'Punk Rock Invasion.' It was at the biggest, most stuck-up rehearsal hall in LA, aptly called S.I.R. (Studio Instrument Rentals). They are still around today. Go see for yourself, and tell them I sent you. The room we rented was the biggest they had, normally used for big time/jerk-off record label showcases. The studio attendant must have known this wasn't the case, by the looks of us. He said he'd keep an eye on us, and throw us out at the first sign of shenanigans.

On the night of the show, we knew we'd need all of our cunning and skill to pull this off. We were becoming experts in this kind of shit, and all the assholes in Hollywood couldn't stop us. To avoid disclosure, Peter and I stood on the opposite corner of S.I.R, and created an imaginary box office. It wouldn't be hard for us to discern who was going to the show – punk rockers who wouldn't object to forking over five bucks to get in.

POSTER FOR THE NERVES AT THE MASQUE WITH AVENGERS, THE ZEROS, SHOCK, AND F-WORD, CIRCA 1977.
courtesy of Paul Collins' Archives

The second and more critical part of our plan required the skills of a specialist. In order to keep the asshole studio attendant occupied and out of the way, we employed the services of our secret weapon: Suzy Headbanger. Suzy was a nice girl, and a groupie who became nationally famous for giving blow jobs to rock stars. We told her what we needed, and she was glad to oblige. We saw neither hide nor hair of the studio attendant all evening.

The lineup was us, The Weirdos, The Zippers, Short Eyes, and The Dils. I remember the Dils, because their original singer Jeff Scott broke the mic. One of the bands stuck a mic up their ass! It was completely fucked up, and then no one wanted to use the mic anymore.

When it was all over and time for me to pay Suzy Headbanger, she undid my belt, pulled down my zipper and gave me my first real blow job. I was scared but it felt good.

Around this time, Peter tried to book The Whisky but Elmer Valentine said no. They would not book 'punk rock.' So on April 16th, 1977, with the last of our money, we held our final pop-up gig at The Orpheum. It was a small theater across from Tower Records, where plays were normally held. The bill was The Nerves, The Zippers, The Zeros, and the debut performance of The Germs, who were added to the bill at the last minute.

We thought we were getting pretty good at this, so we hired two guys as roadies. The Germs were playing, and Darby Crash was going berserk, screaming and yelling. Suddenly, our two roadies ran onstage and started throwing The Germs' gear offstage. They chucked it off to the side, starting with the bass drum. Of course, The Germs ran offstage horrified. They were just kids, you know?

The roadies grabbed the mic and said the next band would be on shortly. We were standing in the back going "what the fuck?" We hired these guys to help things go smoothly, and now they were taking things into their own hands! Then, the roadies told us to come into the office. They were bigger than me, and I was scared. One guy said, "I don't care if any of these bands get paid. The roadies always get paid. Where's our fuckin' money? *We want it now!*"

I said, "Here it is. Can you guys just split and we will take it from here?"

Then, when we were running the box office, the bookers from The Whisky sent some of their people. They said, "Oh, Marshall Berle sent us down from the Whisky. We want to check out the show."

"Fine, five bucks."

"Oh, no man, we're from the Whisky. We don't need to pay to get in!"

"The fuckin' hell you don't need to pay! We can't play the Whisky, so we don't give a fuck about The Whisky! It's five bucks, or get the fuck out of here!"

It got really ugly, but right after that, the scene exploded. Because of these shows The Nerves booked, The Whisky and The Starwood started booking punk, Brendan Mullen opened The Masque, and the rest is history.

While The Hollywood Punk Palace was one of the few ideas we had that actually worked, the problem was other groups got a lot more attention than us. Soon, it was just another idea that got us nowhere. We were flat broke again, and it was time to do something quick.

Jack heard about the record swap meet, a monthly event that took place in the Capitol Records parking lot. Word had it, folks came from all over the country, and it was a good spot to "get it going on." We decided to go for broke, and bring everything we had to sell: our EPs, the original art for the 45, and even the master tapes. Jack had me contact Wakefield Manufacturing. On April 20th, 1977, they shipped us the metal 'mother plates' used to manufacture our EP. We tried to sell those too. No reasonable offer would be refused.

The swap meet began around 4 AM, and the early morning light was like a movie. People in cool cars from the '50s came rolling in, popping open trunks with speakers, and playing records. Looking all dapper in our three-piece suits, we set up on a little concrete square. We were open for business. By noon we were sweating bullets, not counting on the hard brutal LA sun. We hadn't sold much; the collectors just weren't interested in our wares. I felt like I was melting. Why couldn't we just blow the whole thing off and go back home? That was when I spotted The Screamers.

What the fuck were The Screamers doing at the swap meet? They couldn't possibly be buying records, could they? The Screamers were already one of the top new punk bands in LA. They were 'hot-shit' with the kids, and to me, big time. 'Oh shit, they're heading my way! I wonder what they want?' By now a small crowd had gathered, and the 'main' Screamer walked up. I'm pretty sure it was Tomata DuPlenty, but they all looked and dressed alike.

"I want to buy a copy of your record!"

"Sure man, no charge!"

"No man, I want to pay for it, and could you guys sign it, too... *for me?*"

Wow, this was too much. I called out to Jack and Peter. "Hey guys, come over here and sign a record for The Screamers!"

We signed the record. The young man stepped back and threw it on the

From All Ov
Calif. The Nerves

Normalcy fades into obscurity as insurgents seek deliverance. Abruptly the backbeat returns. Then it all seems so clear. The Nerves are at one with the new wave, yet one wonders if the new wave is ready to embrace them. They all sing and compose, saving individuality for guitars, drums, and bass. Their fifteen song set consumes 28 minutes. And no, they aren't the Ramones.

Enough banter. The Nerves are bundled together in San Francisco, drawn together by a cryptic notice on a music store billboard some eighteen months ago. From May-July '76, the band spent forty hours in a recording studio acting as conceptualists, musicians, producers, vocalists, et al. The result: a stunning EP, vital, effervescent and impelling. Each individual Nerve is a fan of AM pop-rock, and it shows. Two of the songs, "When You Find Out," and "Working Too Hard" conjure up early echoes of the Beatles. Perhaps too much so? The band replies, "If we tried, we couldn't be the Beatles, so why even try? We don't. It's just a convenient label, like Punk-Rock. Look, the mechanics are the same — melodies, vocals, basic instrumentation — it's not a slight. If we're gonna be compared with anyone, it might as well be the Beatles. The Beatles started out improvising on their roots, and it's only natural that we do the same."

Recording was a compromise the first time around, everyone in the band concedes. "We listened alot, and then chose a middle line. We wanted something good, clean and not sloppy. We aimed for a true sound, and a relatively total representation of each song. We think we accomplished most of these goals, although we're not totally satisfied." What's particularly refreshing about the Nerves is the fact that they only consider what they're doing now as a starting off point. "We're looking for some professional producer to work with us. We're not trying to be a local band — we're gonna be a national band, with style and energy. We want to have a big sound — the biggest sound around. We wanna make hit records."

Visually, the band is clean-cut, favoring suits "It's not a contrived thing" says drummer Paul Collins, "it just expresses our attitude and tastes. It's just the way we naturally are." The band has been playing around San Francisco for about a year, originally with a keyboard player, and peppering their sets with lots of sixties-based cover material. Guitarist Jack Lee offers, "We stopped doing covers entirely when we realized our originals sounded better than the covers. Since we've become a three-piece, the band is tighter and our sound has crystallized more clearly. People are amazed when they hear what a three-piece can really sound like." Onstage the band usually opens with "Are You Famous," and other group favorites include "Letter To G.," "Stand Back And Take A Good Look," "You Won't Be Happy," and "Will You Come Through," along with the four songs from the EP. "We have 28 finished songs that we're happy with right now," adds Jack.

Hangin' On The Telephone with The Nerves: (L-R): Jack Lee; Peter Case; and Paul Collins.

"Everywhere we went," recalls bassist Peter Case, "people kept telling us 'you can't do this and you can't do that,' but we just kept pushing on. Right now we're all self contained. We own all our equipment, truck, and PA, and we financed our own EP. We worked in a sixteen-track studio in San Francisco, and then mastered the whole thing at CBS. We had delays along the way, so the record wasn't released until December 1976." As to the record itself, my favorites are the two Jack Lee compositions, "Hanging on the Telephone," and "Give Me Some Time." What they may lack in innovative production prowess is certainly overshadowed by the dynamic melodies, subtle musical interplay, and standout vocals. When tracks like these appear, quibbling over something like drum sounds is mere nit-picking. Peter Case's "When You Find Out" is the most Liverpool oriented track, showcasing the Nerves talent for vocal distinction, and Paul Collins' "Working Too Hard" is a concise rocker with a strong chorus.

Soon after the EP was released, the band decided to move their operations to L.A. in an attempt to be closer to the pulsebeat of the music biz. Hopefully the Nerves will attract the attention of major labels, although the band's sights are set on Columbia, because as Paul says, "Columbia is like Coca-Cola. They're everywhere." The band may run up against criticism calling them derivative, but I'm in firm disagreement with that evaluation. The Nerves are going to have their own sound, and it's going to be a hit sound. The band, obviously, feels likewise. "We're not gonna disappear," offers Peter. "We've got staying power" declares Paul. (And yes, they are bored to tears with Peter, Paul and Mary jokes.) Perhaps the attitude of the band was best summed up by Jack when he said, "When the companies call, we'll be ready." The Nerves will be hanging on the telephone alot, because face it, these guys are ready now.

Alan Betrock

The Nerves record is available for $2.25 by mail from: Paul Collins; 7188 Sunset Blvd; Suite 204; Hollywood, Calif. 90046; or in New York at the Golden Disc or Discophile.

ground. He stomped on it with his pointy black boots until the sleeve was ripped, and the record was in little black pieces. The three of us just stood there watching this guy with spiky black hair, a white face, black eyeliner, and a long black trench coat. What the fuck did we ever do him? I don't think anyone knew what to think, and the crowd drifted off in embarrassment.

The guy finished, looked at us and said, "You guys suck!" He walked off and I don't think I ever saw him again. I asked Jack why this happened, and he told me to just forget about it... some things can't be explained.

Everyone in town knew us, but nobody liked us. We were just too against the grain. We single-handedly booked, presented, and spearheaded LA's underground punk movement, but we rubbed everyone the wrong way. Let's face it: the suits didn't help. LA became like a small town where everyone knows your business. In our case, it meant no business, and we were being shut out on all sides. Clubs wouldn't book us, record companies wouldn't talk to us, and bands we helped get started accused us of being shysters.

So here I was at the record swap, depressed and thinking "Man this is getting old, moving to a new town and having to leave again." I'd been doing it all my life, one way or another. I was always on the move and never putting down roots. The big question was, where the fuck could we go now? That was when a smiling handsome young man with a Dutch Boy haircut and a bright paisley shirt walked up and said,

"Hi, I'm Greg Shaw, nice to finally meet you! I'd like to buy 800 copies of your record."

Wow.

Later, The Nerves were at Ben Frank's Diner on Sunset Boulevard. Everyone was there, scattered throughout the restaurant: punk royalty, the chicks that hung out with them, and us sitting off to the side by ourselves. We still *didn't fit in* and didn't have many friends. We knew Billy Shire from The Soap Plant and famed LA pop culture store, Wacko. There was Phast Phreddie, from Back Door Man magazine. Those guys remain our friends to this day.

This was when Jack came up with his last great idea: *Let's do a national tour.*

As usual, Peter accused Jack of smoking too much pot, and I asked how we'd pull it off. We argued about it for three days but came up with a plan. In that respect, we were amazing. Our plans were usually simple, but their success depended

(PREVIOUS PAGE) THE NERVES FEATURE ARTICLE IN *NEW YORK ROCKER* MAGAZINE, BY ALAN BETROCK, CIRCA 1977.
courtesy of Paul Collins' Archives

WHO PUT THE BOMP

THE MAGAZINE FOR ROCK 'N' ROLL FANS

Dec. 29, 1976

Dear Paul,

Gregory Burke at Discovery Books sent me a copy of the Nerves EP because he thought I'd be interested, and I am. It's an excellent record--songs, arrangements, performance, even the sleeve design. I intend to give it a review in BOMP next issue, and also in PRM probably; maybe a few other places. I'd also like to inquire about buying some copies--say 100 to start with, probably several hundred more if/when I get some orders from Europe. I do a lot of exporting of these kind of local 'underground' records to Europe, and sell a lot here as a service to BOMP readers who want to keep up with the latest sounds. I don't know what price you're charging, but if it's within reasonable limits (I generally pay around 65¢, sometimes a bit higher if there are picture covers or other artwork involved) I think I can help you sell quite a few records. Some people try to get away with charging inflated prices for records like these (one group wanted $2.50 a copy wholesale) but they miss the point that the purpose of doing your own record is to get exposure for the group, and the network of dealers that's been growing to handle this stuff, especially in Europe, won't touch it at that price.

Anyway, let me know what your price is, how soon you can send 100 (I'd like to include the record in my January catalog now being prepared) and also let me know if there's going to be any problem if I should suddenly need 500 or so more.

Also, I'd like to know if you have any further tapes, or plans to record any. Where was this one recorded? I'd like to hear demos of any new songs you have; I might be interested in doing something with you guys on the BOMP label at some point, if you haven't got any major label offers by then...

Best regards,

Greg Shaw

P.S. If by some chance you're not familiar with BOMP, it's a rock & roll magazine for rock & roll fans, and you can pick up a copy at Aquarius Records

BOX 7112 BURBANK, CALIF. 91510

The Nerves EP solicitation letter from Greg Shaw at
BOMP! Magazine, December 1976.
courtesy of Paul Collins' Archives

on cooperation from people other than The Nerves. That's something we never got.

This plan was quite simple. We would finally get to play The Starwood in LA, and Mabuhay Gardens in San Francisco. Then our routing would be straight across the middle of the country and back again. There would be no fucking around. I'd contact the clubs, Jack would figure out the expenses, and Peter would take care of mailing promo packets. After smoking a joint, and thinking about it for a few minutes, Jack crunched some numbers. He said we'd need a minimum of $80 a night, a nice round figure, and we didn't have much trouble convincing club owners across the country to agree.

We were nuts, but so fucking what? That was not going to stop us. We would do something no one had even dreamed of attempting – a cross country tour with no manager, no label, and no money.

I think Peter went along with the national tour idea because he didn't think we could actually pull it off. Every time I'd confirm a gig and start jumping up and down, I could see the flicker of fear in Peter's eyes. He was worried that we might actually have to follow through with this insanity.

Peter was skeptical, smart, analytical, and had some semblance of a college education. You couldn't put anything over on him. On the other hand, in his own mind, Jack had already done the tour and was on to other projects. I could see him drifting further and further away. You could tell when talking to him, he kind of looked at you, and then past you. He was a true visionary, but I do think the charm, novelty or excitement of these plans was starting to wear off.

I believe there was an unspoken agreement between Peter and Jack. They kept each other at bay, and wouldn't push each other too hard. I, on the other hand, was the baby of the group. I'm sure they both used this to their own particular advantage. At that point in my life, what I didn't know wouldn't hurt me, *or so I thought*.

I don't think Jack had ever met someone like me. It kind of threw him that I was so trusting and didn't want to take anything from him. I think I became the younger brother he never had. I looked up to Jack and admired him greatly. I think he really enjoyed that.

For an underprivileged kid, Jack could be really nice. He told me his mother had stood on her head all night, to make sure she got pregnant with him. Jack never knew his father and had a tough childhood. Abused and battered, shuffled around in foster homes, he finally wound up in a juvenile detention center. He wasn't bitter, not in the least. He was just going make sure no one ever fucked with him again.

In a weird way, Jack was like the mother and the father in one. One side of him was brutal, vicious, and controlling, and the other side could be gentle, understanding, and encouraging. Jack was the one who inspired me to try and write songs. He had an extremely high standard, and I wanted desperately to achieve it for myself. I learned a lot from him.

Jack was undoubtedly the band leader, but he needed us as much as we needed him.

Since calling clubs all over the country would cost a fortune, I came up with an ingenious plan: I would book the entire tour on one dime. I'm also convinced that I changed AT&T's policy on phone refunds. Here is how it worked:

Me: "Hello operator, how much to call Chicago?"

Operator: "$2.35 for the first three minutes."

Me: "Thank you operator."

Then you hang up and call another operator. "I was just speaking to someone in Chicago and got cut off."

Operator: "I'm sorry sir, how much did you put in?"

Me: "$2.35."

Operator: "I will be glad to reconnect you, thank you for calling AT&T, and have a nice day!"

The only thing was, you had to get all your business done in three minutes or less. As a fast talking New Yorker, it wasn't a problem for me. I don't feel bad, because over the years I've paid astronomical amounts to the phone company.

We were glad to get out of LA. We were relieved to be leaving this city filled with whores, pimps, film stars, rock stars, and managers. There were wannabes, liars, cheaters, hustlers, strippers, punks, dealers, junkies and the one or two nice people that we knew. Fuck LA when you come right down to it. It is a shithole, and it still is today. We refused to let it get us down. We were undaunted, but a good dose of my heart and soul are still stuck to the sidewalks of Sunset Boulevard.

THE NERVES

568 FOLSOM ST.   SAN FRANCISCO, CALIFORNIA 94105

LIVE ENGAGEMENTS
NITE CLUBS: SAN FRANCISCO
LONG BRANCH
WEST DAKODA'S
SAVOY
ROSE & THISTLE

HALLS: SAN FRANCISCO
COW PALACE

TELEVISION APPEARANCES:
SAN FRANCISCO LIVE: JOE BAVARESCO SHOW
CHANNEL 6. SOUNDS OF THE CITY
CHANNEL 3. VIDEO VIBES

RADIO AIR PLAY:
KSAN
KSJO
KIOI
KZAP
KSML
KOME

DISTRIBUTION: THE NERVES MAXI-SINGLE
11 RECORD FACTORY STORES (SAN FRANCISCO TO SACRAMENTO)
RATHER RIPPED RECORDS - BERKELEY
AQUARIUS RECORDS - SAN FRANCISCO
DISCOVERY RECORDS - SAN FRANCISCO

ARTICLES
ROCK & FOLK MAGAZINE, GUITAR CENTER NEWS,
NEW YORK ROCKER, PSYCLONE NEWS PAPER

ENDORSEMENTS:
STEVEN COUNTRY MAN - PRES. RECORD FACTORY
LYNN WIENNER - CBS RECORDS
PAUL STOBBLEBINE - CBS RECORDS
JOEL SELVIN - STAFF WRITER CHRONICLE, SAN FRANCISCO
PHILLIPE GARMIER - STAFF WRITER ROCK & FOLK, EUROPEAN MAGAZINE
BOB McCLAY - KSAN (D.J.)
DIERDRA GENTRY - KSFX (PROGRAM DIRECTOR)
JOE LAIR - KSAN - ADVERTISING
ALAN BETROCK - NEW YORK ROCKER, EDITOR

AREA CODE 415

543-ROCK   'N   543-ROLL

The NERVES one-sheet press kit, circa 1977.
courtesy of Paul Collins' Archives

THE NERVES: Ramones meet Merseybeat

scene. She mentioned the Weirdoes—"If you like the Ramones, you'll love the Weirdoes"— and then came up empty.

I did not get to see the Weirdoes, but there is indeed another band who are, if not punks, a part of the LA scene. Transportation difficulties hampered me not at all when the Nerves came east on their tour to play Max's in May. This band, transplanted from San Francisco, put out an EP (See TP #19) that displayed a light, melodic, Merseyesque approach. Live they threw me for a loop. True, they had the matching Mersey-suits one would expect, but their energy was pure Ramones.

Even with sound problems and superloud volume, the vocals were spot on and the songs distinguishable as solid, enjoyable stuff. In spite of it being the end of a long day, and the crowd being enthused but small, as mid-week crowds are wont to be at 2 AM, the Nerves exuded an infectious energy and refreshing flair for rock 'n' roll at its most basic level. More bands like the Nerves and the Pop! (and, giving them the benefit of the doubt, the Weirdoes) could bring the LA scene into a rock-solid position for contention with NY's.

Nossov, the excellent ex-bass player of the unlikely (let's face it, dumb) monikered Day Old Bread. More news as it happens.

From the depths of Allman/Tucker territory (Atlanta) comes a band positively reeking of Euro-rock influence, the Fans. Led by bass-playing Cuban expatriate Alfredo Villar, the Fans bear comparison to Roxy, Eno, Amon Duul II, early Soft Machine and John Cale (with whom Alfredo has corresponded). Onstage Kevin Dunn, in denim overalls, wrings heavily fuzz-toned screams from his guitar, Russell King whips his drum kit with precise strokes like a mechanical wind-up toy, Michael Green (no relation) sits at his keyboards looking for all the world like a denim-clad Kraftwerker, and Alfredo stands center-stage directing, singing and pumping out a bass bottom.

Their record came out this summer, and while it is not up to expectations (the recording is not the best quality) it does indicate greater things in store. Their version of the Tornadoes' "Telstar" (a pre-Ventures instrumental) is cosmic roller-rink music (make of it what you will; I think it is hilarious and quite enjoyable). "Lonely Girls" and "Ekstasis" are more repre-

THE NERVES FEATURED IN *TROUSER PRESS MAGAZINE* BY JIM GREEN, SEPTEMBER 1977.
courtesy of Paul Collins' Archives

THE BOMP! NEWSLETTER

No. 16   5/9/77

NERVES on the ROAD

LOS ANGELES--A most ambitious undertaking is being attempted by a west coast group called THE NERVES, originally from San Francisco but based for the last few months in L.A. On their own initiative, they've set out on a national tour, hitting every city where there is a 'new-wave' scene, and tying in their appearances with promotions in the local record stores, fanzines/entertainment mags and new-wave oriented radio stations. Although groups from such locales as Cleveland, Washington and Boston have made the trek to New York, this is the first group to attempt to cross the country, entirely on their own with no backing, relying on the underground news network and the awareness of local punk fans around the country to generate sufficient interest to make the tour break even.

    An initial itinerary of more than 20 cities where suitable clubs were located was narrowed down, for logistical reasons, to include a somewhat smaller number of key cities with firm bookings. In most cities contacted, the Nerves' reputation had preceeded them by means of their much-acclaimed 4-song EP, which has been out nearly a year now and is one of the hottest sellers in the new-wave catalog. Awaiting the Nerves on the East Coast are several recording opportunities and a possible tour of England.

    The Nerves have been a strong force in the L.A. scene since their arrival, having promoted a series of concerts at the 'Hollywood Punk Palace', a well-intentioned idea that was plagued by controversy and ended when the third landlord in almost as many weeks denied use of premises. In this brief period, the Nerves had opened up the L.A. scene by bringing in groups from other parts of the state, that few people here had ever seen or even heard of, including such bands as the Weirdos, the Dils, the Zeros, Kid, and Short Ice, that have proved to be significant entries in the new-wave roster.

    In the course of this tour, the Nerves will be supported by some of the most interesting local bands in their respective cities. The possibility has been suggested, after the Nerves have worked their way back to California hitting many of the cities they passed over on their journey east, of combining resources to put on a package tour of some of the best groups from various cities, to do a much more elaborate national tour, using and expanding the channels that have already been opened.

    The establishment of a nationwide circuit for new-wave bands will make it possible for a lot of these groups to reach more of their potential audience, without the support of a major record company. It's the logical extension of the same process by means of which these bands have begun building national followings through privately-issued records. In view of the fact that most of the money in the music business is still tied up in obsolescent forms of musical activity, with each of the major companies having either dismissed it, or satisfied their consciences by signing the most innocuous 'punk' group they could find, it's crucial that the alternative systems be established if the new artists emerging in greater and greater numbers are going to have a chance to be heard. The Nerves have taken a bold and important step. We encourage you to support them by attending their concert when it comes to your area, moreover by pre-publicizing it if you are in any position of access to the media.

    Nerves tour posters, EPs (with a hot picture cover) and additional information are available from us at BOMP. The itinerary below is only skeletal--there are 3 or 4 more presently unconfirmed dates, and others will be added later (we'll keep you informed).

NERVES TOUR ITINERARY

May 2,3,4 - Los Angeles, Starwood
May 5,6,7,10 - San Francisco, Mabuhay Gardens
May 13, 14 - Denver, Wax Tracks
May 25, 26 - Cleveland, Pirates Cove

June 2,3,4,5 - Boston, The Rat
June 6,7,8,9 - New York, Max's Kansas City
June 10,11,12 - Washington D.C. - Rock City

GREG SHAW ANNOUNCES THE NERVES GROUND-BREAKING DIY NATIONAL TOUR IN *BOMP!* NEWSLETTER, MAY 1977.
courtesy of Paul Collins' Archives

AT THE STARWOOD

Dorian Zero — What's in a Name?

In the case of Dorian Zero, who closed a three-night engagement at the Starwood Wednesday, the name says it all. A remnant of New York's decadence syndrome, the roly-poly singer-poseur is comical rather than arresting, recalling John Belushi's Cocker spoof, Monte Rock III's self-spoof, or perhaps Dom DeLuise doing a glam-rock skit on the Donny and Marie Show.

Musically, Zero's raspy shout competes unsuccessfully with his band's high-volume R&B riffs—an ungodly marriage incapable of expressing any genuine thought or feeling. It's all harmless and insignificant enough, except for a rendition of "Bring It On Home" abysmal enough to bring Sam Cooke back to sue for defamation of character.

The second-billed Nerves had the advantage of Zero as the evening's yardstick, by which measure it seemed a highly refreshing and purposeful outfit. The trio, which comes to Los Angeles via New York and San Francisco, sets itself the challenge of doing something original with elements of British Invasion music, and generally succeeds.

The crisp, authoritative, rough-edged sound picks up on early Stones and other English R&B bands (one of the ballads could be slipped onto "December's Children" and even Mick wouldn't notice), with just a hint of Mersey-beat lightness. Added dimension is provided by a distant undercurrent of rockabilly and Chuck Berry.

The Nerves' slam-bang, no-nonsense format—one short song on top of another—keeps the show moving, and the three Nerves wear their matching suits and Rickenbacker guitars without seeming rigid or affected. The main deficiencies are a lack of a distinctive signature in the sound and a stage manner that makes concentration come off as aloofness. —RICHARD CROMELIN

The NERVES live performance with Dorian Zero at the Starwood, May 1977.
courtesy of Paul Collins' Archives

THE NERVES

"Stunningly good...Future hitmakers"
N.Y. Rocker

"Unique style...Electrifying Performances"
S.F. Musicians News

Los Angeles·San Francisco·Chicago·Boston·New York

THE NERVES TOUR PROMO POSTER, CIRCA 1977.
courtesy of Paul Collins' Archives

The NERVES first self-funded DIY national tour route map, circa 1977.
courtesy of Paul Collins' Archives

97

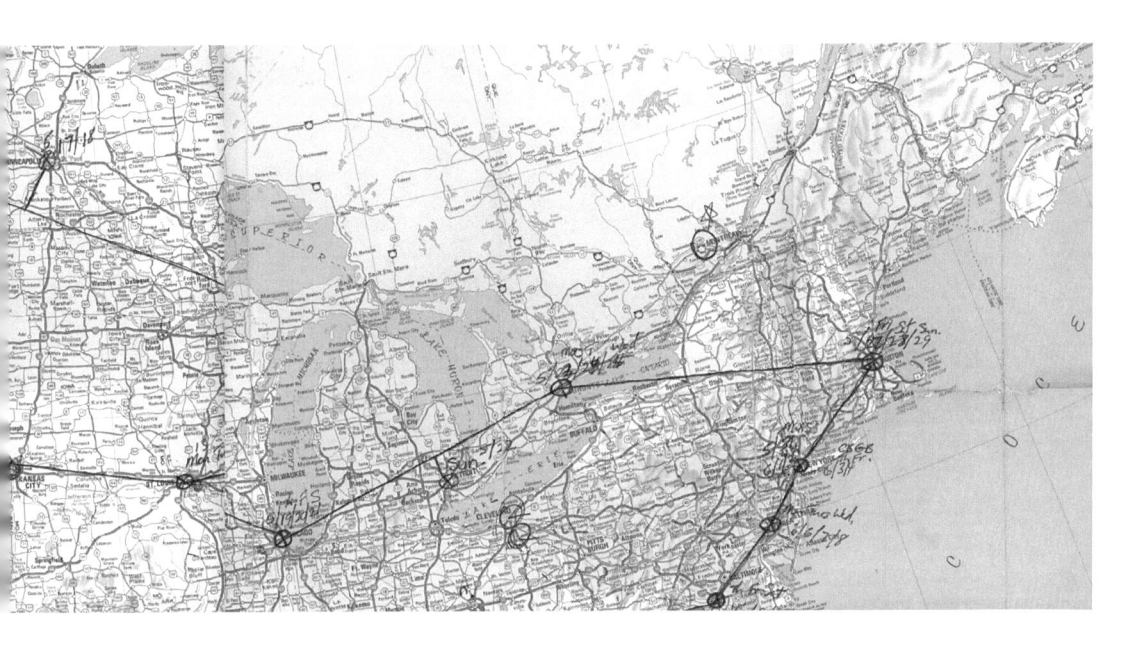

THE NERVES POSTER FOR THEIR SHOWS AT MABUHAY GARDENS, APRIL 1977.
courtesy of Paul Collins' Archives

CHAPTER EIGHT:
One Way Ticket

On May 3rd, 4th, and 5th of 1977, we played three dates with the Dorian Zero Revue at The Starwood. Then we turned the key to the ignition in our station wagon. We were a very small army of three, going into battle against the entire country – pretty lofty and worthwhile shit. The nation was stunned as three of its native sons drove from coast to coast, in three-piece custom-tailored Yves Saint Laurent suits, playing their own particular brand of music to an unsuspecting public. It was one of the most defining moments in the history of America, and in the history of rock 'n' roll.

It was around midnight when we left. The green and red glow from the dials on the dashboard, the smell of cigarettes, joints, the taste of cheap beer all swirled together and created an intoxicating womb-like effect. Our morale was up and our spirits were high. The crushing rejection in LA hadn't taken its full toll, and there is nothing like the open road to lift a man's spirits. We had a long way to go. Fucking A.

I didn't know it at the time, but I'm sure this was going to be "it" for Peter and Jack. So in our own way and for our own reasons, each of us was determined to make this a great trip. In the end, I think it was the ride of our lives. Sometimes you just get lucky in spite of yourself.

In reality, each show was like some hometown band playing a local dive. The tour was in the summer and we were sweating bullets. We were at it 24-7, so after a while we didn't even bother changing our clothes. Our suits were completely soaked, sweat stained, and stiff.

The suits did cause quite a stir though. People would stand there with their mouths open and gape at us. When it was over, they were unsure if they had seen it or dreamt it. But it was real. It had never been done, and when it was over, it could never be done again.

San Francisco was our first stop, and it lived up to everything we hated about the place. Four nights at The Mabuhay Gardens ended up in an on stage brawl between the band and the sound man for the club. We swore for a second time to never come back.

Finally we got the fuck out of California and were really on the road. We drove straight through to Denver to play the Wax Trax record store, on the 13th and 14th of May. We played with The Front and The Ravers, Marc Campbell's early band before he had The Nails.

The Nerves had one fatal flaw. As an adult, I have always been a very punctual person, but Jack was not. Since he was the head honcho, we were always late. It usually revolved around the tuning of the guitars. Back then, tuners were a thing of the future or for the very rich. We'd have to tune by ear. It went something like this. Jack would start by lighting up a joint.

"All right, give me an A."

"You're flat."

"No man, you're sharp."

"No I'm not, you're flat."

"I'm telling you man, you're sharp."

This would go on, and on, until it became an all out war, and we were late. It fucked us up over and over again, and Denver was no exception. By the time we got to Wax Trax, the owners Jim and Dannie were so drunk and pissed off, they said we couldn't play. The place was packed with kids, and after I pleaded on my hands and knees for 20 minutes, they let us go on. We had a great time, and all was forgiven.

The next day, we had a punk rock picnic in the mountains of Boulder, CO, with kegs of beer and huge hunks of BBQ beef. We ate right off the grill with our bare hands, with Ramones and Sex Pistols blasting in the woods from a ghetto-blaster.

The NERVES in front of the original Wax Trax record store in
Denver, circa 1977.
photo by Patty Hefley

We had exactly forty-five cents when we pulled into Chicago. The gas gauge was on empty, it was at least 95 degrees out, and we hadn't eaten or showered in days. I walked up the steps of Huey's Rock Club to see if we could get an advance. I found out we had been bounced from the show.

The manager of Huey's took pity on me, and explained the facts of life: "Chicago is a shotgun town, you got that kid?"

"Yeah, I got that, but if we don't play tonight, we're going to wind up living here until we can scrape up some cash."

The headlining act at Huey's was The Hounds – one of Chicago's heavy metal bands from hell. They had failed to do some advertising, so we were kicked off the bill. Then we were told we could play after all, but after The Hounds at 3 AM. There were five people there and one of them was a journalist. This is what he had to say:

Magical Mystery Tour

"Strange Punks" have entered Chicago city limits! The Nerves have arrived in town, with the promise of something new. The line-up sounds skeletal, particularly in the members' self-inflicted minimalism. But the sparsity of instrumentation is a mere undercoat for one of the most developed harmony teams in rock today. The Nerves have long fashioned themselves as 'the band that could.' Even the most adamant believers couldn't help but question the ambitiousness of this undertaking." - Cary Baker

We played several Chicago area shows, at nightclubs like B'ginnings, and Night Gallery in Waukegan, IL – the territory of Rockford residents, Cheap Trick. They were not only a great band but very cool guys. They all came down to one of the shows, and we felt like rock 'n' roll royalty, signing their copies of our 45. Years later I was told that Bun E. Carlos even had some live recordings of our band in his extensive collection of tapes.

Maybe it was because I was the youngest, or the most responsible in a way, but I was always doing the driving. The trip to Cleveland was no exception and I drove straight through. We arrived at seven in the morning, creeping our way through the foggy grey city. We were a long way from LA and people seemed much friendlier.

At MacArthur Park, we met Crocus Behemoth aka David Thomas, the lead singer of local band Pere Ubu. He took us to breakfast at his favorite greasy spoon, and

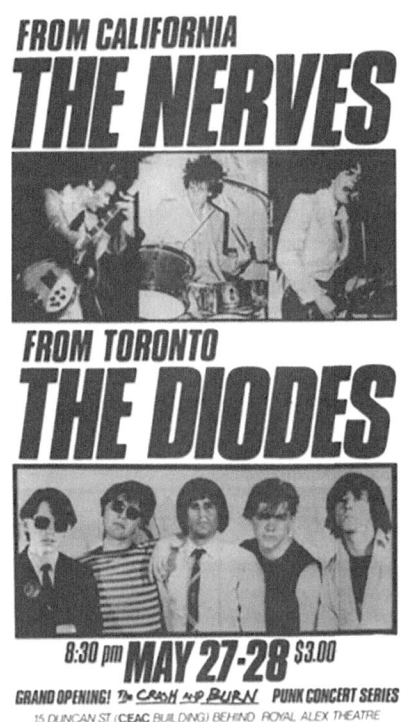

(LEFT) PAUL COLLINS LIVE IN TORONTO AT CRASH 'N BURN. *photo by Patty Hefley*
(RIGHT): FLYER, CIRCA 1977.

filled us in on what was going on in Cleveland. Our car broke down. It would break down in practically every city we hit. John Thompson aka Johnny Dromette spent the whole day with us helping to get it fixed. John was Pere Ubu's art designer and owner of legendary record store Hideo's Discodrome.

That night on May 26th, we played at The Pirates Cove in the flats of Downtown Cleveland. All the up-and-coming bands in town played there. We walked in and the opening act, Devo was already on. One of their songs became our theme song for a while - "Mongoloid, he was a Mongoloid!" Devo had just played Max's Kansas City in New York, and told us there was a real "buzz" about our upcoming show there. I remember Stiv Bators at The Cove, yelling about how his picture was bigger than Johnny Rotten's in *Time Magazine*'s just-released 1977 feature on punk rock.

We left Cleveland in a good mood and headed for Toronto. This would be the only time The Nerves would play outside of the USA. Toronto is a great city, and there was a real scene going on. On May 27th and 28th, we played a place called Crash 'N Burn, an enormous club in the soon to be super-hip Queen St. part of town. The place was packed, and the girls were all beautiful in their fishnet stockings and miniskirts.

THE NERVES (BOTH PAGES) WITH THE DIODES (ABOVE) AT CRASH 'N BURN IN TORONTO, MAY 1977.
photos courtesy of Ralph Alfonso

105

The band was a well-oiled machine by now, and we put on two blistering shows.

This was to be our highest paid gig ever, $600 for two nights. We celebrated by staying at The Waldorf, the best hotel in town. After the last show, we invited everyone to an after show party and didn't say what rooms we were in. Packs of kids were roaming the halls of this very exclusive hotel, trying to find The Nerves.

When we played The Rat, four nights in Boston, we stayed with Oedipus, from the influential punk and new wave college radio station WTBS. We played with DMZ the first couple of nights. I was starting to feel like a real rock star, but the minute we got to The Rat, the place lived up to its name. We were put right back in our place. The crowd ignored us, and the club owner shorted us. Boston has never been one of my favorite places. It's a tough town and it always seemed like a big college campus to me.

We did get one piece of solid advice at The Rat. As we stood in the doorway, a local band dressed in black leather came up to us. Their tall and lanky leader started to give us the lowdown. "You guys are never going to get anywhere like this. What you need to do is get some big time record company to dump a whole bunch of money on you. Then you'll have a chance at making it. What you're doing here is a bunch of

THE NERVES LIVE AT CRASH 'N BURN IN TORONTO, MAY 1977.
photos courtesy of Ralph Alfonso

(ABOVE): THE NERVES FLYER FOR THEIR MAX'S KANSAS CITY DEBUT PERFORMANCES, DESIGNED BY PAUL'S MOM, SICA, JUNE 1977.
courtesy of Paul Collins' Archives

bullshit, playing all these dives. I've got it all figured out. We just signed a big fat record deal. We're going to make it big time!"

"Oh, yeah. Thanks for the tip – and by the way, what's the name of your band?"

"The Cars."

I thought to myself, "What a jerky name! Who does this guy think he is anyway?"

Arriving in New York, I met with Peter Leeds (Blondie's manager) before we played our four nights at Max's Kansas City. It wasn't too difficult to get an appointment. The pitch was very simple, and I gave him our promo package and the 45. He said "Blondie listens to all the bands that want to open for them. They make the decision. I'll give them the package, and I'll let you know what they say." I left.

A couple of days passed and I got a call saying Mr. Leeds would like to see me in his office. In my mind I was going, "This is awesome! We are going to do some shows with Blondie!" Why else would he have me back in his office, other than to give me the good news? I got back to his office, sat down, and Leeds slowly pushed my package across the table to me. He said:

"I gave your package to Blondie and this is what they had to say. You are the

FLYER FOR THE NERVES SUPPORTING THE RAMONES
IN CINCINNATI AT BOGART'S, JUNE 1977.
courtesy of Paul Collins' Archives

worst band they have ever heard, and they would never, *ever, ever, ever* consider playing with you, *under any circumstances."*

He said "ever" like three times. I remember that.

So I was sitting there with my mouth hanging open, dumbfounded. I was in shock, totally unprepared, and I didn't know what to say. I had enough business experience to know that a secretary would usually call and say "Thanks a lot. They're not interested" or "better luck next time." I've never been called back into someone's office to basically be told "go fuck off." I didn't say much, maybe "okay." I picked up my stuff and left.

At the same time we got in touch with Richard Gottehrer, who was Blondie's producer. We gave him a tape of 10-12 live songs, to see if he might produce us. I explained what happened with Peter Leeds, and he said "Oh, don't worry. There must be some misunderstanding. I know Blondie, and they would never say anything like that. I'll see them later, and I will straighten the whole thing out. I will see you at Max's."

Just like Devo said back in Cleveland, there was a buzz about The Nerves at Max's Kansas City. The entire town came out to see the spectacle, Danny Fields, musicians from Patti Smith and Blondie, Greg Shaw, Dan Hartman (guitar player from Edgar Winter), anyone who anybody was there. The place was packed.

Even my mother, who designed the flyer, was there. She really thought we were on the verge, and later told me the feeling in the room that night was one of awe.

I got upstairs and Richard Gottehrer came up to me, handed me the tape, looked me right in the eye, and said "Yes, it's true." He turned around and I never saw him again. I never said anything to Jack and Peter because it was so humiliating. There was no point after all the setbacks. I just kept it under my hat for over 20 years.

I think the first set we did at Max's was probably the best show the band ever did. I remember Suicide played with us one of the nights. This was the apex of the tour. We were white hot, and on our game.

After Max's, we didn't have anything else booked, so we decided to take a two week break. Jack and Peter drove back all the way to LA to be with their (respective) wife and girlfriend. That's how crazy we were. I was to stay in New York with Marci at The Chelsea Hotel, figure out our return, and book us gigs back from NY to LA. *We were staying at the world-famous sleazebag Chelsea Hotel!* It was funky, but I'm glad I got to stay. And on top of that, I wrote "Different Kind Of Girl" in our room on the sixth floor.

During this hiatus, I contacted Danny Fields, manager of the Ramones.

Danny was a lovely guy, and very happy to see me. Just like Peter Leeds, it wasn't hard to get an appointment at his office. He told me The Ramones were the band of the future, and were going to be huge. I said we wanted some shows, and Danny said "Tell you what, if you can book us in Cincinnati, I will give you the Texas leg of the July tour." I had my little diary book with me, with the phone numbers of clubs all over the country. I knew just the place, Bogart's in Cincinnati. I called, and the booker said "The Ramones?" That was when Danny reached for the phone and said,

"Okay kid, I'll take it from here!" That was the first official punk show in Cincinnati, and I booked it.

Danny was good to his word and gave us a string of dates, with Cincinnati being the first. Jack and Peter flew from LA to Cincinnati, and I took the train to meet them. Today, it doesn't sound like a big deal, but back then, there were no cell phones. "Alright man, we will meet at Bogart's at 5 o'clock. See you there!"

On June 28th, I met up with Brad Balfour, a journalist at the *Cincinnati Post*, who picked me up at the train station. We hung out at his office, everything was cool, but it started to rain pretty heavy. Brad got me to the club at 5 PM. I was there in my three piece suit, and there were Tommy, Johnny, Joey, and Dee Dee, who I'd never met. I was a NY guy, but not a real NY East Village scene guy like The Ramones.

Tommy said "Okay man, where's your band? You guys gotta do soundcheck!" I didn't know where Jack and Peter were. I hadn't heard from them. Finally they called Bogart's, told me it was pouring rain and they were going to be late; very late. Tommy was screaming at me now. "Do you think we're going to open up for your fuckin' band? You're fuckin' crazy!" This show went from being our big opportunity, to my worst nightmare. It got so bad that I decided to sit outside the club, underneath the awning in the pouring rain, to avoid the screaming and yelling.

Back in the day, bands always did two sets, and then the venue would "turn the house." We'd play and then the Ramones would play. The venue would empty the club, bring in a new crowd, and we'd both play again. Jack and Peter weren't here, so we didn't play our first set. The Ramones went on to a packed place, and I was sticking my head in every now and again. It was amazing seeing the original lineup.

When Jack and Peter finally showed up, we hauled our gear in as quickly as we could, and threw it up onstage. People were going "You guys had better be good!" I guess we were good, because we were working on gobs of adrenaline. We blazed through our set.

That was our first show, but every single show we did with The Ramones, we were late. It had nothing to do with me, because I am an extremely punctual person. It was just a dysfunction of the band. I won't go into whose fault it was.

The Ramones had an incredible work ethic, and I would see them working

Jack Lee (top), and Peter Case (bottom), live onstage at Crash 'N Burn in Toronto, May 1977.
photos courtesy of Ralph Alfonso

The Nerves In New York

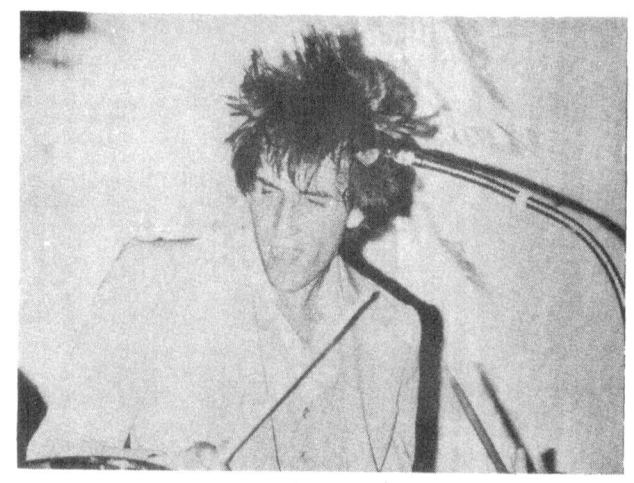

by Michael Hafitz

While awaiting the arrival of The Nerves in the downstairs section of Max's, I was treated to the worst free meal I've ever had. Dried Chic Peas. Even now, the thought of those little, dried spitballs sends my gastric system into fits of disbelief. How could a restaurant build its reputation on those things?

As I was pondering this neo-philosophical problem, a good looking gentleman came to the table carrying two drinks. In return for the Vodka, I told him to avoid the dingleberries.

I had seen The Nerves do two sets the night before and had found their live sound so more more intense than their E.P. as to warrant a brief Q & A

Paul Collins Drums and Vocals

period with bassist Peter Case. Paul Collins(drums) Jack Lee(guitar), and Peter Case met a couple of years ago in San Francisco through an advertisement in a local music store. They spent all their money and time in the studio and eventually released their E.P. on their own label. As soon as the record came out, The Nerves left the limited S.F. scene for the promise land of Los Angeles. As Peter tells the story, "More happened to us in the ninety days that we were in L.A. than in all the time we spent together in San Francisco. We just got fed up with the limited power of the San Francisco record companies. They are all treated as provincial by the main offices in L.A."

In 1977, it seems to be the best interest of any new band to release their own record. While this opens up another branch in the underground network, it does little to promote the scene. On their arrival in L.A., The Nerves decided to inject new life into the laid back atmosphere by opening their own club, appropriately called The Hollywood PUNK Palace. "When we got to L.A., we weren't very excited about what we saw. A couple of clubs folded our first week there and pretty soon only two clubs were left. At the time, neither the Starwood nor the Whiskey were booking anything besides standard record company products. The local groups weren't playing anyplace, so we talked it over and decided to open The Punk Palace. We put on The Zeroes, The Weirdos, ourselves, Zippers, Dils, and the Germs. Along with radio spots(on Rodney's show at KROC) and posters, that kind of

Peter Case Bass and Vocals

Michael Hafitz was the music editor for The University of Rochester's CAMPUS TIMES. Currently our Boston correspondent and publisher of RECORD RAVES.

blew the whole thing open. It really woke a lot of people up. Since we left all the bands have started playing the Whiskey for Punk Rock Weekends. The local bands are finally getting some exposure."

I asked Peter if The Nerves had been approached by anyone in L.A. and received what must be the most common new band response. "Yeah, Kim Fowley wanted us. He said he wanted to change our image or something. We refused, and then he called us the pushiest band in L.A."

Fowley's appraisal wasn't too far off. After nine months in L.A., The Nerves embarked on a coast to coast tour. Not only are they the first of the new wave bands to attempt such an extended trip, but they are also travelling witnout any financial assistance. "We do everything ourselves. Paul handles all the bookings, I do the publicity, and Jack does all the design work. As far as business with the record companies is concerned, we handle that as a group."

Subsistence rock and roll certainly has its finanacial limitations, but The Nerves are already talking about a new "definitive" single. The first EP was an incredible debut, yet they aren't totally pleased with the sound. "We think the first is a great introduction to The Nerves, but it really doesn't capture our live sound. It was made on such a budget...the next single, which we hope to have out in late August, will get that sound more."

The Nerves sound is built on strong harmmonic vocals(they all sing) and catchy melodic hooks. In concert, their material sounds fresh with the lack of guitar leads complimenting the frenzied pace of their delivery. The Nerves have settled into a groove realizing that any solo would detract rather than add to their overall sound. "With our music, we don't think that a solo would say anything. Guitar solos generally don't say anything anymore. You just keep doing it and doing it until you are dead to the feeling--a complete desensitization occurs. Personally, I've gotten to the point where I hate solos. They seem to be used more to fill up space than anything else. Even in the sixties, in the heyday of rock guitarists, there were only a handfull of really good ones. No I think that even they were

only trying to imitate voices. Voices are going to come back. Our music contains an emotional hook in the voices that maybe lead guitar was for awhile. Elvis had it in his voice and The Beatles did too. In our music it is the high blends....the whole rush is right there in the vocals. It's not your basic choir style harmony, where you just sit there and lay on a bunch of voices like CS&N. They weren't interpreting it at all."

The tour has gone well for The Nerves. It has brought them to the attention of many people who would have otherwise never heard of them.

Besides equipment problems in Boston, the rest of the tour has gone smoothly. "The best places we played were Toronto with The Diodes, Cleveland(where Crocus Behemoth from Pere Ubu met us at the Brown's Stadium at 6:30 in the morning and took us to his favorite diner), New York, and Denver. Denver is a really hip town. When we got there, we didn't know what to expect-you know cowboys or something-but there were all these thirteen year olds with The Nerves record! Kids there had Nerves t-shirts on! It was the most enthusiastic reception we got on the whole tour. It just shows you what a record store can do in a particular town. I mean the radio stations won't play anything, so the kids go to the record store to hear the new singles."

The Nerves try to get a visual image as well as a sound image on stage. "Music is entertainment and it has to be all around. I'm not just relating to just music-we are trying to convey our whole world not just the fact that we sit around and play instruments, cause that's really the least important factor. The best band is one who is entertaining. As for our suits, the leather thing has just been going on for too long. It needs something to wake it up. When we put on one of these suits it is really exciting because it sets up a strong contrast between the music and our appearance. I'm just getting tired of people looking so Mondo Deco, man. It is a total effect that we are after."

Jack Lee Guitar and Vocals

Autumn, 1977

THE NERVES FEATURE ARTICLE IN *RECORD RAVES MAGAZINE*, AUTUMN 1977.
courtesy of Paul Collins' Archives

on new songs in the dressing room. I'd walk by, and hear Johnny Ramone screaming at Dee Dee. I thought Johnny was a bit of an asshole, honestly. Joey Ramone was very distant, we never really spoke. I never had much rapport with any of them but Dee Dee, who really liked us, and our songs. When Tommy and Johnny were screaming at us, Dee Dee would say "Don't worry about it man, but maybe, you guys might want to start showing up on time!" This was solid life advice, from Dee Dee Ramone.

Dee Dee Ramone had two jobs in The Ramones, counting off the songs, "1-2-3-4," and jumping up and down while he was playing. One of the clubs had a low ceiling, and every time Dee Dee jumped up, he would hit his head. After a couple of songs, he decided that jumping up and down was not such a good idea. After the show, Johnny was yelling at Dee Dee: "I don't care if you're hitting your head! Keep jumping!" At the next gigs, Dee Dee was jumping up and down again, and hitting his head every time.

The last show we did with The Ramones was in Killeen, TX, at Tremors. It was a weird one, because it was the only place where it seemed like The Nerves got a better crowd reception than The Ramones. Also, the club had a lit up dance floor like *Saturday Night Fever*, which we thought was kind of ridiculous. It was the last time we ever saw the Ramones, or had anything to do with them.

I'm not sure if it's true or not, because it's hearsay, but years later the Ramones were considering recording my song "All Over The World." This would have obviously been awesome for me, but they didn't.

If we had any brains, which we didn't, we would have quit right then and left a good taste in everyone's mouth. But we lived in LA, so that's where we had to wind up. The suits were slowly losing their shape, the shows were few and far between, and our money had run out.

Our last show of the tour was at a biker bar called Debby's Headrest, situated in the middle of a cornfield in Bellevue, Illinois. How the fuck we wound up there is just bad luck, pure and simple. The show wasn't a big deal, because we were completely ignored by the patrons, a bunch of beer-guzzling bikers. The fun started when we tried to get paid.

It was Friday, and Debby disappeared, leaving us a check that we couldn't cash until Monday. We literally had no money, so we had no choice but to stay. We got busted at a dump of a motel, for three people trying to check in as one. When we went back to the club the next night, they saw us coming, and closed it down. We spent two days and nights sitting in our station wagon, in the brutal heat, waiting for the bank to open.

On Monday morning, I walked into the small town bank and presented the teller with the dirty, crumpled check for $80. He asked what happened to the check, and I told him he didn't want to know. He looked at me suspiciously as he counted out four twenties.

courtesy of Paul Collins' Archives

Jack went into a cocoon state; catatonic and staring out the window as the country rolled by. Peter knew it was all over, and dreaded it. I think he would have bailed right then if he could. I just drove.

We took our meals in supermarket aisles, cramming sandwiches down our throats, and checking out with only a jar of Cheez Whiz and a loaf of bread. It was hot in August, and we had a gas leak. At each fill up, one of us would have to slide under the car, and rub a bar of soap onto the leak to stop it. Before long, we looked like punk rockers from hell, covered in grease, with hair standing straight up, and our faces black from road dirt.

By the time we hit Las Vegas we were dead broke, but unstoppable. Jack saved the day one more time, and came up with a plan to get us home: 'The Cigarette Machine Routine.' It was a real doozy. Each highway exit usually had four gas stations, one on each corner. We'd fan out, each of us going to a different gas station. We'd each walk up to the cigarette machine, fake putting some money in, fiddle with the machine, then feign frustration at not being able to get a pack of cigarettes. You'd go into the office and complain to the attendant, who would usually give you your sixty to eighty-five cents back. Jack would usually bypass that part, walk right in to the office, and demand his money back. The startled attendant would usually give it to him.

THE **NERVES** 1977 TOUR PROMO PHOTO.
photo courtesy of Patty Hefley

A gas station in Las Vegas, sometime around midnight August, 1977:

"Sir, I just put seventy-five cents in your cigarette machine and nothing came out. Can I get a refund?"

"Oh, really? I know that machine ain't broke, and so do you. If you want money, go get a job like everybody else."

"I've got a job. It just doesn't pay too good!"

"Kid, get outta here before I call the cops."

"Believe me sir, I would, but we're out of gas!"

"Go peddle it somewhere else. You think you're the only one with problems? How'd you like to meet my wife?"

That's how we got home, from Las Vegas to LA.

The hit song that summer was "Margaritaville," and every time we heard it, we'd drool for a cool drink, but there were none to be had. No one saw us as we crawled, dirty, filthy, hungry, and dejected back to LA. It was worse that no one cared that we had done the impossible, a national cross country tour on our own. No one gave a fuck – and we knew it. Jack said, "Well what did you expect?" I felt like this was the end. I went home, threw myself into bed and cried for a good long time.

Jack never came out and said "The Nerves are over." There was not really a definitive 'end of The Nerves' moment, or incident, but this is how I remember it.

We got back to LA exhausted, like Don Quixote with our canteens, emotionally and spiritually tapped-out. We had done everything humanly possible, exerted an enormous amount of energy, and we were no better off than when we started. It was really crushing, and only Hollywood can crush you on that level.

There was a period of time where we licked our wounds. We went into the studio in late '77, and recorded "Paper Dolls" (Lee) and "One Way Ticket" (Case), with the idea of making a demo to get a record deal. Pranava Studios was a little 8-track studio, and I remember the engineer was this kid in cowboy boots. He had his feet up on the control board, right by the control buttons. I said "Aren't you worried that you might accidentally erase stuff?" He said that's never happened, and right when he said that, he hit the red 'record' button. Fortunately I don't think he erased anything.

(L TO R): PAUL COLLINS, JACK LEE, AND PETER CASE, BACKSTAGE AT THE MASQUE, NOVEMBER 1977.
photo courtesy of Jenny Lens

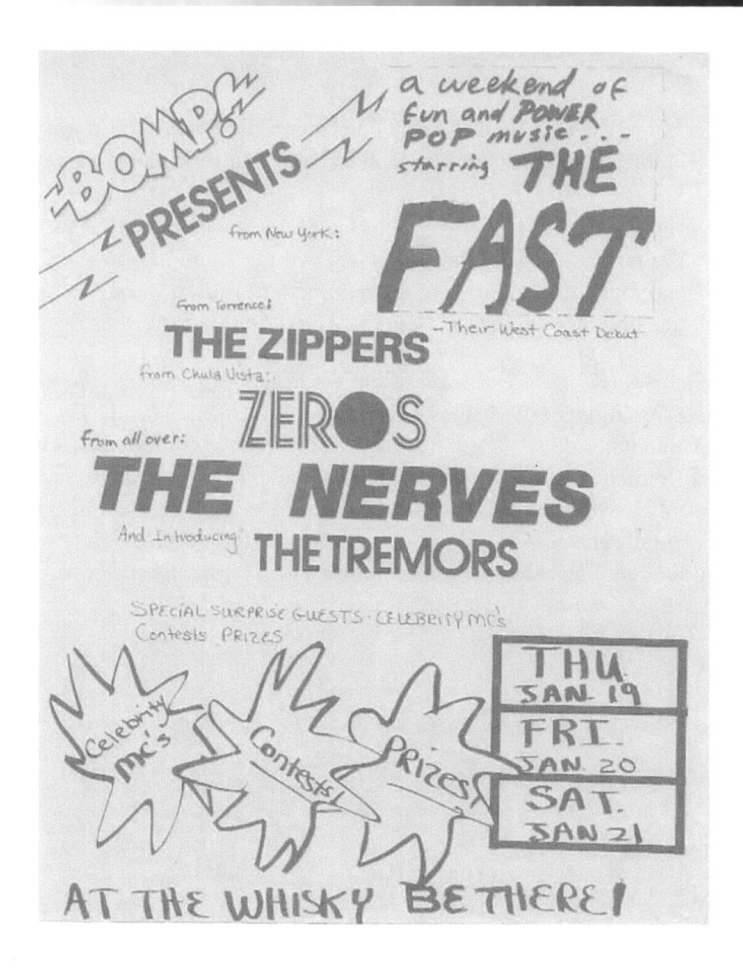

We played a few more gigs. We played LA's #1 punk club The Masque on November 25th and 26th 1977 with The Avengers, and Shock. I believe our last gig may have been January 19th through the 21st, 1978 with The Fast, The Zeros, The Zippers, and The Tremors. We finally got to play The Whisky, as part of a Bomp! Records showcase. All I remember about this gig, was the arm of Peter's suit was so stiff, it broke off.

The next time we got together was at Jack's house on June Street. Jack said "Okay, I know what we have to do. I have these new songs, and this one called 'Sex' is the song that will put us over." This is the way it always was in The Nerves, 'this one song, and all of our troubles would be over.' Peter and I weren't into it, and weren't going to follow Jack's shit on this. This was the first real division. I don't remember what I said, but I was completely distraught about the fact that we were falling apart.

Then, Jack just stopped being reachable. Remember, this was pre-cell phone and Internet. If someone's phone was disconnected, and they weren't in town, you didn't know where they were. Jack just disappeared.

This was when Peter Case and I tried to carry on. We had songs, started cutting demos, and decided to try and mount another group, calling it The Breakaways, in homage to The Nerves.

If there was any definitive "end of The Nerves" moment, it was actually a few months after the formation of The Breakaways, right after Blondie released their LP *Parallel Lines* on September 23rd, 1978. I was driving down Sunset Boulevard and for the first time, I heard Blondie's cover of "Hanging On The Telephone" come on the radio. I literally almost wrecked the car. *Blondie?*

Those motherfuckers *knew* they were going to do the song? Why didn't they want to help us out? It didn't make any sense to me.

Blondie's people were asking around town, "Where's Jack? We need to talk to Jack." I didn't even have his phone number anymore. Jack was a big time guy now. Jack was in the VIP winner's circle.

He was gone, and there we were... *down in the street.*

THE NERVES' JACK LEE-PENNED "HANGING ON THE TELEPHONE" COVERED BY BLONDIE IN 1978 TO WORLDWIDE SUCCESS, INCLUDING EVEN, A COLOMBIAN PRESSING.

Autumn, 1977 $1.00

Record Raves

Jim Sohns
From Out of The Shadows

--PLUS--

Dictators
Nerves
Kiss
Iggy
Fast
Planets

The Nerves

Jan. 21, 1978

(THIS PAGE, TOP):
PAUL ON DRUMS AT THE WHISKY,
JANUARY 21ST, 1978.

(THIS PAGE, RIGHT):
PAUL ON THE PHONE AT WAX TRAX
IN DENVER MAY, 1977.
courtesy of Paul Collins' Archives

(PREVIOUS PAGE, TOP):
PAUL ON DRUMS IN DENVER, 1977.

(PREVIOUS PAGE, BOTTOM LEFT):
THE NERVES FEATURED IN *RECORD RAVES* MAGAZINE, 1977.
courtesy of Paul Collins' Archives

(PREVIOUS PAGE, BOTTOM RIGHT):
POLAROID FROM THE NERVES
LAST SHOW, JANUARY 21ST, 1978
AT THE WHISKY.
courtesy of Marci Marks'

Magical Blistering Tour

Hollywood punk-rock trio The Nerves take on America with a carload of guts.

By Cary Baker

"Strange punks from Hollywood have entered Chicago city limits! Sighted eastbound on I-90 by Austin Boulevard, they are believed to be headed for Rogers Park. We will keep you informed as developments occur. And now, back to our commercial-free hour at the station that plays the long versions of all the songs..."

The Nerves had arrived in town. And a nonsuspecting early shift at Huey's seemed a tad disappointed. There was plenty to drink, but the group onstage appeared to be doing everything wrong. No one looked like Freddie Mercury. The singer didn't sound like Jagger or Plant, but dared to sound a little like Lennon. There were no covers of "Jean Genie," and no one yelled, "Don't it wanna make you boogie!" The guitarist played a dreaded Rickenbacker, a make seldom seen today. And he didn't take more than about four seconds of solo in a 30-minute set.

There were no rave-ups, no commands to get on the floor, no "all-Pink Floyd sets." Alas, no encores. Faint applause.

The group, at 3:30 a.m., looked more like sheepish imps than strange punks from L.A., as they packed and left. They felt the slightest bit defected. Concededly, there may have been little in their set that a dominantly collegiate crowd at Huey's could latch on to. The tailored suits, European flat shoes and Hollies-bent harmonies were straight out of *Mersey Beat* magazine.

The Nerves, our strange punks in question, had taken a risk and perhaps failed. But it's nothing they hadn't done in a dozen other cities successfully.

But wait! What were these shouts of "Play the Nerves' record!" heard two weekends later at La Mere Vipere, a punk emporium that hadn't yet opened when the Nerves were in town?

La Mere, a club once operating as a disco, threw the off switch on Thelma Houston and her ilk right about the time the Nerves were in town. Despite Thelma's protestations of "Don't leave me this way!" Mike Rivers (the club's turntable artiste) proclaimed "Anarchy!", and the closets emptied. The new La Mere crowd has read of the Nerves in *Bomp* and *New York Rocker*, and had pondered the group's nervy *Rolling Stone* ad touting "The record everyone's been waiting for."

With the promise of something new via something old (the British Invasion), the Nerves have risen to the top of the 1977 rock underground, a movement that includes such aggregates as the Tuff Darts, DMZ, the Void-Oids, the Bizarros, the Gizmos and That Hideous Strength. Chicago has caught on slowly, especially in the light of support from smaller Midwest cities (witness Cheap Trick's grassroots following in Rockford). But now the ice is broken. La Mere's full houses prove that.

The Nerves have long fashioned themselves "the band that *could*." Last year, these three Frisco vagabonds migrated to the greener pastures of Hollywood and set up headquarters on the Strip. Long, contemplative walks down Sunset Boulevard (including the obligatory stop at Tower Records) revealed that groups everywhere were pressing up their own 45 RPM singles and displaying them on L.A. countertops everywhere. The Nerves decided to join the ranks. But rather than release a single that looked and sounded as if it were recorded in a basement, the trio decided on an EP (four songs) with a picture sleeve, mastered by no less than CBS. Reportedly, Columbia Records had rejected the Nerves for sounding "too derivative."

Although the Nerves have their sights firmly planted on Columbia (says drummer Paul Collins, "They're like Coca Cola, they're everywhere), their record was recorded and released at the group's expense, on (aptly enough) Nerves Records. The product was advertised in *Rolling Stone*, and the Nerves depended heavily on press mentions and mail order commerce.

"At one point," bassist Peter Case said, "we were in a real state of financial destitution, and sold them on the street."

The record, however, was met with unprecedentedly favorable acclaim, and with good reason. It features four clean, strikingly catch songs, few exceeding two minutes in time. They're so well executed that certain incriminating observations fail to come to light until after several listenings. All four cuts feature minimal guitar work, bass-heavy construction and emphasis on three-part harmonies that bring to mind the Beatles of "Paperback Writer" vintage. Everything seems to be there for a reason, each syllable, each sparse tangent answering directly to the melody line. There are no solos ever; Jack Lee, the Nerves' rhythm guitarist (there's no lead player) often plays a subservient role to Peter Case's thumping bass. Paul Collins, the drummer and one-third of the group's vocal network, brings to mind Keith Clark. He's not out to rival Keith Moon or Ginger Baker, just to contribute to the Nerves' composite sound.

The lineup sounds skeletal, particularly in the members' self-inflicted dictum of minimalism. But the sparsity of instrumentation is a mere undercoat for one of the most developed harmony teams in rock today.

"When the three of us get together, we're very critical," explained Case, over coffee at the Golden Nugget Pancake House on Bryn Mawr. Offstage, in a 9-to-5 shirt and jeans, and a pair of black horn-rim glasses, he looks anything but a proponent of rock's avant-garde. "Everything has to have a good reason for being there."

The Nerves refused, however, to turn sedentary while the record garnered rave reviews. Instead, Paul Collins opened a club, the Hollywood Punk Palace, showcasing new, heretofore unknown local and national talent.

He claims, however, he went through four locations in four weeks.

"More than that, though, we knew it was time to put the Nerves on the road," Collins said. "Success on a local level dictated that we take the next step."

Their biggest step. Without a manager, lacking any record company co-ordination (other than the full co-operation of the Nerves Record Company, a three-way partnership) and concededly un-

cont. pg. 51

Turning Point
- RECORDS
- TAPES
- CAR STEREOS
- CUSTOM INSTALLATION

GRAND OPENING SPECIAL

JENSEN CO-AXIAL SPEAKERS - $39.95

JENSEN TRI-AXIAL SPEAKERS - $59.95

7058 W. 127TH STREET
PALOS HEIGHTS, ILLINOIS 60463
361-2111

---

the RECORD BARREL

$6.98 list LP's still $4.25

620-8020

725 E. ROOSEVELT RD., VILLAGE PLAZA
LOMBARD, ILL.

OPEN 'TIL 10 WEEKNIGHTS
Now open 'til 6 on SUNDAY

E.L.P. SALE!

DURING JULY
ALL $6.98 list
EMERSON LAKE & PALMER ALBUMS
JUST $3.59
TAPES $4.99
WITH THIS AD

Complete Your Collection Now

SUPER SUMMER SALE!

CLEARANCE OF NAME BRAND MERCHANDISE AT DRASTICALLY DISCOUNTED PRICES... HERE ARE JUST A FEW EXAMPLES:

PREMIER 5 pc. DRUM SET... $780.00 – ALEMBIC PRE AMPS
MELLOTRON... $2895.00 – ELECTRO-PRO PIANO... SAVE!
CORDOVOX PIANO... $395.00 – ALL LYLE GUITARS 30% OFF!
WEST 200 WATT STACK... $695.00 – TAMA 5 pc. DRUM SET... SAVE!
ZILDJIAN 14" HI HATS. SAVE! – ORANGE 15" BASS CABINET-SAVE!
KELSEY 20 CHANNEL MIXER. $4950.00 – 32" TAIWAN GONG. DEAL!
SOUND CITY AMPS... DRASTICALLY REDUCED
MOOG SONIC SIX SYNTHESIZER – SAVE!
DEGAS TELECASTER COPY... $149.00
AND MUCH, MUCH MORE AT

ROSELLE MUSIC

217 E. IRVING PARK   ROSELLE, ILL.
529-2031

THE NERVES 1977 TOUR FEATURE BY CARY BAKER IN *THE ILLINOIS ENTERTAINER*.
courtesy of Paul Collins' Archives

Nerves Tour

cont. page 20

familiar with the national club scene, Collins made some phone calls and got some gigs. Soon, he was booked into Max's Kansas City in New York, Huey's in Chicago, the Stone Heart in Madison, and clubs in Denver, Boston and Ohio.

Even the most adamant believers couldn't help but question the ambitiousness of the undertaking. Tours cost money—big money—and the Nerves could barely pay their phone bills. Fortunately, the circuit they expected to play is different from that upon which Foreigner and Supertramp might galavant. Punk-rock belongs to the musicians and the fans, not the industry. And when the Nerves called the Hounds in Chicago, Pere Ubu in Cleveland and the Talking Heads in New York, the groups were honored to add them to standing bills.

The Nerves traveled in a mid-'60s stationwagon, which looked twice its years, with a small U-Haul attachment. They each took turns driving. And they crossed the country inside of a month, playing all the major markets and many smaller ones. They stayed at cheap motels, cooked on a hotplate (concealed whenever the maid was due), contacted the press personally in every city. Many members of Chicago's rock critic establishment came out to hear them with the Hounds at Huey's.

"People at clubs all too often sit with their hands on their chin, as if to say, 'I've assimilated that'," Case said. "There's no surprise left. Rock has become a dictionary of licks that keeps getting wider. Ideally, we can offer some of that lost immediacy."

The Nerves make it no secret that their goal is to make hit records. This is why they don't hesitate to admit that the Beatles, Beau Brummels, Hollies and Badfinger have more to say to them than Pink Floyd.

"A hit," Peter pondered. "To me, a hit jumps off your turntable. Your girlfriend knows. Your father knows."

"The British Invasion groups had hits on the basis of sound, not songs. And Phil Spector's sound was the biggest, baddest sound there ever was, so if the material was mediocre, the production made up for it. We're after that sound too, but we're equally interested in songs."

Although they identify with the punk movement (an encompassing breed that brings together Johnny Rotten and Deborah Harry), Case wonders how much the Nerves have in common with, say, the Ramones.

"The Ramones are honest. I hear what they're trying to do, and I like 'em a lot. But I'm no real fan of their material, especially when they start in on that glue-sniffing business. That's campy. That's an in-joke," he said.

Contrast the Ramones' "Pinhead" and "Carbona Not Glue" with the Nerves' titles: "Working Too Hard," "Don't Leave Me Hangin' On The Telephone," "Give Me Some Time" and "When You Find Out."

"Our records deal with real-life concerns," Case said. "There's nothing bizarre about it, and we're singing to the masses. That's what a hit does."

At time of publication, the Nerves are in their stationwagon heading for California, but not through the

Heartland once again before the tour is through. They're talking with the Hounds and d'Thumbs, and may have some club appearances lined up for July.

The desire to be a hitmaker is not uncommon. Contingent on how many artists will confess to it, the AM airwaves are the ultimate destination for any pop musician. Some, like the Bay City Rollers (and the Monkees in years gone by) have been deemed "manufactured." Others, like Michael Murphey and Henry Gross, are accused of "selling out" when an album cut creeps up the charts by popular demand. But not the Nerves; upfront, they want to make music that everyone can identify with, using melodic nuance that worked for the British Invasion groups in the '60s, and best of all, to get out of their hometown to make or break before the eyes of the nation. This is an uncharacteristically organic quest for popularity coming from a group who would suspect the idea of organic anything.

But there's no Don Kirshner pulling their strings. When the show's over, Peter, Jack and Paul put the equipment into their stationwagon and go on to the next town. And it was Peter's turn to drive as they left Chicago.

MUSIC MAN
INSTRUMENTS AND AMPS NOW IN STOCK

EXCLUSIVELY AT

SUBURBS
MUSIC GALLERY
2558 GREEN BAY RD.
HIGHLAND PARK, ILL.
312-432-6350

CHICAGO
DEVON MUSIC
2700 W. DEVON AV.
CHICAGO, ILL
312-743-1106

---

the flip side INVITES YOU TO...

the flip side IS LOCATED AT:

CHICAGO
3314 W. Foster
478-1490

HOFFMAN ESTATES
Barrington Sq. Shopping Ctr.
Higgins E. of Barrington Rd.
884-9430

BUFFALO GROVE
Plaza Verde Shopping Ctr.
Dundee at Arlington Hts. Rd.
398-6140

DOWNERS GROVE
Finley Square Shopping Ctr.
Butterfield & Finley Rd.
620-6868

WEST DUNDEE
Tonde Shopping Center
Rt. 31 — one mile
North of N.W. Tollway
428-5999

NAPERVILLE
Ogden Mall
Ogden & Naperville Rd.
357-7030

LAKE ZURICH
Main & Church
438-7100

Immerse Yourself

10 C.C. HAVE SURFACED ONCE AGAIN, WITH THEIR DEEPEST ALBUM YET, **DECEPTIVE BENDS.** SUBMERGE YOURSELF IN THEIR SOUND.

$7.98 LIST $4.69 LP OR TAPE

10CC Deceptive Bends
includes the hit "THE THINGS WE DO FOR LOVE"

SEE 10 C.C. IN CONCERT SUNDAY, JULY 31
AT THE AUDITORIUM THEATRE

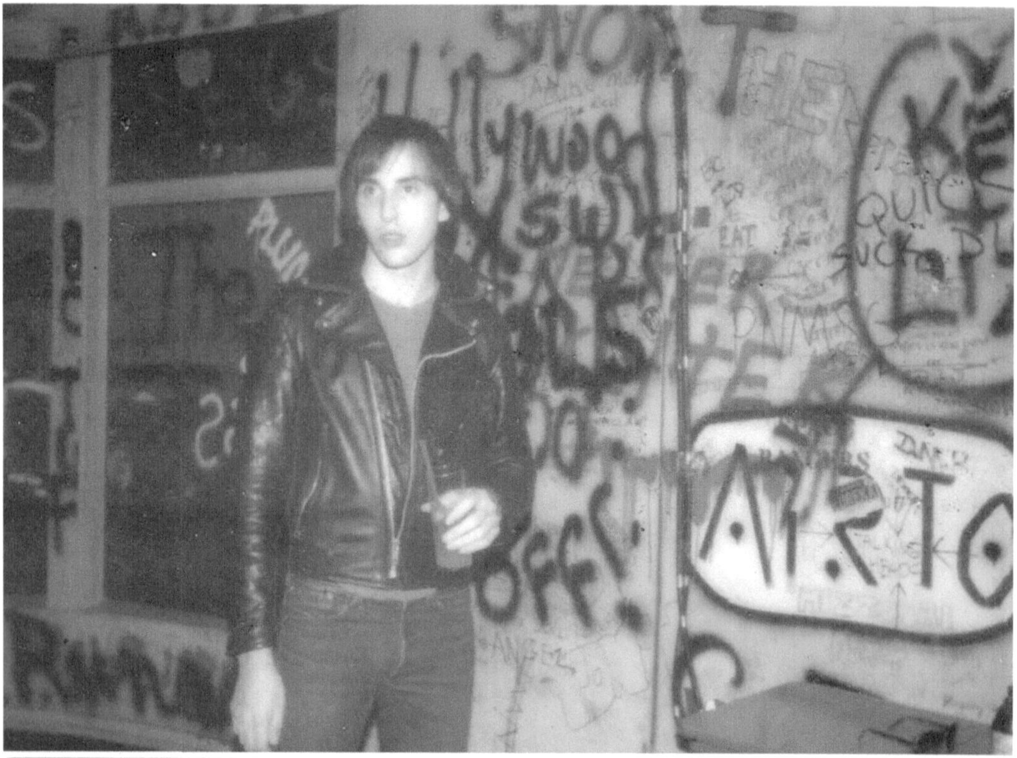
OFF!

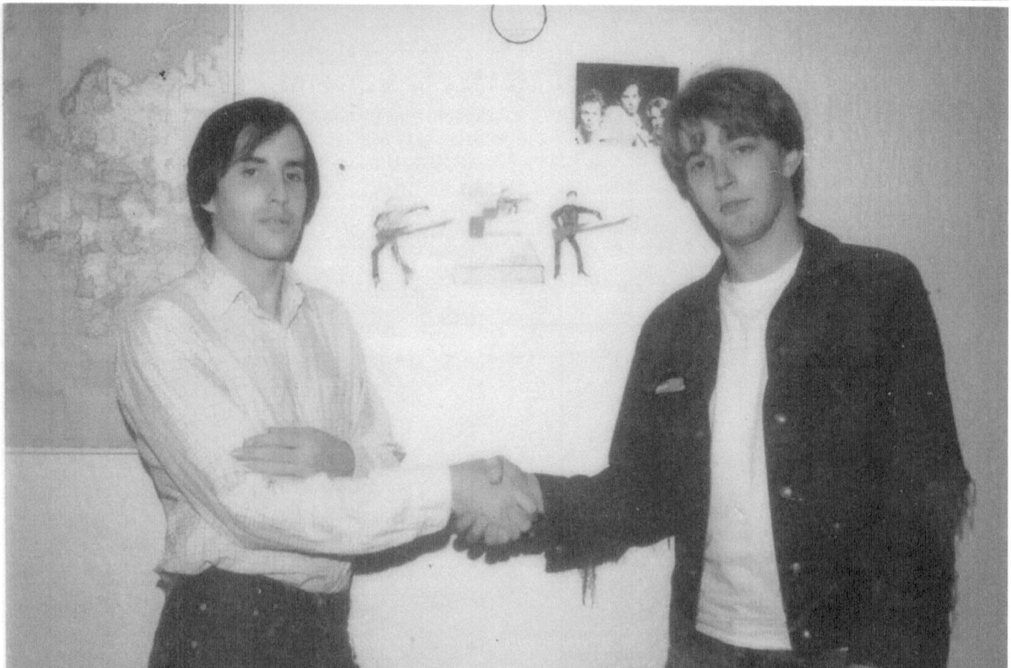

(PREVIOUS PAGE & ABOVE): THE NERVES LAST RECORDING SESSION IN LATE 1977.
photos courtesy of Marci Marks

LOS ANGELES.... LOS ANGELES.... LOS ANGELES.... LOS ANGELES.... LOS AN

• The Nerves (Paul Collins, Jack Lee, Peter Case), somewhere in the midwest on their 1977 tour.

The Nerves

By Kenneth Funsten

Whatever happened to the Nerves?

In the blitzed-out onrush of Los Angeles rock and roll there are always those bands that get left behind in the trenches. But in the legendary past of about 9 months ago, the Nerves had seemed to be at the very center of things here. In fact, anyone who was around way back then will probably find it hard to forget those three loud-mouthed aspirants to musical fame and fortune. And they weren't even punk! In retrospect, the Nerves set the "prototype" for L.A. Power Pop.

Jack Lee on guitar, Peter Case on bass, and Paul Collins on drums are the Nerves. It was these three who rented the dilapidated basement in the tacky movie studio at the corner of Sunset and Gower and dubbed it the Hollywood Punk Palace. From here, the L.A. new-wave was born.

At the 5 Punk Palace shows, the Weirdos, the Dils, the Zippers, the Zeros, the Screamers and many others all received their baptism under public fire. The Nerves, too, gained valuable experience.

Rejecting a loud and trashy punk image, the Nerves dressed in quiet-colored three-piece suits. They looked more like Hoover salesman than rock and roll stars. They played only original material, crisp songs with strong melodies, like "Hanging on the Telephone" and "When You Find Out" off their EP (Nerves Records, dist. by BOMP). Their bare, skeletal sound made every lick seem memorable. They excelled in energy. People compared them to the early Beatles or the Dave Clark Five. And then suddenly, they were gone.

What happened? Were they dead? Had they given up, stopped playing? Or (God forbid!) had they become accounting students, fanzine editors or perhaps something even worse?

None of the above. The Nerves had taken fate in hand and booked their own cross-country tour. During the first week in May, they played 3 nights at the Starwood in Hollywood. Then, loading everything into their black '69 Ford LTD Wagon ("the highest paid member of the touring organization"), the group took off for dates in San Francisco, Denver, Chicago, Cleveland, Toronto, Boston, New York, and Washington, D.C. And that was only the first leg of their trip!

In an article for the *Illinois Entertainer*, Cary Baker called it a "Magical Blistering Tour". The band astounded even themselves by playing in Minneapolis on July 4, and then in Cleveland July 5. At one point they drove from Rockford, Illinois, where they'd been playing with the Ramones, straight through to San Antonio, Texas.

When it finally all came to an end after three whirlwind months on the road, the Nerves were in Chicago playing with Mink DeVille. It was by then the Nerves' third appearance in the Windy City. Altogether, they had logged 25,000 miles and played over 100 twenty to thirty minute sets. Whew!! As Jack Lee said, "We think we've lived up to our name."

And so it all becomes clear now. Or at least evident — the Nerves weren't dead. They were in training!

But in training for what? Since the end of July, the Nerves haven't been heard from. They've been writing new songs, of course, and talking to record companies about an album, but so far there's been nothing definite. "We've just been getting oriented to what our next move is going to be," explains bassist Peter Case. "I mean, say you're a new group, you've released your own record, you've run your own club, and then you went out and did your own national tour, now what do you do after that?"

Pete answered his own question recently at the Masque, the sleazy basement gathering place for L.A.'s young punks. There, the Nerves headlined two spectacular shows with the Avengers, the Zeros and Shock.

Their music is the same — only punchier, more refined, and as high-powered as ever. Of their new songs, "Paper Dolls" ought to become a classic. They picked up a lot from the Ramones ("those guys impressed us"), and they've changed their image some. Now dressed in streamlined, satin jackets and black stovepipe pants they have a very All-American look — that is All-American like some weird Las Vegas bar trio. But don't laugh! This may be the look of the future.

What does Nerves music mean? "It comes from being in the mainline. It's got meaning on its own for collectors," states Peter, "but when you write a song you want the greatest possible number of people to hear it. That's what every writer dreams about, and why not go for it?"

Go for it they will. They've got the brains, and the balls....and the nerve. "We don't want to be part of the scene," warns guitarist Jack Lee, "we want to *be* the scene."

able. Only the Quick and Milk 'n' Cookies have had records released on major labels: Milk 'n' Cookies (like the Mumps) are a transplanted NY band whose album was released on Island *only* in England, and the Quick were victims of misunderstanding in a L.A. scene that is, admittedly, pretty bleak. I can't refute the typecasting by outsiders that L.A. is represented by the Weirdos and Van Halen, but I will vouch for the 7 bands here that make this town's local scene interesting and exciting.

Suggested pick-ups are:
"Youre So Strange"-The Zippers (Back Door Man Records)
"Down on the Boulevard"-POP! (Back Door Man Records)
"Giving It All"- 20/20 (forthcoming on BOMP Records)
"Crocodile Tears"- The Mumps (on Exhibit 'J'/BOMP Records)
"In Tune With Our Times" -The Quick
The Nerves EP (Nerves Records) and forthcoming single "One Way Ticket" (BOMP Records).

WORLD POWERPOP REPORT.... WORLD POWERPOP REPORT.... WORLD POWERPOP REPORT

(PREVIOUS PAGE): THE NERVES FEATURE IN THE 1978 POWER POP ISSUE OF BOMP!.

(THIS PAGE): THE NERVES AT MAX'S KANSAS CITY, CIRCA 1977.
photo courtesy of Nicky Lanzzoni (Lower Third Enterprise)

THE BREAKAWAYS (L TO R): PAUL COLLINS, DANNY BIAZYS, IAN ESPINOZA, AND PETER CASE, CIRCA 1978.
courtesy of Paul Collins' Archives

CHAPTER NINE:
Breaking Away

In 1978, I got a job parking cars at Osko's, Los Angeles' premiere disco club on the corner of La Cienega Blvd. and San Vincente. I thought my life was over. LA is the worst place in the world to be a down-and-out rock star, surrounded day and night by successful people in fancy cars. You can't escape having your face rubbed in it, but I told myself if I can't be a star, I'd be near them. I had to keep trying, but it was eating me up from the inside.

On a Friday or Saturday night, we would park well over a thousand cars. The ten of us were the best there were. Our boss Ernie made sure of it. If you own a fancy car, I'd recommend never leaving it with valet parking. You wouldn't believe the shit that goes on. The guys with seniority got first dibs on everything, and nothing was sacred. Tires, jacks, radios, money, drugs, even doggy bags were up for grabs.

One night I opened up a glove compartment, and couldn't believe anyone would be stupid enough to leave a stack of $100 dollar bills. I couldn't resist, so I palmed a few of them. No sooner than I returned, the owner was back demanding to get his car. I freaked, and thought my goose was cooked for sure. Fortunately at the same moment, another patron was screaming about his stolen radio, and a third customer was accusing Ernie of damaging his car.

A detective from vice squad showed up and started giving Ernie all kinds of shit, but this kind of stuff didn't rattle him in the least. He turned to the cop and in his toughest, baddest, straight out of a B-level TV show voice said, "You wanna fuck with me? Well come on and fuck with me, but you and your boys can get these people their fucking cars!" With that, Ernie took the big board with four or five hundred car keys on it and dumped it on the ground. What a classy guy.

I wasn't out of the woods yet. The cops summoned all the parking boys around the hood of a car and demanded that we empty our pockets. You can imagine my surprise when every last one of us had two, three (or more) $100 bills in our pockets. There wasn't a damn thing they could do. It was one of the few moments where you just had to love Hollywood.

I drifted around, parking cars at various hoity-toity restaurants on the Sunset Strip. I was loaded with money, had all the free drugs I could want, and my girlfriend was a stripper, but I still felt unfulfilled. I was just doing the 'Hollywood Hang.'

I got to work at The Masque as one of the main doormen. I knew the owner, Brendan Mullen, from when The Nerves would play there. Brendan liked me because I didn't let anyone in for free, so I'd be handing him big wads of cash. I disguised myself by wearing a shower cap, a black Zorro mask, and a Sex Pistols-style white shirt with safety pins. I was adamant about not letting anyone know it was me. Brendan also let The Breakaways use The Masque to rehearse.

I had become very seasoned playing in an original band, and was desperate not to go back to being on my own, with no prospects. In The Breakaways, Pete and I were still on bass on drums. We knew that going back to the drawing board with a band was going to be hard. We had a terrible time trying to find people on our level to play with. It wasn't necessarily a matter of chops. You had to have a sound, and we did, but finding other cats who had it was no easy trick in Los Angeles.

I wouldn't dare show my face in any music store. I'd been banned from all of them, so we decided to search the classified ads of the *LA Reader* and *The Recycler*. Throughout 1978, we made contact with a roll-call of musicians who would come over, record, hang out, and jam.

The first lineup of The Breakaways was Peter, Harlan Hollander on guitar, and me. Harlan had been in The Tremors, who were on the bill for The Nerves' last show at The Whisky. This lineup recorded the "Walking Out On Love" demo that a year later, would end up on a couple of Bomp 1979 various artists compilations, *Waves Vol. 1* & *Who Put The Bomp*.

The Breakaways got their first booking, on April 11th, and 12th 1978 at the Whisky A Go-Go, opening for The Pop and The Dogs. The Tremors had a gig that same week and wouldn't let Harlan play, so he quit The Breakaways. Guitarists Ian Espinoza and Danny Biazys joined and played the Whisky gig, but things soon fizzled.

Peter and I decided to switch to guitar, so we began looking for a rhythm section. I was tired of playing the drums and sold them. From then on, I'd think of my life as B.G. (before guitar) and A.G. (after guitar). I bought a Fender Stratocaster for about 60 bucks. Later on, John Carruthers (who is still one of LA's top guitar techs) put his custom neck on it. He turned it into a very cool guitar. I recorded *The Beat*, *The Kids Are The Same*, and many of my other records with that Strat.

One day when we were rehearsing at The Masque, I went out to get some 'ciggies' and beer and I ran into my old pal Eddie Money. He was now a big star with a *Top 10* hit single – "Baby Hold On To Me." He was doing an in-store at Peaches Records, and was surrounded by fans. I wondered if he would remember me, and he did!

Paul Collins (left) in disguise, working the door at The Masque with Trudie Arguelles (right), circa 1978.
photo courtesy of Jenny Lens

"Hey Paulie! How the fuck are you? Wait until I'm done and we can go smoke a joint!"

We went over to my place. On an acoustic, I played Eddie some of my new songs, and he really dug them. He liked a song I was working on, called "The Mystery of Life," but thought the title was a little bogus. "Come on man, this could be really good, but you need to slick this song up! You've got to change the words to the chorus. They suck!" He thought for minute and said, "Hey, I've got it. 'Let Me Into Your Life!' Yeah man, that's it!"

We smoked a joint, played it through a few times, and then Eddie said, "Fuck, this is a good one, man. Let's call up Don Ellis [vice president of A&R at CBS Records] and play it over the phone!" Now I was really freaking out, and about to shit my pants as Eddie dialed the number. Suddenly Don Ellis was on the line. We were playing and singing it over the phone to him, with Eddie doing backups.

"Sounds good, Eddie. Give me a call at the office on Monday, and we can talk about it!"

The Breakaways were falling apart. Nothing was happening, and it looked like Peter was losing interest. I was petrified of winding up by myself, not having the confidence to go it on my own. I knew I needed someone to help me put it all together, and that's when I met Steven Huff.

Steve was the opposite of Jack, mellow, and laid back. He was a total musicologist, who knew everything there was to know - the chord patterns, how to arrange, and how to come up with parts. Steve wasn't looking for the spotlight; he just wanted to play good music. He became the perfect foil for me.

Steve had a home recording studio near Silverlake on 1312 Talmadge Street. He had a Teac 4-track tape deck, and a huge Gibson Magnum amp, with reverb for the guitars and vocals. He was renting a room from a guitar player named David Harvey and his singer Cynthia, who later became my girlfriend. They were in a *Top 40* cover band, and were always out on the road, so Steve would have this big house all to himself.

I had no money, and the walk to his house took me over an hour. For the rest of 1978, I would spend all day with Steve in his living room, working on music, and eating po-boy sandwiches washed down with Lucky Beer (3 bucks a case). It was really good rehearsing the songs over and over, and getting cool sounds on his tape deck.

Soon after I met Steven Huff, Peter quit. I think Peter just decided that he didn't want to be in a band with me. One day he just split, telling us he had his own thing going on. I knew it was coming, but still, I was upset. I thought of Peter and Jack as my brothers, and now they were gone. I felt like my arms were cut off, but Steven

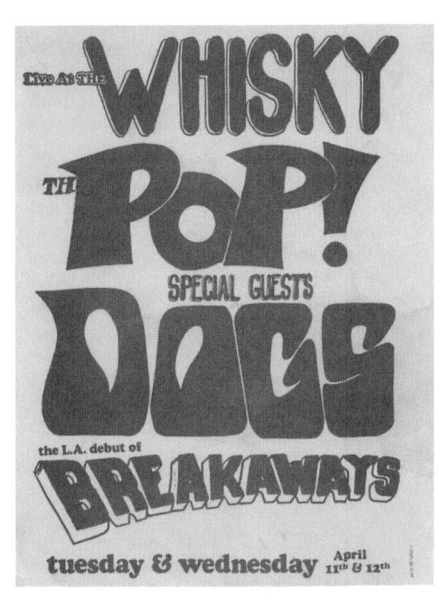

(TOP): FLYERS FOR THE DEBUT BREAKAWAYS SHOWS AT THE WHISKY.
(BELOW): EDDIE MONEY, PAUL COLLINS, AND MARCI MARKS, CIRCA 1978.
courtesy of Marci Marks' Archives

THE BREAKAWAYS (CLOCKWISE FROM TOP): PETER CASE, IAN ESPINOZA, PAUL COLLINS, AND DANNY BIAZYS, CIRCA 1978.
courtesy of Paul Collins' Archives

Huff more than filled the void. We threw ourselves with abandon into making our demo.

During this time, a handful of musicians came over to help us out, including Brandon Matheson. He played with the Rubber City Rebels, and later on he was in Jack Lee's solo band. Irv Kramer, who would go on to play keyboards with The Knack, wrote and gave us the solo on "Work A Day World," for ten bucks! *But still, we didn't have a band.*

Then we met drummer Mike Ruiz who had been in a major label band, Milk 'N' Cookies. He knew The Ramones, who had auditioned him just before he joined us. He had the chops, the vibe, and what's more, he introduced us to Larry Whitman.

Breakaways

ONE WAY TICKET
PLEASE PLEASE ME
DO YOU WANT TO LOVE ME
EVERYDAYS THINGS
LITTLE SUZY
RADIO STATION
WORKING TOO HARD
MR. SANDMAN
BURNING ~~FOREVER~~
WALKING OUT ON LOVE
U.S.A.
COOL JERK

BREAKAWAYS SET LIST, APRIL 1978.
courtesy of Paul Collins' Archives

Larry had a Telecaster and he played the fuck out of it, balls-to-the-wall, heavy-duty rock 'n' roll, which is what we do. This was what we wanted. We didn't want to come across as lightweight. He wrote the solo to "Don't Wait Up," and it just locked right in. *Now we had a band: The Beat!* At this point, things seemed to happen so fast and it made my head spin.

By November of 1978, we were ready. The Beat's demo was recorded and mixed – our twelve perfectly constructed pop songs. This time I was at the helm, but

I couldn't have done it without Steve, I know that. Steve's roommate David Harvey wasn't too happy to come home and find out that his bedroom had been turned into a booth for recording. So not long after that, we were booted out of Talmadge St.

I was about to get really lucky for the first time in my life. Eddie gave our tape to his producer Bruce Botnick (The Doors, Buffalo Springfield). Then Eddie's A&R rep Don Ellis got us on CBS Records, one of the biggest record companies in LA and the world. I was on cloud nine, and it seemed like all my hard work was finally going to pay off. The people at CBS acted like they really loved the band, and we were very optimistic.

Our audition for CBS was conducted one fine Saturday afternoon in early 1979 at The Masque. Bruce Botnick and Don Ellis came down and crammed into our stinky rehearsal room. There was one bare light bulb hanging from the ceiling. We had two Peavy Columns for a PA. Back to back, we blasted through the songs from the first album. When we were done, Don looked at Bruce and said "Sign 'em." He walked out and that was it. We were signed to a major label in the space of thirty minutes. We got what we thought we always wanted. The band was ecstatic.

After years and years of hustling and doing everything we could think of, we played for two of the most highly sought out pros in the music business. We played for half an hour, and that was it!

Remember, this was a time when people would spend tens of thousands of dollars just to make a demo. They would rent the biggest room in town with drinks and catering. They would do whatever it took to get a label to come check out a band, and hopefully sign them.

It's like you burn one joint with Eddie Money and suddenly the world is your oyster.

PART 3:
THE BEAT

The BEAT original lineup (l to r): Mike Ruiz, Paul Collins, Steven Huff, and Larry Whitman, circa 1979.
photo courtesy of Neil Zlozower

CHAPTER TEN:
Dawn Of The BEAT

The beginning of The Beat's major label career was kind of a *Cinderella* fantasy. When CBS/Columbia verbally agreed to work with us at The Masque, it was a package deal. We immediately "got" Eddie Money's record label, producer, and whole team.

I retained Mr. Stan Diamond, Eddie's lawyer and "Hollywood attorney to the stars." At various points in his career Stan represented David Bowie, Van Morrison, John Fogerty, Black Sabbath, John Lee Hooker, Iggy Pop, Marvin Gaye, and many others. Back then, Mr. Diamond made the magnanimous offer of only taking ten percent of my earnings instead of his usual $500 an hour. Things were definitely looking up. I felt like quite the young dude, and we hadn't even made a record yet.

Oddly, while everyone seemed to have the green light from CBS, Eddie's manager Bill Graham hadn't come aboard. Bill was a famed promoter and music impresario who ran the San Francisco music scene with an iron hand. He was a guy you did not want to fuck with. Bill had clawed his way to the top and no one was going to take it from him. If someone tried to put on a show the same night as a Bill Graham show, he'd personally go down to the box office and buy every single ticket. Then he'd say: "Now you're sold out, but no one's going to be there!"

I never told Bill about the first time I saw him. I was still living at home in Leonia and I'd go to his joint in the East Village, The Fillmore East. This is where I saw some of the best concerts of my life, like Jefferson Airplane, Mountain, J. Geils Band, Black Sabbath, Hot Tuna, and Santana's original line up with Michael Shrieve on drums. The Fillmore was the best. You'd get high just sitting in your seat while every possible drug known to man got passed along to you.

One night, I was alone in the can at The Fillmore, when The Hell's Angels walked in as I was peeing. I was like "Oh shit!" Then, this little guy walked in and started screaming at the Angels.

> *"I told you motherfuckers, I don't ever want to see you in my fucking place! Now get the fuck out of here before I have your asses kicked!"*
>
> *Holy Shit! It was Bill Graham himself! I was hoping these guys wouldn't decide to kill him on the spot, but instead, they hung their heads down like little school boys.*
>
> *"Gee Bill, we're sorry! We didn't mean no harm. We just wanted to see the show. We won't cause no trouble, we promise."*
>
> *Everyone left, and I was standing there with my pecker in my hands.*

By April of 1979, I remember it got to the point where CBS said: if Bill Graham hasn't "inked" you yet, then go with another manager. Bill probably wanted to check us out, but waited until the last minute because he knew he could.

Finally, Bill Graham and his people flew down to LA, rented a rehearsal stage in the San Fernando Valley, and had us play for them. Before making any decisions, Bill still wanted to see us perform in front of a live, paying audience. He flew us up to San Francisco. On April 10, 1979, The Beat would play our first actual show at a huge place, The Kabuki Theater. We opened up for Eddie Money.

We were flying out of Burbank, and on the way to the airport, we were all drinking in Steve Huff's car. A cop pulled us over, so we started dumping the beers out on the floor. So, the floor was covered with foam, the glove compartment was jam-packed with Steve's unpaid parking tickets, but when we told the cop that we were going to play for Bill Graham – he let us go!

I don't know how the rest of the band felt at The Kabuki. Mike Ruiz and Larry Whitman had been around the block, so they probably weren't as nervous. I was completely freaked out. I was playing so hard that my strings were breaking constantly. The roadies were frantically bringing up guitars, trying to keep the show going. We went over well and Bill agreed to come aboard. He wasn't sure about me at first, but he taught me a lot and we became great friends.

What management and the label wanted was very simple. They said – Paul, you are the lead singer. You wrote all the songs, so we aren't signing the band; *we are only signing you.* The contracts would be with Paul Collins, and the band was never part of any business agreement. The band would be on salary, paid on a union scale, and would remain that way for the entire time the band was operating on that level. I would be a 'royalty artist' and not get any money until we (hypothetically) recouped. Back then, this wasn't an unusual arrangement. Obviously, the contract for The Cars or Cheap Trick was probably not the same, and it just depended on the situation.

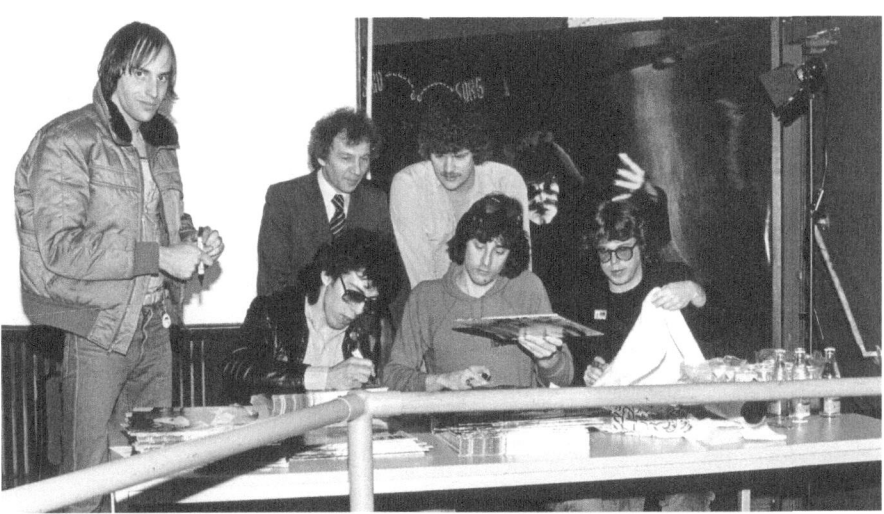

THE BEAT

(TOP): THE BEAT SIGNING COPIES OF THEIR DEBUT LP ON COLUMBIA/CBS RECORDS.
(BELOW): THE BEAT COLUMBIA RECORD PROMO 8x10, CIRCA 1979.
courtesy of Paul Collins' Archives

Also, there was no 'big advance' where I got some big check to put in the bank. The 'deal' was for about $125,000, and $40,000 immediately went into recording the first LP. Around $25,000 went into state-of-the-art musical equipment. The rest would be spent on tour support and the band's living expenses. CBS/Columbia and Bill Graham wouldn't allow us to waste a dime.

I had recently inherited some money from my grandfather, and didn't have money problems then, so I had no problem with the business agreement. Mike and Larry did, but they quickly came around. If anyone should have had a problem, it should have been Steve, who had been paving the way with me for about a year now. Mike and Larry had jumped aboard at the last minute. Steve said "I don't want to wait, give me the money now, and fuck this royalty shit!" Steve remembers making about $6,000 a year back in 1979 and 1980, which is about $21,000 a year in 2020, when adjusted for inflation.

Bill Graham Presents was definitely a real San Francisco tight-knit, family style operation. Jerry Pompili (Bill's right-hand man) had been around since the early Fillmore days, and was also a big supporter of The Beat. Kevin Burns aka "K.B." was another member of Eddie Money's entourage, and he became our road manager. In fact, a lot of Eddie's guys who had gotten in trouble with Eddie or Bill, and were "put on notice," wound up working with us!

I signed with Wolfgang Productions, Bill Graham's subsidiary record label under CBS/Columbia. The way it is in LA, when a band gets signed, the whole town knows about it, clear on down to the guy on the street panhandling. We kind of got the gold star treatment, and everyone treated us 'real nicely,' whether they liked us or not. I'd been shit on, pissed on, kicked around, kicked out, abused both emotionally and physically, and now we were the toast of the town.

Suddenly, everyone wanted to be my friend.

I am not a vindictive person at heart, but who could resist an opportunity? The first thing the boys and I did was go to the biggest, stuck-up music store in Hollywood. We had these assholes haul out every piece of equipment for us to try out, at maximum volume. Then we walked right out, saying "thanks, but we're going to buy our shit somewhere else!" I reminded the manager that I was the guy he had kicked out a year ago. Yeah, I was cocky, but what's the use of being young and signed to the biggest record company in the world, if you can't pull off shit like that? Today, I would use my maturity, reserve, and just let it go, but let's be honest - *who the fuck would want to read about that?*

(BOTH PAGES) LARRY WHITMAN AND PAUL COLLINS, LIVE ONSTAGE, CIRCA 1980.
photos courtesy of Catherine Sebastian

After the band was signed, I was hanging out at the CBS offices all the time. We were like little cherubs to them, sweet rock 'n' roll kids roaming the floors. We would run around, trying to get free records, and talking about music. I became friends with one of the senior promotion managers. One time, I walked into his office, saw his briefcase and said, *holy shit!*

>Do you remember the silver Haliburton briefcase? It was like a Rolex watch. If you were successful in the music business, you had to have one. Most of them were silver, but there was a slightly pink & silver model. It was probably more expensive.

>Well, last year I was still parking cars for a living, and worked for a brief while at The Mandarin - a high class Chinese restaurant. One night a guy pulled up in a Porsche, jumped out, and dashed into the restaurant.

>I sat down in the plush leather seats, and couldn't help but notice the pink & silver briefcase in the passenger's seat. I didn't need any more encouragement, and the first thing I saw was a double-sized vial filled with white powder. Mine!

>Back then I had hardly done any coke; it was too expensive. Steve knew what it was immediately, and knew we could sell it for much needed cash. Well, I sold it... to Eddie Money! We snorted it up and I felt like a cool rock star – but the story didn't end there.

When I saw my promotion manager's briefcase, I knew it was the one. So I asked him, "Uhh, do you ever eat at the Mandarin?"

"Yeah yeah, Paul, I eat at the Mandarin."

"Uhh, do you drive a Porsche?"

"Yes Paul, why do you ask?"

"*Uhh, did you ever lose a big vial of coke?*"

Thankfully, he laughed about it. That's Hollywood for you.

Finally, in June of 1979, at United Western Studios, on 6000 Sunset Boulevard in Hollywood, I was about to make my first state-of-the-art, full-length album. My world class producer Bruce Botnick drove up to the studio in a Mercedes. His license plates said "EARS." My engineer Rik "Aloha" Pekkonen, who did all the Crusaders records, was wearing a Hawaiian shirt. Bruce put together the best guys in the business, top audiophile guys, which is why the record sounds so great today.

Back in 1979, it was the height of studio excess. A studio like The Record Plant had a sauna, a hot tub, private rooms (where god knows what went on), and there was no shortage of cocaine and Courvoisier. In contrast, United Western was an old school, no-frills recording studio where The Beach Boys had recorded. Benny Goodman was next door, rehearsing his band for *Jazz at the Hollywood Bowl*.

We worked 9 to 5, were allowed one dinner with Bruce on the expense account, and there was no partying, drinking, or drugs. Well, Larry was a big weed guy, so he was probably getting stoned, but this was my big break, and I wasn't going to go in there and fuck up. We were the musicians, and CBS and Bruce were in charge. We were smart enough to keep our mouths shut and do as we were told.

In the studio, Bruce Botnick taught me the two most fundamental things about making a good record. He would always say, "Tell me a story and give me a performance." Bruce lined the band up in our prime moment, and preserved our sound with the most advanced technological equipment of the day. Despite that, he didn't want to screw it up with a lot of studio trickery.

The BEAT original lineup (l to r): Steven Huff, Mike Ruiz, Larry Whitman, and Paul Collins, backstage at The Whisky, circa 1980.
photo courtesy of Ron Yocom

Should I dress up, or do I dress down
Should I talk, or should I just frown
I don't fit in, I don't fit in . . . *

Drumming with the Nerves — one of the last gigs at the Whisky

This is Paul Collins, late of the Nerves and between gigs, and still very much a maverick in the musical milieu of Los Angeles. "**I Don't Fit In** is really a personal statement, it sums up my whole situation right now. I don't feel like I fit in with the LA 'hard rock' scene or the 'punk rock' scene. The Nerves never fit into **anything**, we were the weirdest eight-balls behind the whole thing. We had a following, but we didn't reach enough people to really get off the ground. I put more into that band than I put into anything in my life. The three of us put a Herculean amount of energy, emotion and work into it. For four years we really busted our butts. But nothing happened, and this thing with Blondie is kind of ironic."

This thing with Blondie, of course, is the inclusion of the Nerves' **Hanging On the Telephone** on their **Parallel Lines** album. "It's given the Nerves new life," he concedes. "Everytime somebody reviews that ablum they mention '**Hanging On the Telephone** by the Nerves'. It's given the Nerves a lot of press. But when Blondie first heard that song (which was on the Nerves' self-released 45 EP), I was trying to book a gig opening for them, and they said the record was **horrendous** and that we'd **never** play with them. I had that confirmed by their manager and their producer. And now that the Nerves have broken up, they put the song on their latest album and pull it for the single." That first single, of course, failed to receive any stateside airplay, and has since been replaced by the discoish **Heart of Glass**, which apparently is more palatable to the powers that rule our airwaves.

"I'm probably suffering from over-rejection. Every time the Nerves tried to do something, we couldn't get any cooperation or enthusiam." This inexplicably lukewarm acceptance by the public began to take its toll on the trio, and it became increasingly evident in their performing as time and patience wore on. "The last Nerves shows were complete disasters. We didn't know what we were doing, we were groping . . . we were just trying to fit in. We were like chickens with our heads cut off. We were running around . . . we lacked direction . . . and then the group broke up. We'd reached an impass that nobody could

SPIDER

PAUL COLLINS
'I don't fit in'

INTERVIEW BY AL & HEATHER   *I Don't Fit In copyright 1978 Paul Collins get through."

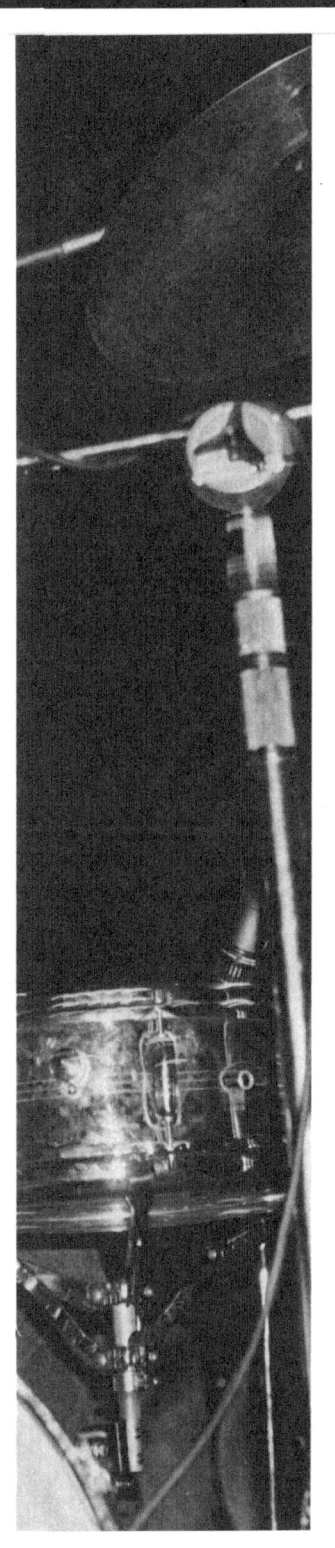

Following the breakup of the Nerves, Paul and bassist Peter Case formed the aptly named Breakaways, while guitarist Jack Lee split off on his own to write and front his own group. "The Breakaways only did two gigs," Paul recalls, "one at the Whisky with Pop, and one at the Rock Corporation in Van Nuys with a couple of 'heavy metal' bands that was a complete flop. The Nerves and Breakaways both had a habit of doing things before they were apropos, the 'in' thing to do. So we never did reap a profit from the whole thing."

There was, nonetheless, the Nerves' cross-country tour, which, amazingly, lost no money and garnered any number of favorable reviews and live receptions. And, of course, there was the EP, which sold well enough to demand a second pressing and is still available at most outlets. "It's a good record," Paul acknowledges, "but the guitar sound is lacking, which makes it a bit thin. That was the biggest drawback of the whole band, that it was basically a bass and drums sound. It was all due to inexperience, really, we just went out there and did it. It was a great little record for the time it came out.

"The Nerves were really rebellious, but the music didn't have that anger in it that the 'punk rock' had. We weren't **that angry**, we weren't trying to get people to go out and riot, we were just trying to get them to listen to some different shit. I learned a lot from that group, I think everybody in it did, and hopefully, the energy we put into it will come back. For me, it'll come back if I can just happen, if I can get my music on the air.

"Right now I'm just getting my material together for an album, arranging the songs, and getting the band rehearsed so we can play live. I've got Mike Rouez, who played with Milk 'n' Cookies, on drums, Steve Huff on bass, with myself on guitar. It's been working out really well, and now we're just trying to find a lead guitar, that fourth member who can fill in what we need." In spite of its reputation as the Musician's Mecca, Paul finds that "Looking for musicians in LA is one of the hardest things in the world. So many of them come here, but I've found that they've all got one really strong area they're into, like a Neil Young style or the 'Southern boogie' style, and it's very prevalent in the way they play. What I'm looking for is the kind of guitar player I grew up listening to, like George Harrison, the kind that really punches out a strong melody. That's what I'm **looking** for," he emphasizes with a tone of frustration, "but probably not what I'm going to **get.** So much depends upon the musicians you work with, they really determine how you sound. I'm not doing the kind of music you can do with session musicians, it's got to come from somewhere gutsier than where most session men are coming from."

By way of example, he clicks on a cassette recorder, which is about the only "furniture" in the room other than his record player. From the first few bars alone, one can sense that Paul Collins' music is coming straight from the gut. Even in this raw, unmixed form, this is definitely AM car radio material. "I'm trying to get a sound that's sort of a mutation of British rock Americanized. The only thing that makes most American rock American these days is that it's very unmelodic and very heavy handed. Don't get me wrong, I like the power you can get with electric guitars, but I want a strong **melody** behind it. The Nerves were into that — what made them good were the songs they wrote. I'm still into those things, but the approach is different. It's still rock 'n' roll, but instead of the 'jackhammer' approach, I'm trying to let it breathe a little. I'd like to keep the Nerve fans with me, but reach a whole new audience as well, an audience that can say, 'This guy's writing about things I like, that I think about, that **mean** something to me.'

"My biggest gripe with the music business is that everybody out there's a bunch of old fogies. I feel that my music is new, young (for the record, Paul's 22), and represents my experience. I want to get it out there, working with people that can make it sound as good as possible. Even with all the mistakes we're going to make, the tunes should be strong enough to get people off."

And what is Paul Collins doing to survive in the meantime? "I'm parking cars. Parking cars to gold records, that's my goal! All the bullshit you gotta do to survive, it really screws you up, but it's just something you gotta do. It gets really frustrating at times, but I've done this too long to stop now."

UPDATE: Since this interview, Paul has found that elusive lead guitarist in Larry Whitman and a manager in Bill Graham. Paul Collins and the Beat opened Eddie Money's San Francisco concert and are currently back in Hollywood recording an album for Columbia.

We had our own stations; the drums, guitar, bass, everything was baffled off. Larry used a small Fender Champ amp, and I was using a Fender Deluxe. Steve and I had demoed most of the songs, and the band was well-rehearsed, so it was kind of like "okay, let's play rock 'n' roll like we've done it a million times before!"

We were getting ready to record, and Bruce and the engineers were in the control room. They kept hearing this noise. They thought it was a technical problem, and were trying to solve it. The way the studio was set up, there was a couch in front of the board, and they couldn't see it. It turned out, that was where our handler & road manager Jerry Pompili was, sound asleep and snoring.

As far as recording specific songs in the studio, I remember Larry was really proud of the fact "You Won't Be Happy" was totally live. My biggest memory was recording the song "Look But Don't Touch." Bruce and Rik said, "hey, listen, we need to do a test to check the gear, but don't play a song that we're trying to record. Just play anything." We played "Look But Don't Touch" for the first time ever, with no arrangement, all the way through. The song went on and on, because we didn't know how to end it. That is why at the very end of the song on the LP, I say to Bruce, "*is that enough for you?*" Bruce left it all right there, and thank god he decided to record it at all. In that sense, it is the most spectacular song on the record.

Then, Bruce said, "Hey, do you guys want to meet Benny Goodman?" We all went next door where he was rehearsing, and he stopped to say hi. I'll never forget meeting him. Here was a jazz legend, taking time out to meet a bunch of kids, who just so happened to be recording in the same studio. The thing that impressed me the most was when he looked me in the eye, shook my hand, and said "nice to meet you son, good luck with your record!" He wasn't too cool for school, which is something that has stuck with me through all these years.

We spent five days total. When we were done, Bruce blasted the whole recording through very expensive speakers, to get the final mixdown. Back then, a lot of records were what they called 'producers records.' Your LP would end up sounding like the producer's other work, and just like every other band. Maybe that would have killed us, or maybe we would have had hits; who knows? In contrast, Bruce let us keep "our" sound, and it was pure analog perfection. He handled us with the utmost of loving care. We were lucky to have someone like him, who actually loved the music.

The first album of any good group is a very special time. It was a wonderful, magical experience, and one of the shining moments of my life. All the stars were lined up, and everything that could have gone wrong, didn't. At that particular moment I was blessed with all the power, strength and reserve that any artist could ask for.

(TOP LEFT): PAUL COLLINS, CIRCA 1979.

(TOP RIGHT): THE MNM'S DEBUT SINGLE, QUARK RECORDS, 1979.

(MIDDLE RIGHT): EDDIE MONEY 'GET A MOVE ON' SINGLE, CBS RECORDS 1979.

(BOTTOM RIGHT): *SPIDER MAGAZINE*, 1979. (ARTICLE IN PREVIOUS SPREAD).

courtesy of Paul Collins' Archives

149

Waiting for our record to come out, I kept busy. I started writing songs with my girlfriend Marci Marks, who always had aspirations of singing. We came up with "Knock Knock Knock" and "I'm Tired." Our two songs became the first single for her new wave band The MnMs. I asked Larry Whitman to help her produce it. Steve Huff ended up playing bass on the recording, and ex-Breakaway Harlan Hollander became her guitar player. The single was released on Quark, which was a subsidiary of Bomp! Records. I was about to leave the LA scene, but was told much later that The MnMs met with some success over in Europe. Greg Shaw put together an MnMs European tour, and instead of Marci, he sent Nikki Corvette to sing the songs over there.

THE BEAT DEBUT LP COVER PHOTO ALTERNATE SHOT, CIRCA 1979.
photo courtesy of Bob Siedman

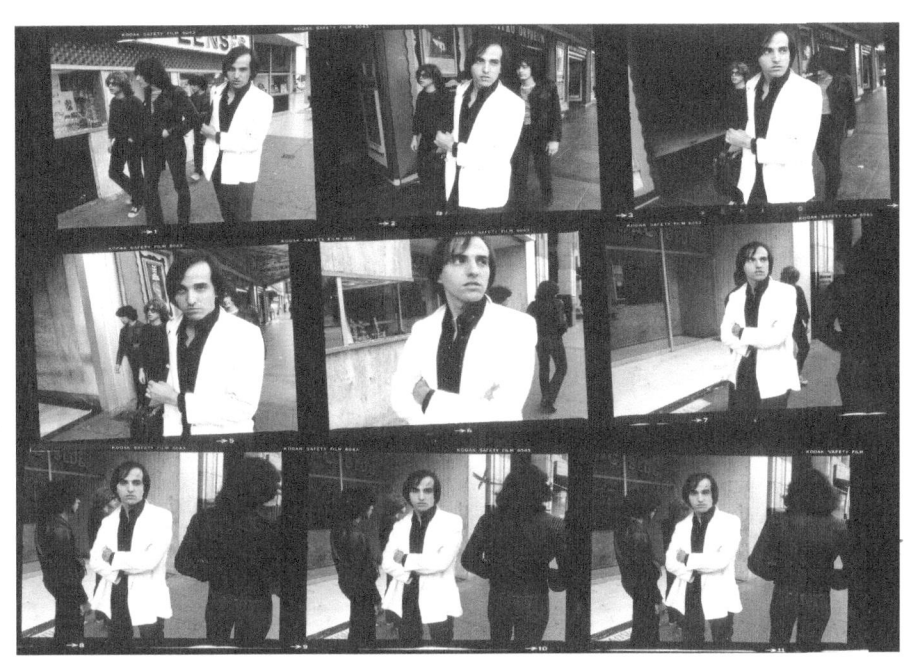

(TOP): THE BEAT DEBUT LP PHOTO SESSION CONTACT SHEET.
(BOTTOM) THE BEAT PROMO PHOTO, CIRCA 1979.
photos courtesy of Bob Siedman

MEET THE BEAT

SAN FRANCISCO—Four disheveled young men, known collectively as The Beat, are onstage in one of the rehearsal rooms in San Francisco's S.I.R. studios. With amplifiers cranked up good and loud, the quartet is pounding through their rock and roll repertoire with the conscientiousness of schoolboys cramming for finals.

Paul Collins, rhythm guitarist/lead vocalist/songwriter, stands center stage as they churn into "Working Too Hard." His slight frame, covered by a baggy yellow T-shirt and blue jeans, accentuates the downbeats with quick jerks. He leans toward the microphone to deliver his vocals, pushing them out over the instrumentation with a dangerous bite.

Steven Huff, his straggly blond hair almost hiding his bespectacled features, lays down bass riffs with a sort of academic detachment. Drummer Michael Ruiz stares into space with a fervid glint in his eyes as he spiritedly flails away. Larry Whitman, the black leather jacketed lead guitarist, grins slightly from beneath his Ramones-style mop top. His crisp guitar work cuts through the nonstop sound with gut-wrenching authority.

The group's debut album, *The Beat*, was released the previous week through Bill Graham's Wolfgang Productions (distributed by CBS). The next step, traditionally, is to push the vinyl with a series of live performances in nightclub showcases and, if one is lucky, as part of a major tour package. The Beat are obviously looking forward to the dates, but realize the absolute necessity of this run-through. After all, they've only played before paying audiences twice during the six months the four of them have been together.

That's an incredibly short time period in which to land a major recording contract. But these guys want to make it clear that The Beat is not, as some wags have suggested, a Monkees-style creation of the Graham machine designed to capitalize on the current roots-rock craze. "We've all been into this kind of music—simple, fun rock and roll—for a long time," says Whitman, flopping onto a couch at the end of rehearsal. "But now people in the business are starting to pick up on the straight-ahead rock that Paul writes so well."

Collins is the 23-year-old creative force behind The Beat's driving sound. A native New Yorker, he began honing his style in San Francisco back in 1974 as part of the pre-new wave outfit, The Nerves. "This city was a horrible place for new bands back then," he recalls. "The club scene was just terrible. You had to play at this beer hall on 17th Street to the bikers if you were going to play rock and roll."

Struggling for survival, The Nerves did manage to pass an audition at the Longbranch, a rowdy boogie bar in Berkeley (since closed) and were hired to open several shows for a then-equally impoverished Eddie Money. When he and Paul hit if off, Eddie invited The Nerves to open several other engagements for him around the Bay Area.

In 1976, The Nerves recorded a four-song EP and moved to Los Angeles. Soon thereafter, they embarked on a self-managed, three-month-long, coast-to-coast tour, where they shared the bill with bands like The Ramones and Mink DeVille. Although the EP went on to sell a laudable 10,000 copies, it's probably best remembered for providing Blondie with their single, "Hanging On The Telephone."

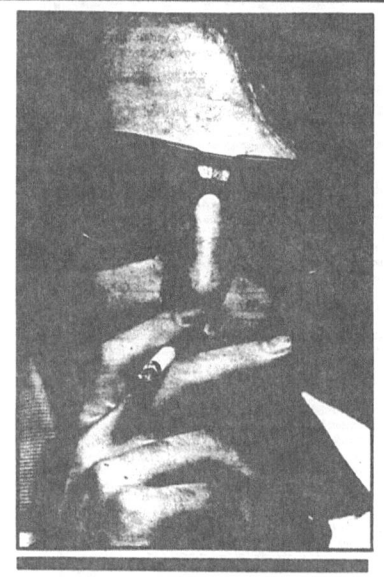

Collins was "very surprised when that song got picked up by Blondie," he says. "The first time they heard it was when I gave them the record, because I was trying to get us a gig with them. And Blondie gave it back to us and said, 'Your band sucks, this record stinks and we'd never play with you, blah-blah-blah.' And six months later, they come out with the tune. I know where *that's* at.

"I look at The Nerves like boot camp," he continues. "I mean, we went out and just busted our butts and got shit in our face every five minutes. But what I'm doing now, musically, is just a continuation of The Nerves. At that time, though, it was like coming out of nowhere—three guys in suits! It was insane.

"When The Nerves started, there was no such thing as power pop, there was no such thing as punk rock. We were sick of hearing what we were hearing, so we formed our own musical style, based on fast rock and roll songs with lots of eighth notes and catchy melodies."

Apparently, audiences weren't quite ready for this sparse style. The group found it harder and harder to book gigs, and in '77 decided to split up. Collins went through a couple of different aggregations before he started forming what would eventually become The Beat.

Huff was the first Beat player to connect with Collins, who describes the bassist as being "tempered by a lot of musical knowledge. He knows everything about jazz, funk polyrhythms—you name it." At first, the pair just sat around and jammed, working out Paul's song ideas in Steve's living room, when the tunes reached fruition, they brought in Ruiz to help record demos. A transplanted New Yorker like Paul, Mike's previous stab at success with Milk 'n' Cookies, whose debut LP was produced by Muff Winwood in '75.

Whitman came into the picture several months later. Ruiz introduced Collins to the lead guitarist, whom he knew from an L.A. band called Needles & Pins. He also knew that Whitman had paid his dues with people like Iggy Pop, Buddy Miles, Jeff Porcaro and even Shaun Cassidy. But through the fall of 1978, The Beat was a trio concerned only with producing a promising demo tape.

Walking to rehearsal one afternoon in August, Collins passed Peaches Records on Hollywood Boulevard and was attracted by a crowd of kids milling near the entrance. There was Eddie Money, signing copies of his top-selling first album. "That day, he came over to my house and I played him this tune that I had written called 'Let Me Into Your Life' [which wound up on *The Beat* LP]. He helped me finish it off and put it together," he recalls.

Not long thereafter, he sent Money a demo tape, and the fast-talking rocker "started hyping it to all these people," says Collins. "Eddie and I are good friends. We both like each other's work and respect each other—at least, I respect Eddie," he laughs. "I look up to him and I think he feels, you know, protective, toward me."

Money introduced Collins' music to his own manager, Jerry Pompili, of the Graham organization, who in turn notified Bill Graham himself. "I don't think Bill really got off on it to begin with," says Collins. "I don't think he quite knew what we were trying to accomplish. But at that point, we were hardly evolved—we were an embryo."

Months went by and Eddie Money embarked on a nationwide tour. As it neared completion, he began pushing to have The Beat open his homecoming show, scheduled for April 10 at the Kabuki Theatre in San Francico. Graham's staff hesitated. So on April 7, when Money was in Los Angeles to play the outdoor California Jam, he persuaded Graham and Pompili to hear The Beat again. They all trooped to the band's rehearsal space. "We really poured it on," says

Beat leader Paul Collins. Photo: Dave Patrick

THE BEAT ARTICLE IN *BAM MAGAZINE*, OCTOBER 1979.
courtesy of Paul Collins' Archives

Also around this time, I had co-written Eddie Money's new single "Get A Move On." I remember coming up with those eighth notes, and the "ba-da" vocal. Then, Eddie continued to work on the song separately with another songwriter named Lloyd Chiate. It entered the Billboard Hot 100 *at #81 on August 25th 1979, finally peaking at #46 on Oct 8th, 1979. The song also appeared on the soundtrack of the 1979 movie* Americathon, *starring John Ritter. I don't remember ever getting any really big money for it, but I did start seeing some royalties.*

What I really remember is, "Get A Move On" was produced by this guy Ron Nevison, who was a notorious drug-addled producer. When they were cutting the record, I got to the studio around noon to do some backup vocals. Everyone was there, I walked in, and Ron was putting the tracks up, finding some problem with every track. So I couldn't do my part because it was all fucked up.

Right then, Nevison went out and took a four hour lunch! They ended up scrapping everything, and I had to come back at a later date, to put my guitar and backup vocals on it. Again, it was just the era of excess; the backdrop of how records were being made at the time. The whole band would be standing around, waiting to record, getting paid triple scale, doing nothing, and then it would be time to have lunch!

In real estate, it's all about location, but in rock 'n' roll, it's all about timing. This ended up being my Achilles heel. A tug of war began between Bill Graham and CBS. Bill wanted our record to come out in September of 1979, and CBS wanted to wait until the New Year - January 1980. I think CBS wanted The Beat to be "new artists" for a "new decade." Why Bill cared one way or another is something I ask myself to this day, but he threw a tantrum. Bill threatened to hold back Santana's new record, and CBS said 'Okay, have it your way.'

So, per Bill Graham's wishes, The Beat's self-titled debut record came out in late September, 1979, to mostly positive reviews. According to someone at CBS/Columbia's publicity department, we had a huge file of glowing press, and the only person with a larger file than us was Bob Dylan.

I could have let it all go to my head, but somehow I knew better.

What I didn't know at the time was, because Bill Graham had waged war, CBS wasn't going to do jack shit for The Beat. They didn't support the record, and we didn't get any senior employees working our record. All the A&R and product managers were first-year guys.

Also, the day my record came out, was right when CBS announced a new 20% return policy. This was done in order to curb spiraling debt, and offset manufacturing costs. Basically, retailers used to be able to return or exchange 100% of what they ordered from the distributor. You could say 'Hi, I'd like to exchange 500 Peter Frampton records, for 500 Kiss records.' Now, retailers could only return 20% of the product that they ordered, so record stores were like 'okay that's fine, give me three copies.' We were a new act, so record stores wouldn't stock our LP and risk not being able to return it. This killed our record. It all comes down to one simple fact: you can't sell records if they're not in stores.

Even the volumes of amazing press we got couldn't prevent the inevitable. As an agent once said to me, "good press and twenty-five cents won't get you a cup of coffee."

We were what they called in the industry, a 'baby-act,' and our first record would soon be a stillborn.

Jack Lee says to me internally... "you have finally made a point."

(ABOVE): THE BEAT ORIGINAL LOGO SKETCHES, CIRCA 1979.
courtesy of Mike Ruiz' Archives

(RIGHT): THE BEAT DEBUT LP COVER ARTWORK, CIRCA 1979.

155

LARRY WHITMAN AND PAUL COLLINS, THE BEAT, CIRCA 1980.
photo courtesy of D.Cooper

CHAPTER ELEVEN:
Goin' All Across The USA

With the record out, it was time to hit the road and promote it. Bill Graham Presents rented a house for us up north, in Oakland. We rehearsed for six to seven hours a day, and became a well-oiled machine. We had an everyday handler, Tom Perme, who drove us around, and everything was paid for. We had money to eat, and to buy all the gear that we wanted. When we went on the road, we had actual roadies – a five-man road crew with lighting, monitors, sound, everything. This was me, going from Nerves/Breakaways-style shit, where you hauled in your own gear, and were lucky if you got a beer.

Now that things were really rolling, we got a ton of work around the Bay Area, playing a lot of shows with Huey Lewis, Eddie Money, and Greg Kihn. We could help these bigger acts sell extra tickets, fill the house, and make it a good show. It was a great slot to be in, and we learned a lot opening for these bands.

In October of 1979, we began our first tour of the USA, opening for Ian Gomm, who had just released his LP, *Gomm With the Wind*. It was a good tour for us to cut our teeth with. Ian's fans liked us, and we went over well. Also, he is a lovely guy, very sweet, and a real gentleman. It was a very comfortable way to start touring, because back then, cutthroat bands would try to sabotage you any way that they could.

In reality it did get embarrassing, when every night we seemed to be blowing Ian Gomm off the stage. Ian had great musicians with him, from his former band Brinsley Schwarz, so it's not that they weren't good. The kids were just more into what we were doing – the new, hot, up-and-coming, loud and aggressive rock 'n' roll band. Ian Gomm was still playing English pub rock.

For me, the highlight was when we played Boston toward the end of the tour. We were all backstage after the show, and Ian Gomm and his band were all asking us, "Did you guys see the ghosts on stage?"

"What do you mean, Ian?

(TOP LEFT): POSTER FOR THE BEAT WITH BRINSLEY SCHWARZ' IAN GOMM AT THE WHISKY, NOVEMBER, 1979.
courtesy of Paul Collins archives

(TOP RIGHT): THE BEAT AT A LAUNDROMAT, CIRCA 1979.
courtesy of Paul Collins archives

(LEFT): PAUL COLLINS AND MARCI MARKS, CIRCA 1979.
courtesy of Marci Marks

"What? You didn't see the ghosts on stage? They were trying to push us off the stage, man, it was incredible!"

Keep in mind, they were drinkers, but they weren't drunks. They really did seem to think there were ghosts on that stage! Maybe there were? It was a really old theater, so who knows.

Our first tour was right at the apex of an evolving scene, where everything was still fresh. The further we got away from the major American cities, the cooler it got. In contrast to the punk scene, the new wave-power pop scene was optimistic, the kids were fantastic, and everyone dressed in bright colors. In those days, you could tell what kind of music someone liked, just by their clothes. Our scene was good, clean, fun, which in the end, may have been its downfall. It wasn't dangerous. How can you threaten someone with upbeat melodic pop songs? Therein lies the rub.

In the beginning, one of the hardest things for any band to do is to come up with a name. Jack had come up with The Nerves, so The Breakaways just seemed obvious. But when it came time for me to come up with a name for my new act, it was very difficult. Mike Ruiz says he actually came up with the name The Beat, so maybe he did, but when I decided to call the band The Beat, I was petrified. I thought everyone would rip us to shreds, comparing The Beat to The Beatles. That never even came up, but in late 1979, I got a call in the middle of the night from some English lawyers.

"Mr. Collins, we have a problem. There's a ska band here in England called The Beat."

While our first self-titled album was released all over the world, Columbia/CBS had dragged their feet releasing our record in England. It wasn't a priority for them, because in those days, Europe was very nationalistic about their music, especially in the UK. They didn't care for a lot of American acts, so it wasn't a huge market, even for bands like Journey or The Eagles.

Just when our LP was about to be released in the UK, an English band also called 'The Beat' had already put out their first single ("Tears Of A Clown" b/w "Ranking Full Stop") on Nov 23, 1979. By December of 1979, it peaked at #6, and was a hit. According to international commerce and trade laws, the UK band had usage rights to 'The Beat,' and could prove it.

November 29, 1979

Mr. Myron Roth
Vice President
CBS Records
1801 Century Park West
7th Floor
Los Angeles, CA 90067

Re: "The Beat"

Dear Myron:

I am enclosing a clipping from the November 10, 1979 issue of Melody Maker containing an article on an English group named "The Beat". I am also enclosing a clipping which indicates that their first single "Tears of a Clown" on 2-Tone Records was released on November 23, 1979.

I would appreciate your bringing this to the attention of CBS International and the London office, so that perhaps legal steps can be taken to protect the name in that territory. Please give me a call and let me know your thoughts.

I am still waiting for the tape for David. However, my plans were slightly changed and we won't be going back until December 16th.

I think it is terrible that we have not had lunch for several months and suggest we get together one day next week.

Kindest personal regards.

Sincerely,

DIAMOND & WILSON

Stanley J. Diamond

(BOTH PAGES) LETTERS SENT TO THE BEAT FROM CBS & ARISTA RECORDS REGARDING THE UK BAND ENGLISH BEAT AND THE PROPOSED LEGAL DISCOURSE, 1979-1980.
courtesy of Paul Collins' Archives

February 15, 1980

President
Arista Records
6 West 57th Street
New York, New York 10019

Gentlemen:

We have exclusive recording rights with the group known as the BEAT, which group has recorded and released a number of popular records.

It has come to our attention that your company may have entered into a recording agreement with a British group also known as the BEAT or the U.K. BEAT. Since you have not as yet released any recordings of that group in the United States, we are advising you that in the event such recordings do appear, we plan to assert our prior rights to such name.

In our opinion, the respective names the BEAT and U.K. BEAT are confusingly similar, would lead to confusion of the public, and use by your company would cause us and our group substantial damage. At this point, it should not be difficult for you to make certain that a substantially different name is adopted for your group.

We have advised the Managing Director of your British affiliate of our objections to their use of the name in the United States.

Our companies have always maintained a close and amicable relationship and we believe it would be unfortunate to engage in any misunderstandings over this matter.

Please advise us what action you propose to take in view of the likelihood of confusion between the names of the respective recording groups.

Very truly yours,

Richard G. Rowe

RR/kp/ag
REGISTERED MAIL - RETURN RECEIPT REQUESTED
cc General Counsel, C. Levison

bcc T. Bowen, N. Clainos, M. Cohn, S. Diamond, A. Gerber,
     M. Hyman, A. Marks, T. Tyrrell

THE BEAT LIVE ONSTAGE, CIRCA, 1980.
courtesy of Paul Collins' Archives

Over the years, rumors started, saying there was a lawsuit, but that never happened. To make a long story short, the lawyers said 'here's the deal:'

"You own the name The Beat everywhere except for in England. You can keep using the name if you want, but not in England. You're going to have to change the name of your first album, if you want it released in England. You can call it The American Beat, Paul Collins' Beat, or whatever you'd like."

Since our LP was already printed, and out all over the rest of the world, the record company didn't want us confusing anyone, by having any kind of UK success under a different name. So I used the old showbiz adage; 'if you have to use anything, use your own name.' We became Paul Collins' Beat, and the UK band became The English Beat. Any subsequent copies of the first LP released in the UK were repressed in Holland with 'Paul Collins' Beat' on the cover.

A few years later, when our second record came out, CBS told me to just call ourselves Paul Collins' Beat everywhere. It was a bad decision; because it caused a lot of confusion for me in all the places we had established the band as The Beat. I should have only used Paul Collins Beat in England, and kept The Beat everywhere else. Apparently I still legally own the name, even though I don't use it.

On December 13, 1979, we did a high profile gig at The Palladium in New York called the '$5 Rock 'n' Roll Show.' For one low price, you could see The Beat, along with up and coming power pop bands The Sinceros, Bruce Woolley, and 20/20.

The gig was important enough for Bill Graham to show up, and I heard that Paul McCartney was in the crowd. Mick Jagger actually came backstage in disguise, with a fake beard, and said hello! We knew he was just there to meet and do business with Bill, but we were certainly impressed. Well, apparently Steve wasn't impressed enough to give Mick one of our last two beers he had stashed backstage.

Right before we went on, Bill and Steve were battling. At the time, it seemed like the entire BGP (Bill Graham Presents) office was involved in figuring out how to "dress Steve." Steve wore jeans, t-shirts, sometimes a country style button down shirt, and that was it. He had his own look, and they should have just left him alone, but Bill would give Steve all kinds of shit. We would be going to all these clothing stores, and it was hard. Steve Huff was one of those guys, kind of like Joey Ramone, where nothing seemed to fit him.

THE BEAT LIVE ONSTAGE, CIRCA, 1980.
photo courtesy of D. Cooper

I loved Bill, but he was prone to throwing tantrums. At the $5 Show, he took his own shirt off and ordered Steve to put it on. Then, Bill actually 'fired' Steve that night, but this lasted maybe 24 hours. Bill didn't hold a grudge, and sent Steve an expensive bottle of champagne at the Santa Monica Civic Center, where on December 31st, 1979, we closed out the decade. We welcomed in the New Year opening up for John Waite's band, The Babys.

Unbeknownst to me at the time, we were getting many offers from bookers up and down the east coast. For whatever reason, this information was kept from me by management. These shows could have cemented my future on the east coast, which I could be working off today, if we had established ourselves.

1980 started off well with The Beat taping our appearance on *American Bandstand*, about a month before it actually aired on March 8th. The night before, we had played a show at the Old Waldorf in San Francisco, and had to be up very early, in order to catch a plane to Los Angeles.

According to Steve, he and Larry had met a drug dealer staying at our hotel, who was in town, awaiting his sentence in a federal trial. He had a lot of coke, so Steve and Larry decided to pull an all-nighter, doing three foot lines on a full length mirror they had ripped off the wall. They were still snorting when road manager K.B. woke me up to go to the airport. Larry looked so wasted when we arrived at the ABC Television Center, that a CBS rep gave him a bump just before we went on. In those days, cocaine was everywhere.

To tell you the truth, the taping was over and done with before we knew it. We had to be there by 8 AM and were out the door by ten. The *American Bandstand* crew was so professional, with everything all set up, so before you knew it, you were on stage lip-synching.. Dick Clark came up with his microphone, and interviewed Mike, Steve, Larry and me. He asked great questions, and was being very complimentary. It was exciting, the kids were screaming, but suddenly you're back in the dressing room, and it's over.

Honestly, back then, I didn't realize what a big deal it was, but people still come up to me and say, 'you did *American Bandstand?* Man, that's epic!' Thanks to YouTube, now we get to post it, and you can see what a consummate professional Dick Clark was.

For me, guys like Dick Clark, Roy Rogers, and Benny Goodman are hallmarks of show business – all smiles, all positive, no negative, and no slagging. It was all about entertaining people, and that's the kind of showbiz I remind myself to aspire to. That's what my true interest is, in all of this.

The BEAT performing on *American Bandstand*, March 8th, 1980.
photo courtesy of Richard Creamer

    Our second tour of the United States was with The Jam, in February and March of 1980, on their *Setting Sons* tour. We ended up playing really big 3,000 seat venues. Back in The Nerves, Jack Lee turned me on to The Jam, a UK band, and we saw one of their earliest shows in LA. They were on fire, with their presentation, stage moves, sound, songs, and the suits. I was blown away, and loved their single "In The City."

    When the news hit that The Beat would tour the USA with The Jam, I thought it would be a lot of fun, but when we got to the first gig, it was like, oh boy. Right off the bat, we got this sheet of rules, of what we 'can and can't do' in our own dressing room. We weren't allowed to have any contact with The Jam, and they would have no contact with us. They refused to meet us; we never even got to say hello.

    I can remember being a little envious, seeing huge road cases coming in, and being opened up. Unlike The Nerves, The Jam's suits had arrived from the dry cleaners, neat and all wrapped up in plastic.

MUSIC

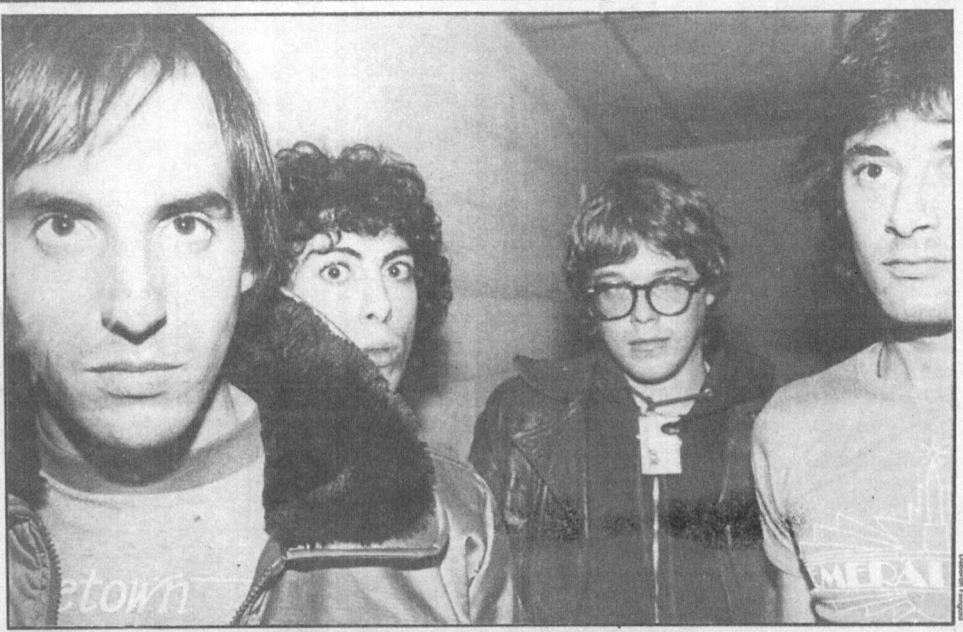

Paul Collins (l.) and The Beat: "Being lumped in with these other bands, it's like throwing mud against the wall."

BEATING THE RAP

Debra Rae Cohen

The Emerald City in Cherry Hill, N.J., looks like a sound stage for a Ken Russell movie: the dance floor is vast, ringed by a cushioned landscape; conversation pits loom like prehistoric pools. It's raining hard in the New Jersey shopping-mall belt, and the small crowd that's braved the weather struggles incongruously about, dwarfed by the flashing Bride of Frankenstein neon and a pulsing chandelier that's enough to make you renounce geometry for life.

Out in the lobby, jagged glass fronds turn pillars into mirrored palms. This place was once the Latin Casino, where Frank Sinatra and others crooned; its new-found thyroid-condition opulence — intended for an ill-timed disco — now serves as a setting for rock 'n' roll. All in all, it's a perfect place to see the Beat, a band with its own involuted ironic images.

First off, there's the central irony (it seems to me) of the new pop: that its state-of-the-art innocence and retroactive teenage dreaming imply a sort of rock 'n' roll perpetual adolescence. You can't believe in teenage passions if there's no hint of adult bittersweet, if you know these guys are *never* going to grow up. At its most calculated, pop turns adolescence into a static condition — about as far as you can get from a tormented phase. The Beat seems less like teens-in-aspic than most of the new bumper crop; the songs by vocalist/guitarist Paul Collins have enough energy that the problems they bring up seem to seek solutions rather than hover in perpetuity. (Also, as critic Tom Carson has pointed out, Collins writes about work as well as love.)

But all that only underscores the other odd twists to the Beat and their history: that the post-Knack vagaries of the music business have resulted in their being lumped together with a slag heap of blatant poseurs and anonymous no-talents; that Collins anticipated and predated the whole pop revival (American wing) in his work with Jack ("Hanging on the Telephone") Lee in the San Francisco-based Nerves; that the new wave-derived Beat got their signing push from Collins' pal Eddie Money and now share his manager, Bill Graham. Add to the list that the Beat make their New York debut this week on a bill with three other CBS pop-rock acts at the Palladium — a double-edged marketing concept if ever I've heard of one.

"Initially I was against doing it," admits Collins, "but now I feel the adversity is good. We'll work harder with the odds against us." Collins has the dark, eager good looks of a young waiter tapped for movie stardom. Talking rapidly, looking intently at the opposite wall of his dressing room, he sits still except for one hypertense knee. If you didn't know that, at 23, he's been in the business for years, that he set up a nationwide tour for the Nerves at only 21, you might even think he was nervous. Just another little irony — and Collins is well aware of the others.

"Being lumped in with these other bands," he muses, "it's like throwing mud against the wall — the good stuff will stick. The most important thing we can do is take this music and drop all the classifications like 'new wave' and 'power pop' — call it rock 'n' roll music, which is what it is. The masses aren't going to accept new wave, or power pop, because the terms are something they don't understand. People just don't know what you're talking about. Those terms are fine to spice up an article, but they don't do the scene any good."

But if Collins resents the pop category, he's always loved the pop single (he calls growing up with WABC his greatest influence). "I always thought of it as controlled improvisation — like an inspired moment captured and put into a controlled situation," he exults. "That whole idea really excited me." Collins was educated at Juilliard — "Jazz, atonal music, modern music, I can do all that stuff," he says. "But at a certain point I had to say, 'This doesn't apply to my life at all. If I can write a rock 'n' roll pop tune, it'll be a hell of a lot more satisfying.'"

Collins is perfectly happy with the constraints he's chosen. "We're a *rock 'n' roll band*," he says. "We realize what our parameters are, and we stay inside them. Once we step outside we're lost. We wouldn't try to play reggae music, because we can't. We wouldn't try to play a disco-oriented thing, because we can't. What we do best is play simple rock 'n' roll: two guitars, bass and drums."

Talking about the Palladium show, Collins sounds like a populist garage-rocker — or a Marxist ashamed of his aristocratic ancestry. "I basically didn't want to play New York until we'd played all the small clubs," he explains, "because that's what we did on the West Coast, and it was very effective. I wanted to play where every other band would start out playing. I didn't want to use the fact that we were managed by Bill Graham, CBS, to play a big show. The reason we should play a big show is because we've proved ourselves to the people in that area."

With only one live gig to their credit before they were signed, the Beat are starting from scratch. "That's what's *weird* about this band," says Collins. "We had *no* following." But he's looking for that legitimacy — what better way to be vindicated of pop calculation? "I'd rather take a year," he says seriously, "get a following of people who'd seen us in dingy little joints and be pushed further along by their patronage of what we were doing."

Okay, it's easy to say. And the Emerald City's hardly dingy. But the backdrop of glass bricks and glitz makes the band on stage look younger, rougher. Collins wears a T-shirt displaying the universal price code. As I watch, he reminds me of Tom Petty — not just in the ringing, guitar-based sound of his music, but in the endearing, awkward edge to his stage presence, the erratic vigor of the band. Like Petty's Heartbreakers, the Beat is a cohesive group whose exuberant missteps simply seem to add to their promise. You can see how good these guys are going to be after a few more laps around the field, and they don't seem the type to get winded.

With 100-or-so people bellied up to the stage, the crowd's only a couple of rows thick. While it means he keeps peering down like a parrot, Collins tries to meet everyone's eyes. It's what makes him, finally, convincing: He's working to win them, one by one.

The Soho Weekly News December 13, 1979 23

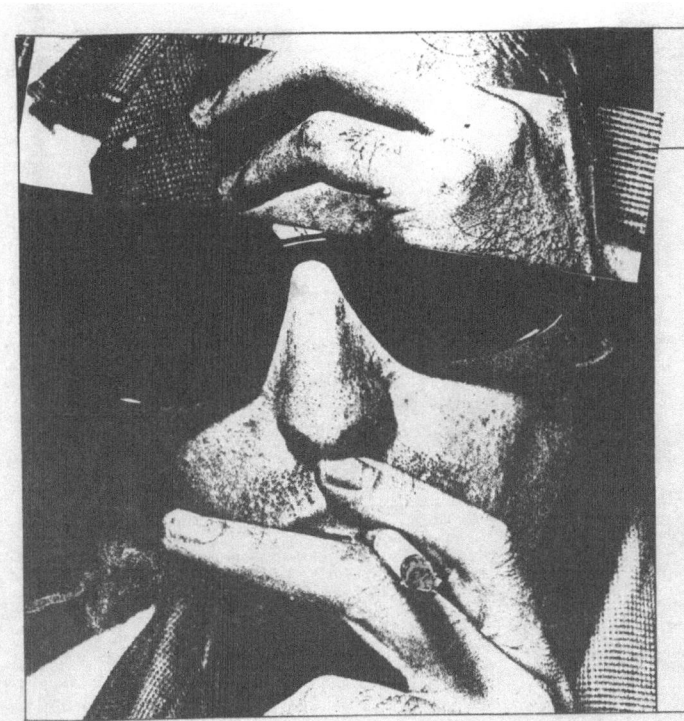

PAUL

From The Street to The Beat

COLLINS

by Michael Branton

HOLLYWOOD—Paul Collins stands in the middle of a tiny recording booth in the maze of United/Western Studios on Sunset Boulevard. Head bowed, eyes hidden behind dark glasses, he listens attentively to the full-tilt pop strains of "Rock 'n' Roll Girl" blasting through high-tech speakers. The bouncy vocal harmonies ride a sharp, melodic base with controlled hysteria. "You Won't Be Happy," another Collins original, follows with crashing guitar chords and an echo-laden Dwight Twilley-styled lead vocal.

Collins looks up and smiles imperceptibly. He and his band, the Beat, have spent all morning laying down the first rough vocals on an album that is nearing completion. *I Don't Fit In*, produced by Bruce Botnick, is being readied for a tentative early August release. Today's results gleam with the edgy, teen-angst drama that dominates most of the 23-year old songwriter/vocalist's work.

The tape grinds to a finish and Collins picks up his guitar and grins. "You know, I did an interview for the very first issue of *New York Rocker*," he says. "Alan Betrock did it long distance from New York. He saw our ad in *Rolling Stone* for the Nerves EP and called me up for a story."

Although the Nerves' one and only recording included three other originals and sold nearly 10,000 copies, it is probably best remembered for providing Blondie with "Hanging On The Telephone" (by Nerve Jack Lee). Paul says he was "surprised when that song got picked up by Blondie. The very first time they heard it was when I gave them the record, because I was trying to get us a gig with them. And Blondie gave it back to us and said, 'Your band sucks, this record stinks, and we'd never play with you, blah-blah-blah.' And then six months later, they come out with the tune. I know where *that's* at!

"I look at the Nerves like boot camp," he continues. "I mean, we went out and just busted our butts and got shit in our face every five minutes. But what I'm doing now is just a continuation of the Nerves. What I do comes naturally—it's never premeditated."

Paul Collins can afford to look back on his career with a mixture of wry cynicism and scrappy pride. The Nerves were one of the very first American new wave bands to record and release their own record, and *the* first unsigned group to undertake a cross-country tour they'd booked themselves. Since the Nerves's demise, Collins has shopped his songs all over the record business, cut numerous demos, and had one track, the rollicking, "House On The Hill," included on the Bomp *Waves* anthology. After struggling amidst the West Coast rock scene since mid-'74 (Collins was raised in New York), he's about to sign a management and recording deal with Bill Graham's Wolfgang Records (distributed by CBS). The only point still up in the air at press time was the specific name the newly-recorded group will use: Paul Collins & the Beat, The Beat with Paul Collins, or simply the Beat are all variations being bandied about. "It's not really like Tom Petty & the Heartbreakers or the Patti Smith Group, because we are a band," Collins explains. "Everybody is irreplaceable. It's my conception, but the band lend their personality and really make it happen."

The only time I—or anyone else, for that matter—saw the Beat onstage was on April 10 of this year, opening for Eddie Money at the Kabuki Theater in San Francisco. Just returned from a national tour, Money threw his considerable weight behind the Beat when he introduced them to his Bay Area fans. "These guys are friends of mine," Eddie announced, "and they are real, real good!" The band—Larry Whitman (lead guitar, backing vocals), Steve Huff (bass, vocals), Michael Ruiz (drums) and Paul Collins (guitar, lead vocals)—had the SRO crowd on its feet and sweating by the time Money rejoined them for a rousing encore.

As we step out of United/Western Studios into an overcast L.A. afternoon, heading for a nearby restaurant for beers and chatter, Collins acknowledges that "Eddie and I are good friends. We both like each other's work and respect each other—at least, I respect Eddie." He laughs. "I look up to him, and I think he feels, you know, protective toward me."

Collins met Money in 1975 when the Nerves were hired to open several shows for the Money band at the Longbranch, a rowdy boogie bar in Berkeley, since closed.

"Then we moved down here in December of '76," Collins says. "I didn't see Eddie for two years after that. In the meantime, he cut his album and started

Cont. on next page

(TOP): THE BEAT LIVE, CIRCA 1980.
(CENTER): CBGB's POSTER JAY THOMPSON AND STEVE HUFF MADE IN SICA'S STUDIO IN NEW YORK, 1982.

(LEFT): THE JAM / THE BEAT 1980 US TOUR POSTER.
courtesy of Paul Collins' Archives

In those days, a lot of things went on between bands and their opening acts. A headliner would take bandwidth out of the PA, so you wouldn't sound as good. This happened to us on The Jam tour. We weren't allowed to touch anything, or change the monitors. Then, The Jam would come out, sound great, and play so loudly that an MC would come on stage beforehand, warning the crowd to use earplugs.

Also, we would walk on to a huge stage for sound check, yet there was no room. My foot would be six inches from the bass drum. I said "This is bullshit! It's a deliberate attempt to sabotage our show!" I told our road manager K.B. to call the office and talk to Bill Graham. The next night, suddenly we had all the room in the world.

That was the power of being managed by Bill Graham.

When The Jam tour entered Texas, a legendary LPM (local promotion man) who called himself Stormin' Norman picked me up. He said "Listen man, there is someone I want you to meet, but you have to promise that you won't tell anyone that I'm taking you here."

So he took me, by myself, to 'The Eagle,' a Parallel One radio station, which was one of a group of the biggest, most influential stations that determined what songs would become 'national breakouts.' If a Parallel One station in Texas started playing your record, then the Parallel One station in California went on it, then New York, and so on, and so on.

Stormin' Norman led me into the building, into a room, and said "I'll see you later. I'll pick you up when you guys are done." I wondered what the fuck was going on, when The Eagle's program director walked in, shook my hand and said:

"I really wanted to meet you, and tell you that I think your song 'Don't Wait Up' could be a *Top 10* hit, but I can't play it."

"What are you talking about? Why not?"

"Well, we called Columbia, told them we want to start playing "Don't Wait Up," and they told us to forget about it. They say they are 'pushing,' Billy Joel's *Glass Houses* this year, and that's all they care about. For that reason alone, I can't play your record, and run the risk that I'm the only Parallel One station playing it. I can only play records that are getting a national push from their record company. *I just wanted you to know that.*"

FFFFUUUUCCCCKKKK!

Obviously this crushed me. It drove me crazy, and for the rest of the tour, I was screaming and yelling "What the fuck is going on here? Why are we getting tour support, when no one is promoting the record?"

This was when I learned the sad truth about the music business, and it seemed like the writing was on the wall. Last year, Bill Graham had declared war on CBS/Columbia over our LP release date, so in retaliation, now we were on a 'token tour.' This is when your record company merely goes through the motions. CBS/Columbia had the ability to make "Don't Wait Up" a hit, and chose not to.

A hit record would have changed my life, or as a good friend of mine once told me, "You probably would have died from an overdose."

Right after that, on the road, I found out that our tour was abruptly over. On route from Houston to Austin, The Jam found out that their single "Going Underground" had debuted at #1 on the UK charts. They said 'fuck the United States,' headed straight to the east coast, and took a Concorde back home. All of this had obviously soured my enthusiasm for being a Jam fan.

We played a few gigs in smaller clubs, in cities where The Jam had cancelled. We ended up in New York, laid up for about four days. This was where I met my next girlfriend, a gorgeous blonde, at our gig at the original location of the famed NY nightclub - Tramps. At the time, she was estranged from her husband, a very famous singer-songwriter in the '60s and '70s. She had been running around the country with all kinds of rock stars, like Phil Seymour, and David Coverdale, and taking pictures of everyone. John McEnroe was there that night too, so maybe that's why she had come to our show.

In the coming year, we had a torrid affair. I wound up chasing her all over the country, from the west coast to the east coast, and back again.

I think I had more sex with her than anyone I've ever known in my life. She was into coke, and in no amount of time, so was I. 'It's free, so what the hell?' is how I thought, but this was when I began to go off the deep end.

After this short stay in New York, we flew to Europe, for a tour that had been given to us as a gift by Columbia's International Department. They had travelled to the USA, checked us out, and offered tour support - hotels, transportation, absolutely everything. The tour wouldn't go against our expense account, or royalties.

They did it just because they loved The Beat.

(TOP): LARRY WHITMAN AND (BELOW): STEVE HUFF, THE BEAT LIVE, 1980.
photos courtesy of Catherine Sebastian

PAUL COLLINS, CIRCA, 1980.
photo courtesy of Rob Overtoom

(TOP): THE BEAT PROMO PHOTO, CIRCA 1980. *photo courtesy of Neil Zlozower*
(BOTTOM): LARRY WHITMAN AND PAUL COLLINS, THE BEAT ONSTAGE CIRCA, 1980.
photo courtesy of Tom Sorem

THE BEAT, CIRCA 1980.
photo courtesy of Neil Zlozower

CHAPTER TWELVE:
Europe

On the evening of March 29th 1980, we arrived at the Orly Airport in Paris. Our guide, a guy named Andre, hardly spoke English, but he was hysterical, and we had great fun with him. Back at the hotel, despite being very tired, I couldn't fall asleep.

The next morning, I was really spaced out. I had to get my shit together, but there were no drugs, not even a joint. What would I wear for the first gig? I decided to be cool and downplay it, by not dressing up. A jacket, t-shirt, and jeans would do.

After breakfast, we were off to the Pavillon Baltard, a fairly large auditorium that held about 800 kids. We were playing with eight other bands, and immediately, we were all on 'drug recon,' looking for anything to get high on. We checked out a couple of ska bands, and I met a photographer, who introduced me to a guy from one of the other bands. Finally, we went to the boy's room and I smoked my first joint in Paris. Ahh... it was great!

A little later, Larry and I were in a tavern around the corner, listening to French rock 'n' roll on the jukebox. We met up with some reps from CBS International, named Suzy and Jon-Jacque. We met two crazy American chicks, Jon-Jacque's friends, and one of them had a huge block of hash. She told me to keep it! Now we had enough hash for the whole trip, and my voice was getting pretty shot.

It was show time, and Steve and I were having trouble tuning our guitars. We were getting worried, until we realized we were a whole key up! I hoped we wouldn't get booed off stage, but thank god for rock 'n' roll. The kids dug us and we got the first encore of the day. Europe here we come!

When we arrived in Madrid, Spain, we were met by the CBS reps. One of them, named Paco, was so excited to meet us, he kept forgetting his English. We went straight to the Hotel Claridge, had a drink at the bar, and Paco gave me some Spanish lessons.

I did some interviews and the only thing the reporters wanted to know was, "what do you think about The Knack?" I told everyone that I didn't think about them. One of the journalists, Jesus Ordovas, told me about a nearby club called the Esacalon. The scheduled band had cancelled, but had left their equipment there. When I told Jesus that we could do a surprise last-minute set, everyone thought I was nuts. Jesus went about setting up the show and I went all over town promoting it. In Spain, Jesus Ordovas went on to become one of the most influential radio journalists of all time. Many years later, I wound up living down the block from him in Madrid.

After the interviews, we did the *Aplauso* TV show, and it was perhaps the funniest TV show that I will ever do. Every time we were supposed to start, this little fat man, who spoke no English, started jumping up and down, and playing an imaginary guitar. Larry and I were just cracking up. We performed "Rock 'N Roll Girl," and "No Me Esperes," the Spanish version of "Don't Wait Up" we released over there as a 45.

Then it was off to Radio Madrid, where we found out "No Me Esperes" ("Don't Wait Up") had been #1 on their playlist for two weeks. It was a great interview, and I got my first taste of what it's like being a rock star. I can't begin to describe how good it felt in that hot little studio, drinking Bacardi and Coke, with the outer room just jam packed with kids. Someone told me they had waited four years to ask me questions about The Nerves, as the DJ segued from The Nerves' "Working Too Hard," right into The Beat's version. It was a good interview, and on the air, I told everyone about the impromptu gig that evening. After signing a few Nerves and Beat records, we were off.

By the time I arrived at the gig, I was pretty drunk, and I worked my way through the dense crowd, toward the stage. I found out that the rest of the band was likewise, completely smashed. The equipment was bad, Mike was babbling about the shitty drums, and Larry was screaming at me, "How the hell did you get us into such a mess?" Surprisingly, Steve had it together, and was getting things organized with the soundman.

I looked out into an audience; the likes of which I had never seen. It was like an Agatha Christie movie, with people from all over the world, Spaniards, Germans, Americans, punkers, bikers, you name it. I don't know how, but this ended up being the best show we had done, to date. It sounded great to me on that stage, and it was one of the few times where I could hear everything. The crowd was going nuts during "Don't Wait Up," drowning us out by singing along to the chorus. A guy from the radio station had tears running down his face. Back at the hotel, I stayed up until the wee hours of the morning, drinking champagne with Jenny Bier, head of CBS International. What a night... I will never forget it.

We made some real fans that night in Madrid, and believe me - The Beat had no problem communicating with a Spanish-speaking audience. A few years later, when Steve and I returned to Spain, we found out that we had become true rock stars. That

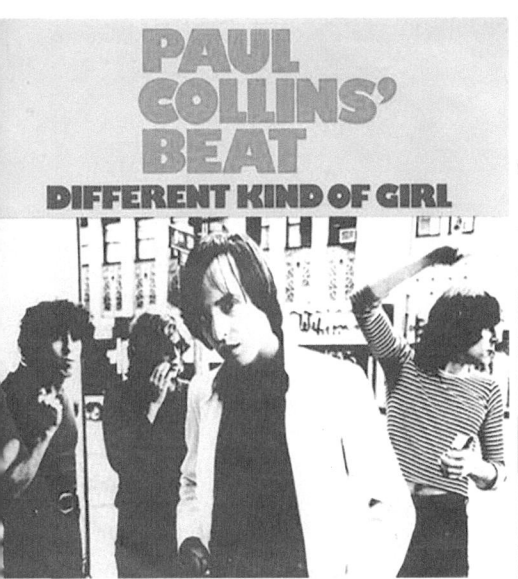

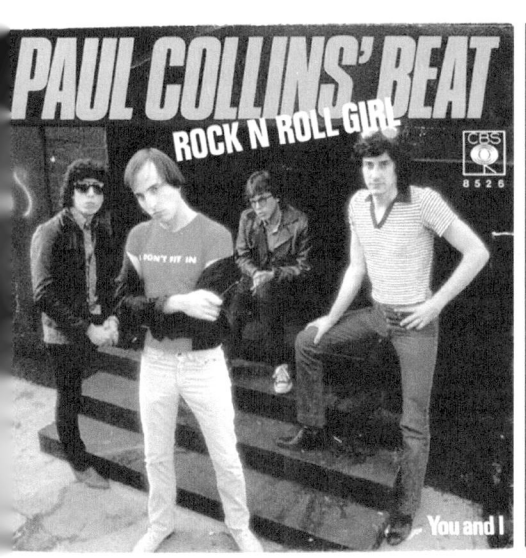

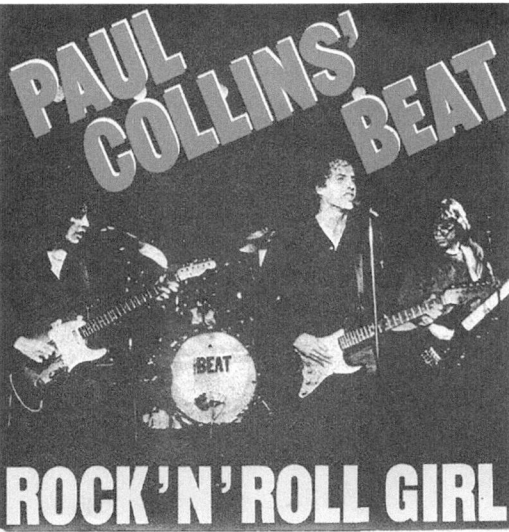

PAUL COLLINS' BEAT EUROPEAN-ONLY 7" SINGLES.
courtesy of Paul Collins' Archives

first show at the Escalon had become legendary; a permanent part of Madrid's rock 'n' roll canon. For me, this one last-minute show paved the way for a lifetime of high-profile, lucrative gigs in Spain.

In Hamburg, Germany, we played at Onkel Po's, a fondly remembered club from the the late '70s/early '80s. They were able to stay open as late as they wanted, and there were no liquor laws, so once again, we ended up getting very drunk. Somehow we made it back to the hotel, but Larry and the road crew were 'looking for a little action,' so they went to Reeperbahn Street, a notorious German red-light district. When they got back, Larry didn't seem too impressed, and K.B. ended up with a black eye, after an attempted mugging in front of the hotel.

In Paris, we did a live show called *Chorus TV*. Our sound was critical to us, and using rented equipment didn't help. It was frustrating speaking through interpreters, but it ended up being, perhaps, our best live performance on video.

For the last day of the tour, we went out with a bang, opening up for The Police at the Palais des Sports in Paris. It was the biggest show we'd ever done, a 6,000 seater, and there was a lot of electricity in the air. No one expected us to get any reaction from The Police's fanatic fans. We went out there undaunted, and kicked ass. We nearly got an encore, but at the last second, the house lights came on. The reps from CBS were pleased with us. To top everything off, Stewart Copeland of The Police, a very nice guy, came back to our dressing room, and chatted with us.

So that was it: 16 gigs in 17 days, in six countries; a total blow-out. We were living the dream, but now it was time to start worrying about our next record.

Just as we were about to fly back to the USA, I received some bad news.

At the time, the mindset of the music business was, when an album was a big success, it was because the record company and management did a great job. But if an album was a bomb, and didn't sell, they blamed the producer. So our record label and management had decided to fire Bruce Botnick, and somehow convinced us that it was the right thing to do.

I was still a kid, and assumed that guys like Bill Graham, or the CBS reps knew everything. I felt like I had to listen, but for anyone to say Bruce did a lousy job producing us, would be insane. That first LP was the best possible recording any band could have ever hoped for.

Bruce was a sensitive guy, and was legitimately heartbroken. He didn't just like the band – he loved us, and treated us like we were his kids. Bruce took me out, and bought my clothes for the first tour, including a leather jacket, saying 'it's going to be cold out there, *and they fired him.*

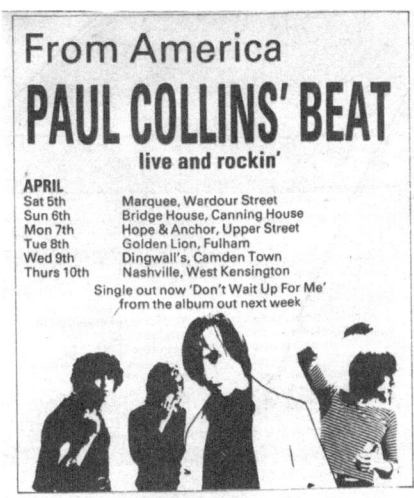

(TOP LEFT): FLYER FOR THE BEAT IN SPAIN, CIRCA 1982.

(TOP RIGHT): THE BEAT 1980 UK TOUR ADVERTISEMENTS.

(LEFT): PAUL COLLINS, CIRCA 1980.
all courtesy of Paul Collins Archives

THE BEAT, LIVE ONSTAGE, CIRCA 1980.
photo courtesy of Catherine Sebastian

I was upset, but we needed another producer. I asked management if we could work with whoever produced The Clash's *London Calling* – an LP I was absolutely in love with. Management did some research, and got back to me.

"Well, Guy Stevens is credited as the producer, but he's a total alcoholic. The guy who actually produced *London Calling* is Bill Price, who is listed on the LP as the engineer."

The rest of the band flew back to Los Angeles. Management arranged for me to meet with Price at Wessex Studios in London, where The Clash, The Pretenders, and the Sex Pistols had all recorded.

For three days, in a small, but very posh London hotel, I was holed up, waiting, alone, and bored out of my mind. I was very excited when the driver finally arrived and took me to Wessex Studios. I told the English secretary that I was here to meet Bill Price. She said 'Please take a seat,' and I waited there for about 40 minutes.

What is this bullshit? Bill Graham management set this up! This guy knows I'm coming!

Finally, a guy came out of the control room and said "Hi, I'm Bill Price. I don't know why you're here. Your management sent me this cassette tape and it's blank." He handed me the tape, said "I'm not a producer, so I can't help you" and he went back in the room.

I flew back to the USA, wondering, "What the fuck? How much money did this whole ridiculous charade cost, the hotel, the driver, going to the airport...?"

I didn't know it at the time, but the troubles of recording The Beat's 2nd LP were just beginning.

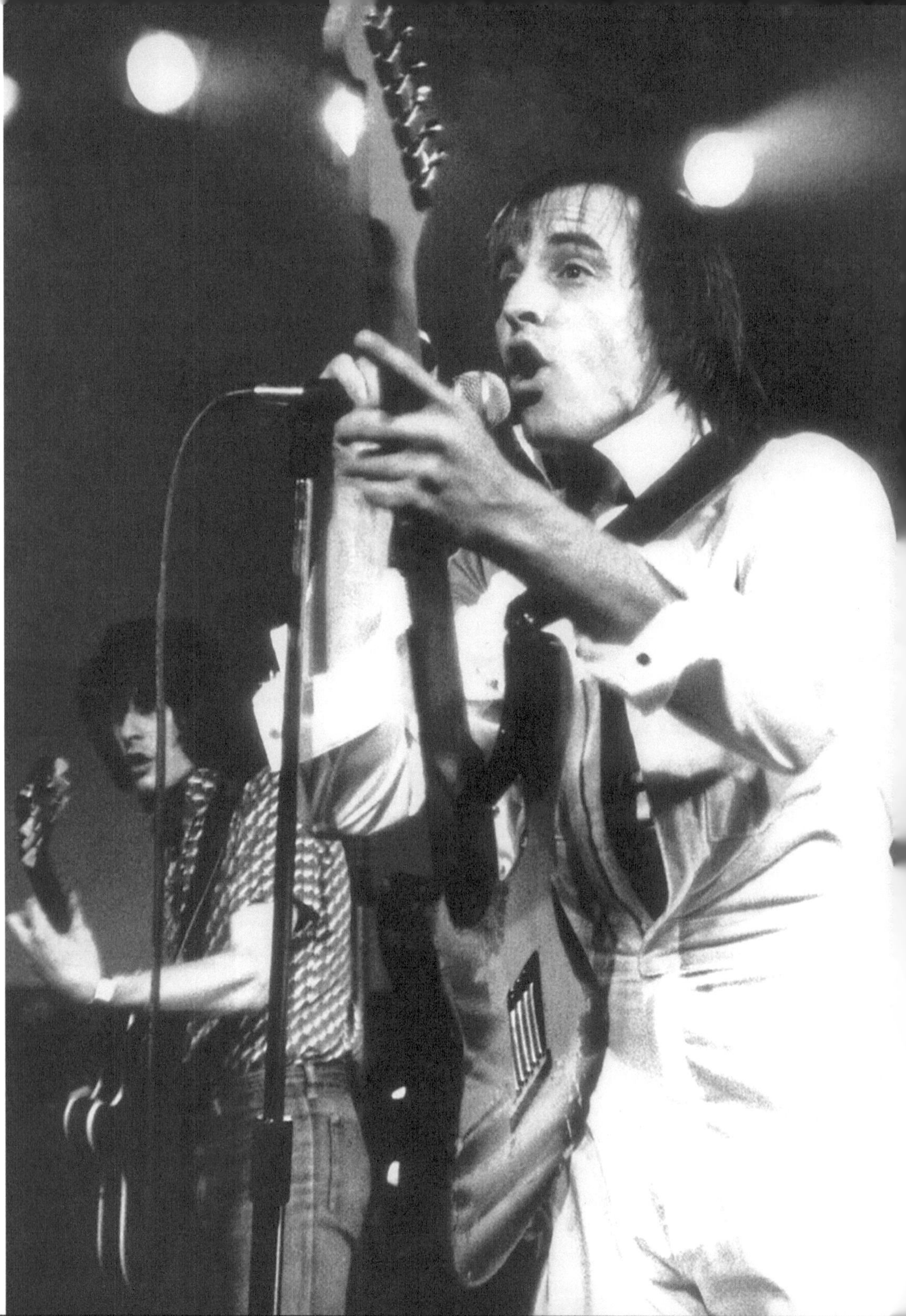

THE BEAT

Anyone who's heard them knows.
Everyone who's seen them agrees.
The Beat is not going to wait for anybody.

Listen to the new single from The Beat: "Don't Wait Up for Me."
Play it loud.
See The Beat on "American Bandstand," Saturday, March 8th, on ABC.
"The Beat." On Columbia Records and Tapes.

(PREVIOUS PAGE:) LARRY WHITMAN AND PAUL COLLINS, LIVE IN EUROPE, CIRCA, 1980.
photo courtesy of Rob Overtoom

(THIS PAGE:) THE BEAT DEBUT LP PRINT ADVERTISEMENT, CIRCA, 1979.
courtesy of Nathan Webber archives

The BEAT, recording *The Kids Are The Same* at 20th Century Fox Studio, 1981.
photo courtesy of Catherine Sebastian

CHAPTER THIRTEEN:
Will You Listen?

Album number two was the most difficult album I've ever made. It was recorded *three* times, and a lot of bad stuff went down. It was a long process of the whole thing unraveling. I felt like the whole thing was over and done, yet no one was pulling the plug on us.

The first LP tours had gone well, critics and audiences loved the band, but we weren't making a dent on the radio. You still couldn't find our first record in the stores, so we weren't making mega-sales.

In retrospect, I should have gotten on my hands and knees and begged Bill to get involved, and do what everyone else did back then. Bill had told me he thought our first record was a masterpiece, and that every song was a hit. Everyone in the business expected Bill to do with The Beat, what Capitol had done for The Knack. I should have begged him to do the same for us, because in the end, that was how the business worked.

I learned the hard way that success had very little to do with the actual record. I should have told Bill to get CBS to spend as much money on parties, cocaine, and free trips to Hawaii as it took for program directors to put our record on the air. Bottom line, if you didn't pay for promotion, the record died. This was true for all the bands, big or small, even Michael Jackson.

When I flew back to LA from my useless meeting in London, Marci Marks and I broke up. I had really loved Marci and we had a lot of fun together. She was a great companion and we made quite the couple, but we were young and we got tired of each other. Since I had met that 'gorgeous blonde' on the road, it wasn't exactly a clean break. I remember Marci calling me:

"I guess now that you have a deal, you have all this money! You were living with me, you owe me, and now I'm going to sue you!"

I never had someone threaten to sue me before. It really caught me off guard. What would she sue me for? I felt guilty so I agreed to give her some money. I paid her rent for a while, and then it all went into the wash.

Now I was about to get knee deep into the Hollywood weirdness. I moved in with the gorgeous blonde I had met at Tramps. She was living alone, in her estranged rock star husband's million-dollar home on Sunset Terrace, right above where Tower Records used to be. She was a total coke fiend. It was a dysfunctional, drug-fueled relationship, and she became more and more distant and uncommunicative. She'd go for days at a time, and I'd be all alone in her husband's house.

Time was dragging on. We needed to make a new record before everyone got bored, and forgot about us. Management lined up a New York producer for us: John Jansen. I didn't know it at the time but he had some very impressive credits to his name. Bill Graham wanted to keep his eye on us, so they flew Jansen out to San Francisco. We would record at The Automatt, the very same studio that The Nerves had been thrown out of years before.

In the studio, there were all kinds of inter-band politics going on and tensions were running high. Larry and Steve couldn't get along, yet they would both gang up on Michael, accusing him of speeding up or slowing down. Larry and Steve were threatening to leave if I didn't fire Michael, and John Jansen seemed to be encouraging this.

Also, our management team BGP saw musicians as cattle, and thought that if someone wasn't working out, you just fired and replaced them. It was ridiculous... first Bruce Botnick, and now Michael? I was really depending on Steve, but he wasn't coming to Michael's rescue, so I felt like I had no choice. On July 4th 1980, I called Steve and Larry and told them that we were letting Michael go. It was all just stupid, fucking dumb, punk kid shit, but the situation became intolerable.

I'm not blaming anybody for what happened, and I blame myself to a certain extent. I wish Bill Graham or his right hand man Jerry Pompili, a guy who really knew us, would have just told us to 'Shut the fuck up! You have a great opportunity here, more than you'll ever see again, so set aside your differences, and get down to business. Don't fuck it up over petty disagreements and arguments!' It seemed like no one with any sense was in earshot of us, so it just fell apart.

I was a huge fan of Prairie Prince from The Tubes, so we called him up immediately and he agreed to record with us. Prairie's a big, muscular, Billy Cobham-type drummer with chops up the wazoo, *and we were doing blow.* The tempos for that session were through the roof. We just played faster and faster, in order to get the tracks

PRARIE PRINCE, (OF THE TUBES) RECORDING WITH THE BEAT AT THE AUTOMATT.
courtesy of Paul Collins' Archives

over with, so we could go and snort some more blow. Prairie had the stamina to keep up with us; it was insane.

We finished recording, and Jansen seemed to think everything was fine, but he wanted to mix the record in New York. "We really need to mix the record at Sterling Sound!" Unsurprisingly, that's where Jansen's girlfriend was. I'd heard of Sterling Sound, so I said okay, but I didn't like the idea of Jansen wanting to be in New York by himself, making my record without me. I convinced management to send me along.

In 1980, America was firmly entrenched in FM Rock, and everything had to have that big rock sound, like U2 or Tom Petty. In contrast, our new record was sounding thin and one-dimensional in the studio. Why did a monster track like "The Kids Are The Same" sound so wimpy, when Prairie Prince was beating the shit out of those drums, and Larry was on 10 out of a Marshall... *what's going on?*

I called the office and said "I don't know man, the recordings sound bad! I don't think this guy's got it."

Then Jansen called them up and said "Listen, I can't deal with this Collins guy in the studio, he's driving me nuts! I can't mix the record with him here."

photo courtesy of Rob Overtoom

So management said "Paul, just stay in the hotel, Jansen is going to mix one or two songs, send them to us, and then we will decide what to do." Now I was going really crazy; banned from my own mix session! Jansen mixed the songs, sent the master tape back to the office, *and management fired him.*

"You're right Collins, this sounds like shit!"

I suggested getting the tapes back to LA, and having Andy Johns, who I had met through Eddie Money, mix them.

> This is another great Eddie Money story. Back when we first reconnected at the Peaches in-store in 1978, Eddie called me up, said "Grab Marci, and meet me at the Record Plant. We are going to a mixdown of a Rod Stewart song." We showed up, and Eddie said "Don't say anything, just stand in the corner with your girlfriend, and look cool!"
>
> We went into the studio, and Andy Johns was mixing "Do Ya Think I'm Sexy?" Andy had lost most of his hearing from skeet shooting, so the way he

mixed records was with a bottle of Jack Daniels, and he turned everything up so loud, you could feel it. He said "Paul, you have to feel it!"

Rod Stewart walked in, and the first thing he said was "Okay Andy, what do you got for the drums?"

Andy said, "oh, I've got drums for ya, man, huuuge fuckin' drums!"

Andy Johns made platinum records in his sleep, so I thought if anyone could salvage our second LP, Andy Johns could. We went to the Record Plant. Andy had his bottle of Jack Daniels, and he asked "Who the fuck recorded this shit? Sounds like he had a wet blanket on the bass drum! How am I supposed to mix this?" He was yelling, screaming, and did a couple of mixes, but it didn't sound much better. No one was sure what to do.

In a nutshell, losing Bruce Botnick and Mike Ruiz ended up sending the band into a long tailspin. I felt like I was watching my life go down the drain. We were supposedly looking for a drummer and producer, but honestly, we began doing the whole 'LA rock 'n' roll excess' trip, partying, carousing, and spending money. We were floundering, not playing gigs, and not being productive.

So I was driving up Sunset Terrace Drive, heading home toward the 'gorgeous blonde's' house, and I passed by another beautiful house, with a limousine parked in the driveway. The initials 'RTB' were on the license plate. My management had recently told me that they were in discussions with famed producer Roy Thomas Baker (Queen, The Cars, and Journey), for my 2nd LP. Could this be?

I saw a woman standing on the walkway in front of the house, so I stopped, rolled down the window, and asked "Is this Roy Thomas Baker's house? This cute, blonde, older European woman walked up to the car, stuck her head in the window and said:

"Who's asking?"

"Me... Paul Collins!"

"*Ohhh,* so you're Paul Collins. *They've been telling us all about you!*"

It turned out this was Roy's estranged wife, and they still lived together, but separately. They were still business partners, and she was the one behind the scenes, who had made his career. The next thing you know, I was sleeping with her! I moved in with The Bakers, and my torrid affair with the 'gorgeous blonde' finally went up in smoke. It took me a solid year to get over her.

Roy was into younger women, so he didn't mind that I was giving it to his estranged wife. In fact, I remember one morning we were all in the kitchen, and Roy said to me:

"Just because you're sleeping with my wife, doesn't mean I'm going to produce your record!"

This was when I started hanging out with the jet-set, driving around in Roy's Rolls-Royce, and having $250 dollar lunches. Meat Loaf was coming over for dinner, and Alice Cooper (*Flush The Fashion* LP era) would show up looking for drugs.

One night, The Bakers had a dinner party with Meat Loaf, his wife Leslie, and me. Mrs. Baker had gone through the trouble of cooking up a huge platter of roast beef for Meat Loaf, which she carried from the kitchen, toward the dining room. I heard the now familiar sound of a plate crashing to the floor, and knew that dinner had just been ruined. Poor Mrs. Baker was distraught, but Mr. Loaf, ever the gentleman, went into the kitchen, picked up the roast beef, right off the floor, put it on a new platter, and we all sat down to eat!

I was knee-deep in the whole Hollywood-gonzo thing, and between the drugs and the wives, I was losing it. Like most good things in life, it didn't last long. So when things fizzled out, with Mrs. Baker's help, I finally found my own place on Franklin and La Brea.

Around this time, Buzz Clic of The Rubber City Rebels held a weekly Thursday night poker game at his place. It would go on all night, and then Doug Fieger of The Knack started showing up. This was after their second album, and the Knack backlash had happened. Doug had a ton of money and was just hanging out in Hollywood, so he would come over and play cards with us. Buzz would tell him, "Okay man, you've got to bring some blow, and if you want to ante up, you've got to throw a couple of grams on the table!" Doug was a very nice guy, and I missed really being able to sit down and talk with him. I regret not getting to know him outside of those card games, which could get pretty ridiculous.

Toward the end of 1980, I was hanging around CBS's office in Century City, where everyone was trying to figure out what to do with us. There had been another record company change of guard, and Michael Dilbeck was now in charge. He saw me in the hall, cornered me, and said "I don't know what the hell you're doing. Call Bruce Botnick, get back in the studio, and make this record with him! He loves you, understands your sound, and he's the guy. Why are you screwing around with all this other stuff?"

photo courtesy of Rob Overtoom

I said "Wait a minute, I didn't fire Bruce, you guys did!"

Dilbeck said, "I don't know who fired Bruce, but you guys need to get it together."

So I got in touch with management, who agreed that it was a great idea, but said "There's no way we can call Bruce, because we fired him." So it would be me, who was going to have to talk to Bruce. I went to his house, and on my hands and knees I said:

"Bruce, I'm begging you; the whole thing's a mess! Please come back and help us finish this record."

To his credit, Bruce said yes.

Since we didn't have a drummer, Bruce called Gary Mallaber, who had played on many platinum records, with acts like The Steve Miller Band and Van Morrison. Bruce figured we could finish the record with Gary, and then we could go find a permanent drummer.

We did some initial sessions with Mallaber at CBS's rehearsal studios. Bruce said "Paul, you know how to play. Can you get behind the drums, and show Gary how 'On The Highway' is supposed to go?" I got behind the drums, showed him, and Mallaber said:

"Oh, if you want me to make it sound stupid, I can do that!" Not *exactly* what we had in mind, so we decided that Gary Mallaber wasn't exactly the right fit.

After around 5,000 more drum auditions, we finally met Alice Cooper's drummer Dennis Conway through Mrs. Baker, who knew everyone. She had met Dennis through Elton John and his crowd of musicians. When we found out Dennis had played a gig with Elton at Wembley, we were duly impressed. Dennis was an easy going guy, but he was married to a woman who wouldn't be settling for the life of a struggling musician.

Then, on December 8th, 1980 with producer Bruce Botnick, and new drummer Dennis Conway, Paul Collins' Beat began our 2nd round of recording sessions at the 20th Century Fox motion picture soundstages. I drove my car into the studio, that's how big it was: an enormous room, all wood, with a 4000 foot high ceiling, and a huge silver screen where they projected movies for an entire orchestra. You can see the studio on the back cover of the second album.

This was the only time a rock band had ever been allowed to record in this

(RIGHT):
PAUL COLLINS' BEAT
PROMO 8x10, CIRCA
1981.

(BELOW): THE BEAT,
RECORDING *THE KIDS
ARE THE SAME* AT 20th
Century Fox Studio,
CIRCA 1981.
*photo courtesy of
Catherine Sebastian*

STEVE HUFF   DENNIS CONWAY   PAUL COLLINS   LARRY WHITMAN

BILL GRAHAM MANAGEMENT

PAUL COLLINS' BEAT

193

(TOP): THE BEAT, SECOND LINEUP PROMO SHOT, CIRCA 1981.

(LEFT): *The Kids Are The Same* LP (COLUMBIA/CBS, 1982.)
(RIGHT): "THE KIDS ARE THE SAME" DUTCH-ONLY 7" SINGLE (CBS, 1982).

courtesy of Paul Collins' Archives

room. Normally, they only did film scoring there, but a musician's strike was going on in Hollywood, so the soundstages weren't being used. Movie scores were being made in Italy, because 20th Century Fox couldn't come to an agreement with the musician's union in Los Angeles. Bruce had all the right connections to get us in the room.

I will never forget that first night, recording with Bruce at 20th Century Fox, because someone called us, and told us that John Lennon had just been shot. We all just stood around in the studio, not knowing what to do. *One of our heroes was gone.* Finally, Bruce called the session and we all went home.

Bruce wasn't really sure if he could trust the monitors or playback in the 20th Century Fox control room, so he decided to take the recordings over to Cherokee, another top-notch studio. Bruce mixed the record down, turned it in, and CBS rejected it, saying they didn't hear any hits. We were stalled once again.

Then, I got a phone call from BGP:

"Listen Paul, take two weeks, and write some hits!"

What was I going to say to that? So Steve and I bought a whole bunch of blow, speed, pot, booze, beer, 20 cartons of cigarettes. We holed up in Steve's apartment for two weeks, writing like mad dogs. We made and sent in demos of three songs; "That's What Life Is All About," which ended up being the first song on the album, and "It's A Matter Of Time," which CBS thought could be a hit. The third song we wrote, called "Give Me The Drugs," was rejected. I would have loved to have seen their faces when they heard it. "Give Me The Drugs" would later come out on *To Beat Or Not To Beat.*

At Chateau Recorders in North Hollywood, we recorded the two new 'hits' we had just written. Then we took the tracks from the previous sessions, the Jansen-Automatt tapes, the Bruce-20th Century Fox tapes, and mixed everything down into one album. When we finished, the record company said "Okay, you've got it! We're going to release this."

The Kids Are The Same LP was mastered at Capitol Recording Studios in Hollywood. Grammy-winner Mick Haggerty did the album cover. He also designed *Ghost In The Machine* for The Police, Bowie's *Let's Dance*, and LP covers for the Go-Go's, Hall & Oates, and other top acts. We were getting the big guns again, the big treatment, and the record was going to be great.

Because I had made so many good friends in Paris, I decided to go back, just hang out, and enjoy myself while CBS prepared the new LP for release. Soon, I was drinking champagne with my friends Jean-Jacque and his lovely wife Michele, at their

The Beat road trip, promoting *The Kids Are The Same* LP
in Juarez, Mexico, 1982.
photos courtesy of K.C. Webb

fabulous apartment. Michele knew the real Parisian high society, people like the owner of Cacharel clothing, or the vice president of Moet Chandon, and I felt like their resident pop star. We sat around, getting high, and I'd do things like making a bong out of tin foil, or smoking hash inside of a Marlboro. Michele always got a kick out of that.

One night after dinner at an exclusive Parisian restaurant, Jean-Jacque and Michele begged our forgiveness, and said they had to retire early. Jean-Jacque whispered in my ear, "Don't worry you are in good hands!" The remaining guests at the table were the owner of Trident Studios in London, and two very attractive French ladies.

Everything was prim and proper, so I thought we would have our coffee and cake, and that would be the end of the evening. Nothing is ever what it seems. We ended up back at the ritzy home of one of the women, who turned out to be one of most successful madames in Paris. Her old millionaire husband didn't seem to be anywhere around. The other lady was the bored wife of a French military general. The Trident studio owner pulled out a huge bag of 99% pure cocaine, and all hell broke loose. We did all the coke, and I got to screw both women – not at the same time, and thanks to the coke, not very well. Ah, gay Paree!

Then management called and said:

"Get back to New York immediately! It looks like the record is going to be a big hit!"

What happened is, *The Kids Are The Same* LP had come out in early 1982, and no one was saying anything. Then a new guy, hired at the CBS New York branch, heard "On The Highway" for the first time, and said "This is a smash hit! I want this out as a 12-inch immediately!" Most of people at CBS, and our management were bored of "On The Highway," since we'd been playing it live since 1979. This is a good reason not to start playing the new stuff too soon. So right out of the box, CBS got the newly pressed "On The Highway" 12-inch single on WPLJ, a major New York radio station. They had recently started mixing new wave into their AOR format. At last, we were being played on a Parallel One station! Management was all over it, so we thought it was finally going to happen.

We were going to be rock stars, and everything would be just fine.

No sooner than I landed, I went to the CBS branch in New York, and told them I had an idea. I would get in my car, by myself, drive across the country with copies of my new 12-inch single, and do a radio tour. I'd promote "On The Highway" while I was on the highway. Just like in The Nerves, no one was going to do anything for me, so I'd do it myself.

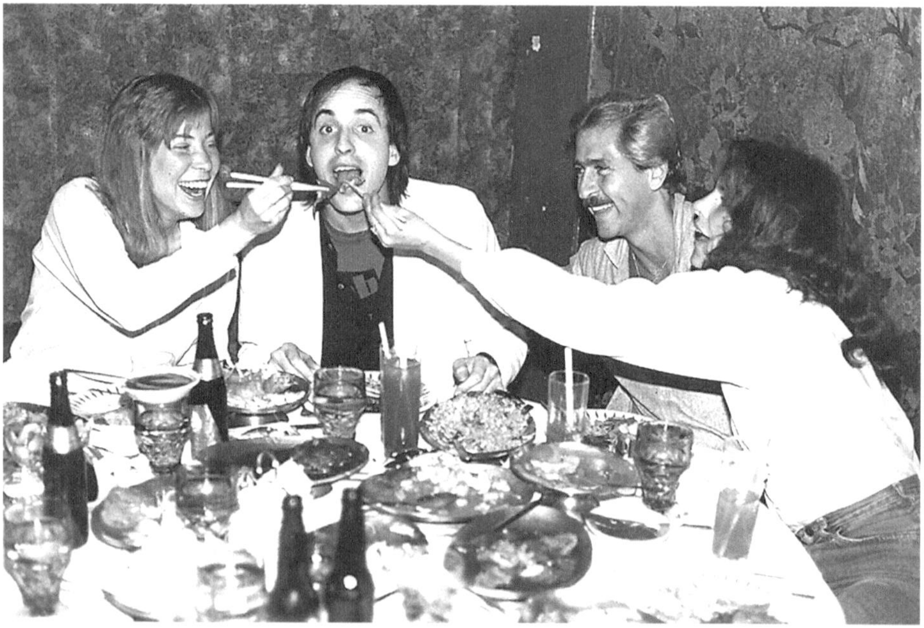

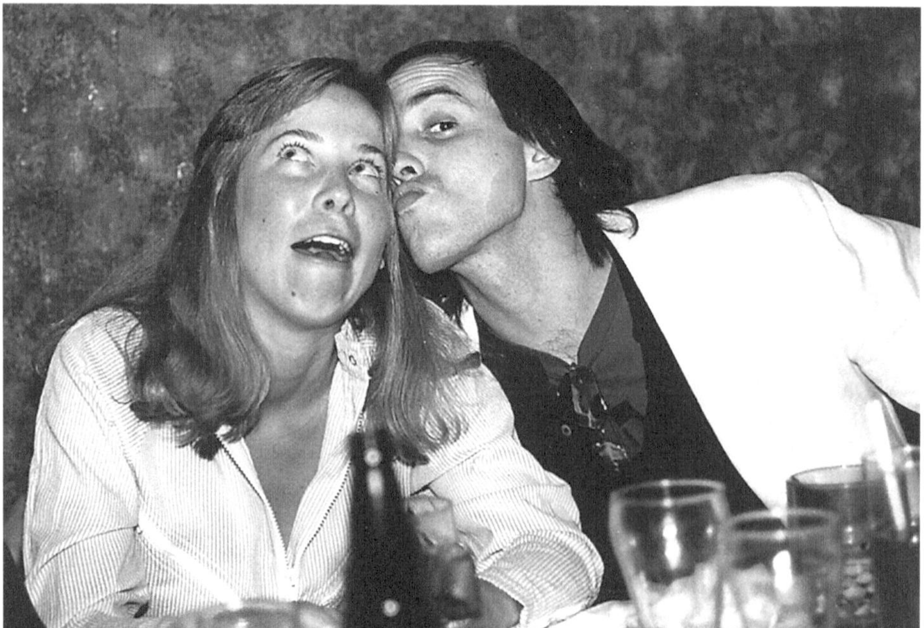

When I told CBS my plan, they go "Whoa, whoa, we can't just have you riding around the country by yourself ! No, you're a CBS recording act, managed by Bill Graham; we've got to make this official." So now they really liked the idea, and decided to go the whole nine yards. They would rent a car, hire photographers to take pictures of me 'on the road,' where I'd go to three radio stations a day, and do meet-and-greets. Not only that, they would fly Larry out, to go with me.

So east to west, we started driving. It was good hanging out with Larry, but he and I always had a very volatile chemistry. The room would heat up sometimes with the two of us in it. Larry had recently made a record with his girlfriend, Susan Lynch, released that year on Epic Records. He was making snide remarks, comparing our record to hers. It was very touch and go, with us arguing, but then going out every night, hitting the bars, and having fun.

The farther we got, the more we started to realize this record just wasn't happening. They were not playing it. We were not getting the big push. We went all across the country, did all this promotion, and got back to LA. Management called, and said:

"We have some bad news. There was a big meeting at Columbia Records. They made a decision to drop every single band that has sold less than 600,000 units...

...and you're one of them."

(PREVIOUS PAGE): PAUL WITH BOB CONRAD (CBS), LORI PETERSON. (SOUNDWAREHOUSE RECORDS), AND ARIN MICHAELS (DJ) PROMOTING *THE KIDS ARE THE SAME* IN JUAREZ, MEXICO, 1982.

photos courtesy of K.C. Webb

THE PAUL COLLINS' BEAT, 1982.
photo courtesy of Randy Bachman

CHAPTER FOURTEEN:
To BEAT Or Not To BEAT

With The Nerves, I came to Hollywood too soon, and with The Beat, I stayed too late. I should have arrived the day before I got signed to CBS, and left the day after I finished my first record.

It seemed like the end of the world. My heart was bleeding, my psyche couldn't take it, and I went crazy. I started to lose my hair, and I was snorting massive amounts of cocaine attempting to numb my feelings. Nothing worked, I was losing it, and everyone in Hollywood knew it. I couldn't go back to being in the Sunset Strip gutter again, *anything but that.*

I had busted my ass, and gotten so close, just to watch it all go down the drain. I had scaled the Ivory Towers. You couldn't get any higher than CBS and Bill Graham Management; it was the top-of-the-top. I couldn't understand how or why this was happening. Why the fuck did everything always go wrong for me?

What would Jack Lee say?

"Stop exaggerating. Put a cork in it, will you? Worse things are going to happen." Jack wants to know if this is a soap opera, and if so, he is leaving. Okay, I'll snap out of it. "Fine," he says, "just watch your step."

"I will Jack, I will."

When we got dropped, management really downplayed it. Columbia had dropped 600 acts, and that kind of softened the blow. It wasn't just us. Bill Graham Presents told us "Don't worry; we haven't given up on you. We will get you on another label," but from there it just all went south.

We told management we were a working band, and weren't going to go on hiatus, like we had done before we recorded our second LP, *The Kids Are The Same*. We would keep touring, so BGP pitched us down to the junior employees at the company. These were novices, people almost like interns, but they would work with us on the live circuit, while BGP figured out their next move.

We still had friends at CBS, people like Burt Baumgartner, who kept supporting us at the risk of their jobs. I don't know if they would have been fired, but they certainly would have taken a lot of flak for helping out a band that was no longer on the label.

My 'lawyer to the stars' Stan Diamond must have been really disappointed, and regretted ever offering me such a good deal for representation. With Bill Graham Presents, there was never any real absolution or dissolution. Their involvement just got less, and less, until we finally had no choice but to strike out on our own.

That's when I bought all my publishing back. I lucked out in this regard. Even though I had a contract with CBS, at the end of the day, I was able to get my publishing back through Bill Graham's subsidiary label, Wolfgang. I asked Nick Clainos, Bill's business manager, and BGP sold the publishing back to me for one dollar. I'm guessing they didn't think it was worth anything. It's also tribute to the fact that I always maintained good relationships with people. I never burned bridges, or told people to fuck off.

So we toured, toured, *and toured* in support of *The Kids Are The Same*, even though we weren't on the label anymore. We went all across the United States, east to west, LA to Seattle, up and down the west coast, into Canada, and back again. Larry and Dennis had their quota, where they had to make a hundred bucks a night, *and we paid them*. We kept going, and made a living, but the returns got smaller and smaller, as did the crowds. It became an exercise in futility.

We would drive a thousand mile drives at a clip. I'd be so exhausted, Steve would take the wheel so I could rest my eyes. Once, in one night, we drove from Grand Junction, Colorado straight through to Champaign, Illinois. On the advice of some truckers we cut up through Kansas to avoid the cops. We floored it all the way, doing coke to stay awake. While I drove, Steve held the wheel and my knee down on the gas pedal, so I could take a hit. That's when I fell asleep and the cops pulled us over.

My hands were shaking so bad I could hardly get my license out. The cop asked where we were going in such a rush. I told him and he said, "You're never going to make it," but we did, and on time. It takes more than a thousand miles to fuck us up. We were determined to run this thing as far into the ground as we could.

In the end, CBS and Bill Graham abandoned us, leaving us out to dry like so much dead meat.

We were off of CBS, but had made friends with Gail Sparrow at MTV, right at the beginning. I did one of MTV's earliest interviews, with J.J. Jackson. We were not giving up, and had a couple of hundred bucks to spend, so why not make low-budget videos for "The Kids Are The Same" and "On The Highway" on our own steam? We knew MTV would play them.

We used Mike Pinera of Iron Butterfly's video production studio. During the shoot, Dennis Conway decided to quit. I think you can even see it in the video, when Dennis just started packing up his drums. We had told the camera guy "Just keep rolling!"

Dennis' wife was there, saying "We deserve better than this!" They were from a different world. She wanted Dennis touring with Alice Cooper, hanging out with people making millions of bucks, and here he was in some fucking band looking to make two-hundred a night.

Deborah Newman (Director of Artist Development & Video at CBS) saw the video and said "What are you doing? MTV is never going to play this! You need to spend 25 grand on a video." Then she played me a clip from Foreigner. CBS told MTV not to play it, but MTV said "Excuse me, but we decide what we play, and what we don't play!" I think they played it just snub CBS, and to show they wouldn't be told what to do.

I was writing new songs, like "All Over The World," and "Dance, Dance." Larry said "Listen man, I'm only here to promote our records, so I will only play the songs from our two albums. I'm not getting paid to play anything else."

I said to Steve... *"We really need to get out of this place!"*

***

For Christmas 1982, I went to New York to visit my family. I was hanging out at CBGB's, and met Jay Dee Daugherty from Patti Smith Group, Jimmy Ripp from Kid Creole and the Coconuts, and Fred Smith from Television. These cats were looking to do something, and in their eyes, I was probably somebody.

We put together a surprisingly well-received New Year's Eve show at The Peppermint Lounge. The place was packed, and it felt good to be playing with these top-notch musicians. It was a much needed infusion of excitement and energy for me.

One of my fonder memories of that show was when someone came onstage to tell Jimmy that his girlfriend, Holly (of Holly and The Italians) was on the phone. She was about to throw all his stuff, guitars included, out the window! He took the call, pleading with her to wait for him. That's how crazy it was in those wild New York nights.

New York seemed like an oasis after years in the burnt-out wastelands of Los Angeles. We had burned every bridge, so I decided it might be a good idea to relocate. I convinced Steve to join me, and we set up shop in NYC.

For a brief time we lived a double life, going back and forth, playing with two different backup bands. We would play with Jay Dee and Jimmy in New York, and Larry (with whoever was available on drums) on the west coast. Our west coast shows had little or no spark to them. I couldn't believe after all of our hard work, we were playing the music like we were going to work in an office. All the life had been beaten out of the band, and it was time to retire it for good.

At the last minute, just before Steve and I moved, I remember saying to Larry "You don't want to do new songs, so we're working with other people, and we're moving."

Larry goes "Well I never said that!" I had to laugh.

"Yeah Larry, you did man. *Yeah you did!*"

Steve stood by me, and I must give credit where credit is due. Not once did he turn his back on me. We continued to work together for years, trying to salvage that one moment of glory. We never could.

We moved into my sister's loft on 6th Street and 3rd Avenue, right up the block from CBGB's. There were two Korean girls who lived downstairs, and we immediately adopted them as our 'Seoul Sisters.' They were cute as the dickens, but Steve and I were too shy to get anywhere with them.

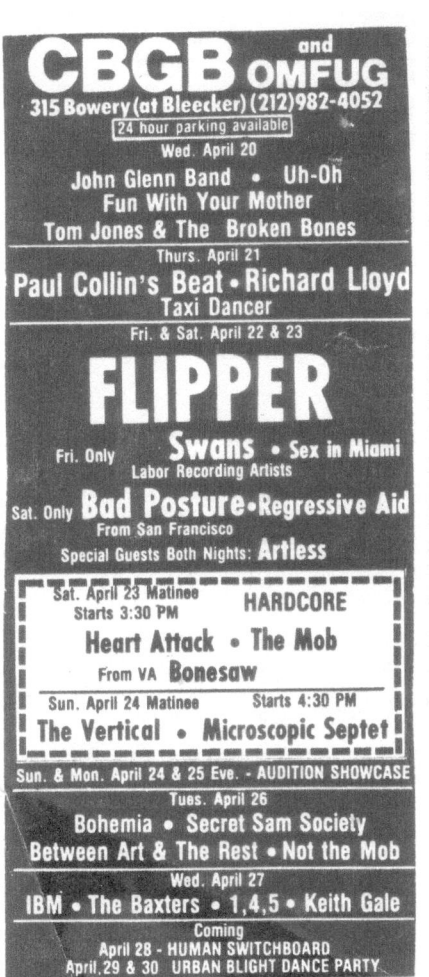

THE PAUL COLLINS' BEAT IN
CBGBS ADVERTISEMENTS,
CIRCA 1983.

courtesy of Paul Collins' Archives

When it came to girls, The Beat were gentlemen. We always had a coterie of girls who came to our shows, and we looked out for them. In fact, we would give preference to the girls who otherwise might feel left out, and for that reason, we've kept our fans for a lifetime. Everyone was welcome backstage, guys too.

At night, we could rehearse with Jay Dee Daugherty and Jimmy Ripp, at my mother's art studio loft on 19th street, or at rehearsal halls, which were still affordable. We were all set up.

It was when New York was still fun. We just blew it out, partying until the wee hours of the morning, and sleeping all day. People liked us, and we made a lot of friends. There were all these nightclubs, the rent parties, and Jay Dee knew every after-hours joint in New York. He would take us to some luncheonette at 8 in the morning; stoned out of our minds. Some guy going to work would be drinking a cup of coffee, and we'd be having vodka tonics.

Danceteria became one of our favorite places to hang out. We would roam around floor to floor with Sirius Trixon, a madcap rock 'n' roller from Detroit, in a band called the Motor City Bad Boys. Every night in his rock 'n' roll garb, Sirius always had a smile and a big hello for us. There was also this guy Frank; always walking around bent over, scouring the floor for money or drugs that people would drop. "Hey Frank, how much did you find tonight?"

We could actually get work, gigging at CBGB's, Hitsville, Peppermint Lounge, and Webster Hall. We pretty much supported ourselves playing gigs, since our overhead was so low.

There was one drawback; the coke was shitty and expensive. When we found out that you could cop ten dollar bags of heroin in Alphabet City, it was a no-brainer. I never thought I'd try heroin, but there I was snorting that brown shit right up my nose. I was afraid of needles, and never even remotely interested in shooting up. I was just looking for cheap thrills.

In those days the cabs wouldn't go past First Avenue, so we would walk the rest of the way. It usually went something like this:

"Hey Man, you got any dope?"

"No man, if you wanna cop some dope, you gotta talk to The Wiz."

"Oh yeah? Where's he at?"

"You gotta stand in the shadows, if you wanna talk to The Wiz."

The Wiz was one careful dude. He'd always start out by telling you that if you were a cop, he was going to blow you away. I would always say, "If I was a cop, don't you think I'd be ready for something like that?" He'd never answer me. Business was business, even in Alphabet City.

One time, due to my already fucked up condition, I dropped the little white bag of heroin. It was always dark 'in the shadows' and I couldn't find it, so I started to make a scene, crawling around in the rubble. The Wiz and his crew couldn't believe it.

"These white boys are fucking nuts!"

It looked like I'd never leave, and this could be bad business for The Wiz, but someone finally produced a flashlight. We found the little white bindle of heroin in the rubble, at 4 o'clock in the morning, on Avenue D and 3rd, in Alphabet City. Go there today and you wouldn't recognize the place.

***

One night Steve and I were trying to pick up this Russian chick in a downtown nightclub. She took us to her place, and after a few straight vodkas, started telling how she had spent her life studying the best ways of committing suicide. She described the pros and cons of each method, but her main concern was what effect each method would have on people with the bad luck of finding you. She didn't want to leave a bloody mess. After much research, she decided that sticking your head in the oven was the most efficient way. Steve and I left wondering, *what happens if the person who finds you is a smoker?*

We documented our stay in New York by recording a five song EP called *To Beat Or Not To Beat* at a small studio in midtown called The Ranch. For five thousand bucks, we produced it ourselves, and shopped it around to small independent labels. We had given up trying to break into the big leagues. Marty Scott, from a small independent label out in Jersey, loved it, and on September 7th of 1983, Jem/Passport released *To Beat Or Not To Beat* in America.

"All Over The World" began getting airplay on KROQ in Los Angeles, so Steve and I decided to visit the west coast, to see what we could make happen. Marty came out and we had a big record-signing dinner party. We felt like rock stars again.

We invited Don Bean, a promoter from Fresno, where The Beat had done a lot of shows. Don wanted to start managing bands, and had the good sense to think The Beat would be a good one to start with. He was impressed with Marty, and the strength of our deal with Jem/Passport, so he agreed to underwrite the band coming out to the west coast.

It didn't take much convincing to get Jay Dee to pack his bags. He and Steve had become great drinking buddies. We lost Jimmy though, who had too much going on in New York, and we would never have been able to pay him enough.

We met another hot shot guitarist, Werner Fritzsching, who wanted to travel. He had played with Hall and Oates, and that was good enough for us. We wound up living at a cool motel in Fresno, with a nice pool for us to relax by. For some reason it felt like we were in Vegas.

This was when we made our one and only big production video for *To Beat Or Not To Beat*. Don hired the director of a local TV station, which instantly gave us access to the TV studio's gear, including cameras and personnel. We even had a crane for the opening shot. We got the whole town in on it, about 50 kids. We spent the night at a cafe in Fresno filming "Dance, Dance," while most of us consumed copious amounts of beer and cocaine. MTV played it for a while, so I guess it was worth it.

Don got us a string of dates in Canada, playing for a week at each club, in four different cities: Edmonton, Calgary, Vancouver, and Victoria, at the world famous Harpo's. The gigs were something else, with built-in crowds, terrible accommodations, and the food was worse. What started out as spaghetti on Monday, would wind up as Sloppy Joes on Sunday.

We spent a week at Harpo's, where we stayed at 'the band house.' This made such an impression on us, that Jay Dee and Steve wrote their potential 'hit single' "Band House." It was a catchy number. 'Band house! Band house!' We should have recorded it.

Jay's drinking hit an all-time high here. I think he was drinking a six-pack before breakfast. Soon, he slipped in the shower, cracked his ribs, and we got him to the hospital where they fixed him up for free. This is the first time I got an inkling of what good health care means. There's not much you can do for cracked ribs, so they bandaged him up, sent him on his way, and told him, by all means, don't laugh. Of course, a few days later we were all walking down an empty street, when one guy started heading our way, and bumped into Jay Dee. This started us all laughing, including Jay Dee while he hollered in pain.

(TOP):
To Beat or Not To Beat
EP, US edition (Passport Records).

(below left):
To Beat or Not To Beat
EP, French edition
(Closer Records).

(below right):
To Beat or Not To Beat
EP, Spanish edition
(Record Runner).

courtesy of Paul Collins' Archives

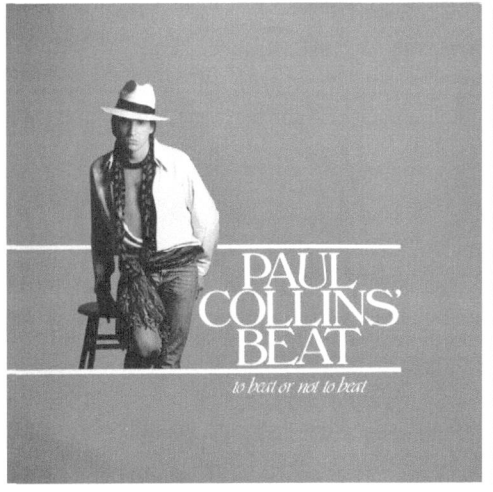

We went back to New York, and Don Bean agreed to pay for one more recording session. We cut "Always Got You On My Mind" at Media Sound, one of New York's bigger studios. We got that big sound, and the song was added to the European releases of *To Beat Or Not To Beat*, but it wasn't enough to put us over.

The EP ended up selling somewhere between 10,000 to 15,000 copies, which is great by today's standards, but not in 1983. The problem was, the industry as a whole had moved on, and decided that the type of music we played was not going to happen. They gave up on it, and shifted into indie-rock. I remember going to a music industry symposium back then, where some big indie-radio guy was saying:

"Fuck Tom Petty, he's not indie-rock! R.E.M. is indie rock, and that's where it's at, maaan!"

The American record industry thought The Beat were archaic, and wondered why we wouldn't go away. Yet we kept trying, and it got embarrassing...

> ...just like it was in San Francisco 1974, when Jack and I went to see Peter Case playing at The Wharf. I'm not kidding. Back then, people said "Fuck The Everly Brothers and Chuck Berry!" I sat there thinking – "You can't tell me this stuff is shit. I'm not buying that!"

"All those great songs, the harmonies... things like that."

Once again, our kind of music was considered taboo.

photo courtesy of Catherine Sebastian

The Paul Collins' BEAT onstage in Europe, 1984.
courtesy of Paul Collins' Archives

CHAPTER FIFTEEN:
Madrid Me Mata

My mother was having lunch with an art gallery owner and her daughter. Since moms are always so proud of their sons, my mother brought me up in conversation. The gallery owner's daughter became ecstatic. Her boyfriend John Pita, and his business partner Pepe Ugena had been trying to find me for six months. They owned two record stores called The Record Runner – one in downtown New York, the other in Madrid, Spain.

They wanted to bring The Beat to Madrid and were willing to pay us a lot of money, including an advance. The big shows were set for September 6th & 7th at Sala Star in Madrid. We heartily agreed, neglecting to tell them we didn't have a backup band at the moment. Jay Dee and Werner had moved on to greener pastures, but for Steve and I, this was just a minor detail. We knew we'd figure out something when the time came.

So in August 1984, with the advance money for Madrid, we packed our bags, and bought tickets to France. We ended up staying in Europe for almost three years.

My brother Patrick had a French girlfriend, Laurence, living with him in New York. We rented her small flat in Drancy, outside of Paris for $80 dollars a month. This was the same amount of money The Nerves hit the road with on our 1977 DIY tour. After all these years, that number was still following me around.

In eighth grade, I had taken French as my second language, but now I wished I had paid more attention. The extent of my French was 'oui oui,' 'bonjour,' 'comment allez-vous,' and of course, what practically every radio listening American knew - 'voulez vous coucher avec moi;' (the chorus of the 1974 hit, "Lady Marmalade" by LaBelle). In time, my vocabulary got better, but at the moment, it didn't help us negotiate at the Charles de Gaulle airport. The French aren't known for their hospitality to strangers, especially Americans.

We missed three trains, unable to figure out how to open the doors. In France, you had to push a button, or lift a lever. You'd think other people coming and going might help us, but not in the dead of August. Being Americans, we thought the whole world functioned as it did back home – one global world so to speak. It took a few years, but eventually we learned that life in Europe was completely different.

We finally made it to Drancy, infamous for its Nazi internment camp during the occupation. Now it was just a rundown north-east suburb of Paris. We lived in Laurence's small, simple apartment above a pasta factory, in what seemed to be a ghost town. We saw and heard no one, except for the workers underneath us. Apparently, some part of the pasta making process involved counting. Every morning at 8 AM., the workers would count to ten in French, there would be a loud 'thump,' and they would start all over again. After a while, this began to really piss Steve off. He would scream "Shut up!" but the guys down below paid him no mind.

We spent our days working on songs, and at night we would go out looking for bars. We hadn't figured out yet that in August, every self-respecting European goes on holiday. One night we just kept walking, and thinking "We are in France for Christ's sake. We know they like to drink!" Eventually the cops pulled us over, asked us what we were doing, and told us we needed to go to Paris for that.

Paris was grand, and I enjoyed it to the fullest, but I think Steve was homesick. He was getting drunk every night, and only eating at McDonald's. One evening we had to take a cab home. When we arrived, I got out first and went upstairs, assuming he would follow. I waited, fell asleep, but soon woke up to find three Gendarmes, and Steve completely covered in blood.

"Is this your friend, Monsieur? You should take better care of him."

I told them I would, so they left, but I'm glad they didn't see the hash pipe on the small table beside the bed. It turned out Steve had started a collection of posters for *Le Nouveau Detective*, a French weekly magazine known for its lurid photos and headlines. He had fallen down and busted his lip trying to rip one down from the wall of a newsstand.

I was getting worried he might not make it to Madrid.

Our records had been well received all over Europe, so it paved the way for us. We made friends and travelled in all kinds of circles. I was always hustling my shit, and got an appointment with CBS's international office in Paris. Unlike Americans, Europeans don't think you are a worthless piece of shit when your label drops you. I was graciously received by my old friend from when I was a little pop star, Jean-Jacque Gozlan, who was now the head of creative affairs.

PAUL COLLINS BEAT BACKSATAGE

Record Runner

He took me out to a sumptuous and very expensive lunch; no doubt paid for by some other artist's record sales. He immediately agreed to help, and thanks to his efforts, we were able to release *To Beat Or Not To Beat* on Closer Records, a very cool French label, run by Philippe Debris. It may not have been the big time, but at least we were in Europe where the coffee was good, and the croissants were fresh.

Closer did as much as any small label could. We got on radio shows and made TV appearances, some of which are still floating around on the Internet today. Closer eventually got picked up by Virgin Records, which gave us even more publicity.

We needed to work, so I booked some gigs with Alain Lahana, a French promoter I knew. We picked up a French band - Olive, our junkie guitarist, Plume, the drummer, and for the first time, a keyboard player named Rudolf. We thought it might modernize our sound, but it didn't. Rudolf's main contribution was always wearing a trench coat, looking like a cheesy Frank Sinatra. I have some of our shows on cassette. It's not my best work, but there were some moments, and it did have that Euro-sound with the keyboards.

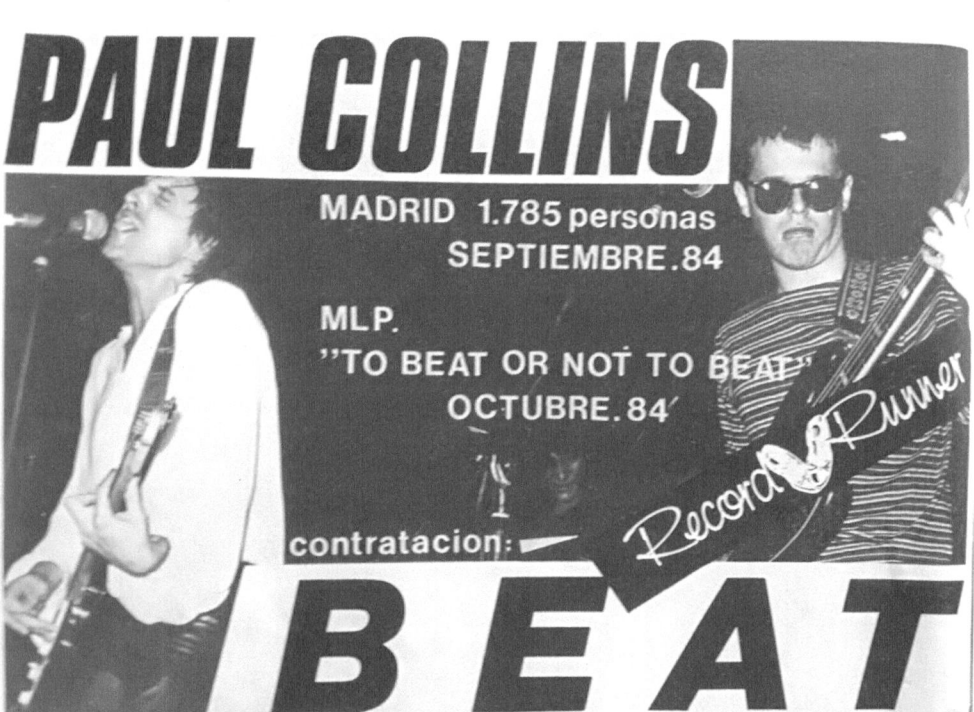

(TOP): PRINT ADVERTISEMENT FOR 3RD LP & SPAINISH TOUR, CIRCA 1984.
(BELOW): PAUL COLLINS' BEAT EUROPEAN PROMO POSTCARD, CIRCA 1984.
courtesy of Paul Collins' Archives

While we were rehearsing at Le Studio Parisien in Paris, The Eurythmics were down the hall recording. We thought they sounded great, and had the new sound everyone wanted. We thought we were heading that way too, but it wasn't the right fit for us. The Beat are a rock 'n' roll band through and through.

Touring was nothing short of hysterical. No one knew where anything was, or how anything worked. Everyone was always late, and no one seemed to mind. Directions were usually wrong or non-existent, so getting to a gig could take hours. Sometimes we would see the place, but couldn't get there through the maze of one-way streets and dead end alleys. In the end, we would have one guy catch a cab, and the rest of us would follow them to the gig.

One night we pulled up and began to haul in our gear. A few older men standing around asked what we were doing and I said "We are the band for tonight."

"No, no" they said, "there's no band tonight, this is a VFW hall!" It turned out the gig was nearby, so we had to pack up, and get on down the road.

Finally we were flying to Spain, for a madcap weekend in Madrid at Sala Star. The highway from the airport was lined with huge posters of us – it was wild! The shows were packed with rabid fans. My mother and brother Patrick showed up from New York, and my French girlfriend Silvie flew in from Paris. Our guitarist Olive was completely fucked up on smack, and his English was bad. He told us he was going to "make fuck" onstage, which is exactly what he did. We sounded horrible, but everyone loved us. The shows were considered a huge success, especially by the guy who brought us, Pepe Ugenda of Record Runner.

Madrid was happening for us, and we were sad to leave. We got back to Paris, did a few more shows and decided to call it quits with Olive, Plume, and Rudolph. We went right back to Spain, to try our luck in Madrid.

***

We hit Madrid at the perfect moment. Once again, we were the toast of the town, and were treated like royalty on the Spanish rock scene. Spain was coming out from almost 40 years of the Francoist dictatorship that had shut them off from the rest of the modern world. The whole town was busting out. They were in the bars, at the clubs, or just out on the streets promenading. I have never seen anything like it, before or since, and I doubt that I ever will. It was one big beautiful party that included young and old alike. Even Steve seemed to be enjoying himself.

Neither Steve nor I had ever taken Spanish in school, so for the first few months we went around saying "si" to everything. Since we were rock 'n' roll stars, and the Spanish loved to drink, we would get very drunk. I couldn't understand them, and they couldn't understand me. I was caught between two worlds.

The people we met were warm, and very generous. They would show you around town, introduce you to their friends, invite you in for a drink, take you into their homes, stay up all night, and fall down laughing, listening to records. They would spend two months at the beach, riding Vespas, kissing everyone they met, smoking hash, and swapping girlfriends.

They were also very sharp dressers, men and women alike. The girls were cute, really fucking cute, and the way they looked, dressed, and acted drove me nuts. Why hadn't we heard of this place before?

The first time I went to a swimming pool, I thought I had died and gone to heaven. I grew up like any other red-blooded American, to worship tits, ass, and money. My Spanish friend took me to the University pool on a nice hot day, and I had never seen so many beautiful naked breasts in one place in all my life. I got such a hard-on, I thought it was going to fall off. My Spanish friend, sensing that I was having trouble breathing, smiled and said, "Oh this is nothing special, you should see the girls when you go to the beaches down south."

You sure could have fooled me.

Since The Nerves and The Beat were very popular in Spain, we ended up staying in Madrid for a few years. There was no shortage of work for us. We made shitloads of money, touring Spain up one end and down the other.

There were no highways there, only little two-lane roads with European truckers in their eighteen-wheelers, barreling down the road. I would witness horrific accidents as we toured the country, and we never slept once while the van was moving. "All lanes now open," as cars and trucks would fan out in all directions.

Our new touring band had my brother Patrick, from New York on guitar. We also found the fabulous drummer Fabian Jolivet from the Spanish rock band Los Pistones. Our first gig together was December 1984 on this huge TV show called *La Edad De Oro (The Golden Age)*. We got paid 350,000 pesetas. As I left, I felt like a millionaire, cramming money into my bulging pockets.

In early 1985, after months of drinking and touring, we decided to go to London. It was our drummer Fabian's idea really. He had friends there and he was sick of Spain. We booked a show in Le Havre, home to our French label, Closer, and

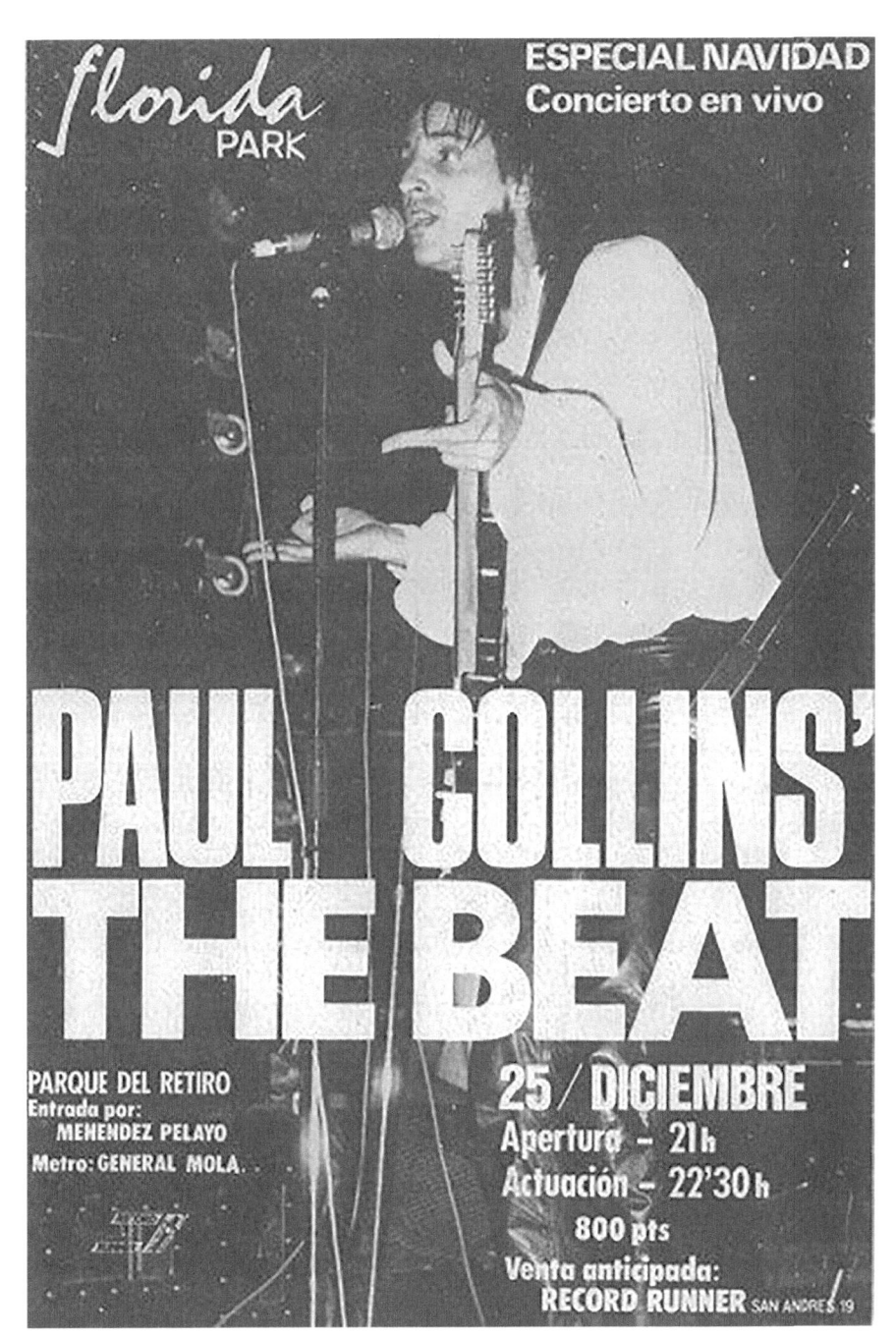

PAUL COLLINS' BEAT SPANISH TOUR ADVERTISEMENT, CIRCA 1984.
courtesy of Paul Collins' Archives

then booked a passage to London via Portsmouth.

What we didn't know was that Fabian really had it in for my brother, and was convinced Patrick was not up to snuff. It became a 'him or me' showdown in Le Havre. It came to a head by the time we got to London, and after constant fighting between Fabian and Patrick, my brother decided to leave. Understandably he was pissed off that I didn't stand up for him. Once again – just like it was with Michael Ruiz in the original lineup of The Beat, I gave into band politics. I let my brother go for 'the good of the band' and it was an extremely upsetting experience. I remember getting drunk, calling my mom in New York, and crying to her about what a shit I was.

It was a terrible time, and I hated everything about it. Once we were in London, it became apparent there was little to no interest in the kind of music we were making. It was also one of the coldest winters on record. Fabian didn't last long, as we froze our asses off in a London bedsit. Fabian had a lot of contacts, but when they all fizzled out, he split back to Spain.

Steve and I would try to make friends, but we didn't fit in on any level. We were broke, which only made matters worse. In London, if you go out with your mates for a drink, each bloke has to buy a whole round in turn. That was a disaster for us, as we could barely afford one pint.

We put out a few ads in *Melody Maker*, and met the very lovely drummer Paul Bultitude (from The Jet Set, and Mari Wilson). He was enthusiastic, and introduced us to guitarist Jim Barber, who worked for The Rolling Stones. They both dug our music and wanted to play out, so we finally had a band with English cats!

Phillipe of Closer told us he would finance a recording in London, with Lucas Fox at the controls. Lucas was the original drummer of Motorhead, which didn't mean anything to me. In the spring of 1985, we went into Easy Hire Studios in London to record the *Long Time Gone* mini-album in five days. The record was a kind of fusion between American power pop sensibilities, and a decidedly British production style and musicianship. Both Paul and Jim brought their English roots to the sound.

Lucas was consuming so much pot, he lost track of time. On the last day, he desperately tried to mix the 6-song record down in a few hours. Phillipe accepted the recording, and had it remixed in France, where it came out on Closer.

We toured a bit with Paul and Jim, but it seemed like we were spinning our wheels. We went back to the easy life in Madrid to make more money, and plan out our next move.

Steve and I wound up living at the home of my Spanish girlfriend Helena in Majadahonda, a suburb of Madrid. She was a model, fluent in English, and a huge rock 'n' roll fan. Helena introduced us to a lot of the cool bands that lived in Madrid. Los Secretos, Nacho Pop, Elegantes, and Pistones were all friends with her. She knew almost everyone there was to know on the Spanish rock scene. Thanks to Helena, we got to hang out and play with a lot of the great Spanish bands in Madrid.

We continued touring with two fantastic musicians – Manolo De Palma (drummer for one of Spain's first big rock bands, Tequila) and guitar-slinger Emilio Huertas (from the Spanish new-wave band Flash Strato). This was the band we recorded *Live At The Universal* with, released a year later in 1986.

These were some cool cats. Emilio was like a Spanish Keith Richards. One time a fan laid out some lines for him on the side of the stage. He jumped offstage, snorted the lines, and jumped back in time for his solo! Manolo had that Spanish

BACK COVER PHOTO FROM *TO BEAT OR NOT TO BEAT* EP, 1984.
courtesy of Paul Collins' Archives

(TOP): PAUL COLLINS WITH HELENA.
(BOTTOM): PAUL COLLINS, JUAN CARLOS, RICARDO, SPAIN 1984.
photos courtesy of Gabrielle Hernandez

Gypsy vibe, kind of like Mink Deville, with slicked-back black hair, a suit, frilly white shirt, topped off with stiletto boots.

One time in the north of Spain, we did a sound check that lasted seven hours – the longest of my whole career. There was only one sound company in the area. You used them, or you had no sound. The guy who owned and ran it was about sixty years old, and had probably spent most of his life herding sheep. In the end, Manolo's girlfriend, who had no experience and wore a bone through her nose, ran the soundboard.

***

Year by year, Spain modernized, and the more it tried to be like the rest of the world, the worse it got. Spain is the only place in the western hemisphere that I know of, that went through that kind of change. In a way, it was like my own life. Trying to be hip is the worst thing that can happen to you.

For some reason, Franco the Spanish dictator never wanted public awareness about the effects of drugs. Rockers consequently thought shooting-up was the same as smoking a joint. People started dying. Between the overdoses and the road-kill, the rock scene in Spain was littered with carcasses.

Still, there was an incredible optimism here, the arts were flourishing, and everyone was going to do something. We were incredibly lucky to have been there at that precise moment, which is today lovingly remembered in Spain as *La Movida* (*The Movement*). Filmmakers, photographers, painters, and musicians were all on the rise. Almodovar (who was just starting his career as a filmmaker) had a rock band, and we played some shows with him.

But we were living in a fantasy world, and I knew it. Sometimes, driving through some absolutely spectacular countryside, I would have to pinch myself. What I should have done is slapped myself.

Being an expat was starting to get old and we longed to be back among our peoples. It must have been some kind of genetic programming. For some ungodly reason, we felt that being *somebody* in Spain wasn't enough, and we needed to reclaim our rock-stardom back home.

PAUL WITH DRO RECORDS STAFF, CIRCA 1984.
courtesy of Paul Collins' Archives

We did one last tour and we left Spain in a blaze of glory, our pockets full of money and our heads filled with the completely absurd idea that maybe, just maybe, we could make it, back in the States.

> *I have done some stupid things in my life, but this was one of the worst. We were living in a paradise, but maybe like Adam and Eve, having it all wasn't enough.*

Spain was a place where people were trying to figure things out, but having fun. Isn't that the point, in life? After many years I am still trying to grasp that. I lost a lot by not knowing it then. I comfort myself with the saying, better late than never. I am starting to think that all those stupid corny sayings you've heard all your life, are true.

Jack would probably say "There is a reason why you heard them in the first place."

My mother used to recite really obtuse sayings her father told her when she was a child. When she asked him what he meant, he would say, "When you're older, you'll understand." My mother would respond to us the same way. Maybe this is just a way for people to hold onto things, and pass them from one generation to the next.

Jack would tell me "Maybe I should leave this to the experts."

As Steve Huff would say, "Keep on rocking," and in a perfect world, I'd be inclined to agree with him. At the time, this would have been the end of my book, the perfect capper. It seemed so simple, and it summed everything up nicely for me.

I don't live in a perfect world, and I never have.

The BEAT with STEVE MARRIOT of the SMALL FACES in ROUEN, SEPTEMBER 1984.
courtesy of Paul Collins' Archives

(LEFT, L TO R):
STEVE HUFF, PATRICK
COLLINS, PAUL, AND SICA
(PAUL'S MOM) BACKSTAGE
AT SALA STAR SEPTEMBER 6,
1984.

(BELOW, L TO R):
PAUL, JAVIER BOLIDO, AND
SICA (PAUL'S MOM), BACKSTAGE
AT SALA STAR SEPTEMBER 6,
1984.
*photos courtesy of
Gabrielle Hernandez*

PART 4:
Paul Collins Solo

photo courtesy of Kike Jimenez

CHAPTER SIXTEEN:
Work-A-Day World

We went to Redding, California in early 1987 to plan our assault on the West Coast. Steve was from there, so we could stay for free. I arrived with my Spanish girlfriend Helena and her young son. To put it mildly, Redding was a strange place. It all really hit home, when we saw a young couple having their wedding reception at a Chuck E. Cheese. Helena began to understand the tradeoff she had made in coming to America.

I went from living like royalty in Europe, to grubbing for handouts in California. These were going to be hard times, no doubt, trying to have some kind of family life while crashing at people's houses.

In order to get Helena a green card, we got married, and she slowly became immersed in the American way of life. One time when we were on the Embarcadero, Helena walked into a trade show for psychics, and that was it. She became sufficiently enlightened at the Berkeley Church of Psychics, another place I was banned from. They told me I brought a black cloud over the building, and asked if I'd be so kind as to 'get the fuck out.' I was starting to think I had bad karma.

Steve and I put together a band with Hector Toro and Jeff Leeds, guys we had found through an ad in *BAM*. It wasn't long before we were back in action, but the only work we could get was in the tertiary markets. At first it was San Jose and Fresno, but then we had to go farther afield. We wound up in places like Telluride and Ketchum, Idaho, famous for being the place where Hemingway killed himself. Ketchum is like that town in Peter Bogdanovich's *The Last Picture Show*, where the wind always blows in the same direction. That thought crossed my mind once or twice while I was there.

We even started to tour up in Canada again. In the dead of winter, we made it as far as Saskatchewan. We spent a week at the Saint George Hotel without going out once. The Queen of England had stayed there a long time ago, but now it was a shit-hole.

We were sliding into the deep abyss. The American music scene had changed once again, and it slid into apathy. I was getting into my thirties and it didn't look good. I had spent the better part of my life trying to make it in show biz and I was no closer than when I started, all those fucked-up years ago.

We recorded the *One Night* album at Astral Sounds in San Jose with David Hayes, bassist and band leader for Van Morrison. He did a fabulous job producing, and got us to use instruments we normally didn't use. Bongos, dulcimer, and keyboards were all used to great effect. When the record was done, we couldn't get it released in America, and it came out in France (Stoneage) and Spain (Twins) in 1987.

Everything fell apart after that. Steve and I began to slowly part ways. I really could not blame him. We had done everything. We did shows until it dwindled into nothingness. It had gone from the sublime to the ridiculous.

I got a telephone sales job, selling office supplies worldwide. I stuck out like a sore thumb. Their motto was 'Get a guy to say no ten times, and on the eleventh time, he will say yes.' Surprisingly, it worked most of the time selling pencils and paper clips, but never in my own life. After a while it got to me, so I stopped showing up.

I'm sure Helena and I were equally responsible for making a mess out of our marriage, and now she wanted a divorce. It was the only thing I had left to give her, so I did. I was broke, so I went down to the county clerk's office, and filled out the paperwork myself. Thirty days later, we were divorced.

I got a room with two other guys on 16th and Church. After many years of living with band mates and being married, I was back to living on my own, defeated, and totally unhappy.

At about this time is when I found God. 'God' came to me in the form of a sailboat. Yes-sir-ee Bob, I was walking down on the Embarcadero, not feeling too pleased about things, and I met a man who sold me a boat.

> *"Hold on a minute there pal; let me see if I got this straight. You are jobless, penniless, wife-less and some guy sells you a sailboat that you think is God?"*

Well, in a manner of speaking, yes.

I loved the water, always have, but I had never sailed. My old dad had been dead quite a while, so I called my new dad (who wasn't actually so new anymore) and asked him to lend me a thousand bucks. He did and I bought myself a 21-foot beautifully-proportioned, and very stable sailboat. She had a red hull and white topsides. I named her The Big Dipper.

I went to the library, took out all seven instructional books on sailing, and taught myself how to sail. Sure, I fucked up all over the place. I even rammed my boat into the Oakland Bay Bridge, but in the end, I taught myself how to sail in thirty knots of wind, and that is no small feat.

Sailing was probably the best thing I did for the whole fucking time I was in California. I felt like I was a failure at everything else, so this was something I could control, and accomplish in my life. Of course I didn't really think my sailboat was God, but it did give me a new lease on life. It gave me back some self-respect, taught me to believe in myself, and, as far as I can figure, that's what God *should* be doing, so ergo...

One evening, I was trying to bring The Big Dipper back in during rough weather, but was forced into the adjacent marina. As I tied her up, a fellow sailor happened upon me. He could see I was drenched and exhausted, so he invited me over for a hot toddy.

He had a magnificent boat that he had built himself, and we sat around getting drunk. Little by little, each of our stories came out. I started lamenting about how heartbroken I was over my failed marriage. He told me his war stories about the women he had left back home in Sweden.

I told him how much I loved European women, which was why I had married one from Spain. "Spain?" he asked, "What a coincidence, I just met this broad from Spain over in Berkeley." He tells me they had really hit it off, and that he was having a hell of a time *banging the shit out of her.*

"So Paul, what does your wife look like?"

I told him, and it got real quiet. We looked at each other, and we both knew. I said goodnight and went home drunk, soaked, and feeling like shit.

***

I managed to convince my label in Spain, Dro Records, to finance a recording. They thought I was as much of a big shot in America, as I was in Spain. I was living in San Francisco, surrounded by tons of great musicians, and thought – wouldn't it be amazing to get them all together on one record? I had fifteen thousand dollars to work with, so I got in touch with producer Norman Kearner, who knew most of these great musicians personally. He agreed to orchestrate the whole thing.

CYRIL JORDAN OF THE FLAMIN' GROOVIES WITH PAUL COLLINS, CIRCA 1989.
photo courtesy of Pat Johnson

With everyone's schedule, it wasn't easy getting people in the studio, so the recording took a while. In the end, the *Paul Collins* self-titled LP became a who's-who list of great Bay Area musicians:

- Cyril Jordan (Flamin' Groovies)
- Greg Kihn
- Chuck Prophet (Green On Red)
- Dave Immergluck (Camper Van Beethoven)
- Kenny Dale Johnson & Rollie Salle (Chris Isaak Band)
- John and Hilary Stench (Pearl Harbor & The Explosions)
- Jill Olson (Movie Stars)
- Chris Solberg (Santana)
- Jeff Trott (Wire Train)
- Chris Von Sneidern (Flying Color)

And last but not least – my good buddy Steven Huff joined me for a few backup vocals. It was a dream come true, working with all these fabulous cats!

This was my record, and it was really important for me to break away from The Beat. The music was firmly rooted in the emerging 'Americana' genre, but I felt that the main song "Another World" was my power pop masterpiece. But this was a songwriter's record. I had the material to delve into a lot of different subjects. "Dream A Little Longer" was about being trapped in one place, and wanting to go to another. *Take what you need, but meet me at the border.* "Can't Go Back" summed up what was happening to me, coming back to America. "Aswan To Luxor" was about a trip I took to Egypt. It wasn't just a straight up power pop rock record.

The deal with Dro was a fifty-fifty split. They went to Midem, a big international music industry event, to cut a distribution deal. When they got there, grunge was in full swing, and no one wanted to hear about some fucking guy from San Francisco who wrote songs on a sailboat. The record came out in 1992 in Spain and Italy, where it enjoyed modest success.

One night I doused my sailboat with gasoline and torched her. I could not think of having her in anyone else's hands. The next day I left San Francisco and California for good, and drove across the country for thirty days. I had no plan but to get to the other coast. Along the way, I would visit some of the places where The Nerves had played, but nothing was the same.

I was traveling with my good buddy Chris Von Sniedern and we had a short lived acoustic group, The Wandering Minstrels. We played all over the country, doing open-mics and pickup gigs. In Austin we did the Songwriters Circle at Threadgill's Old #1 with Jimmy Dale Gilmore and Butch Hancock. That was a good one. They gave you a three-course meal for playing three songs, and man, we were hungry. We ran into all kinds of folks I knew along the way, who would let us stay in their houses. In 30 days on the road, I don't think we spent more than one night in a hotel.

I arrived in New York City, and it was raining cats and dogs as I drove down the Great White Way. I did not have a single idea in my head, other than remembering Jerry Pompili (my handler from Bill Graham Presents) telling me not to quit my day job, as he laughed his ass off.

On the staircase of my mother's New York apartment was where I met my second wife Pilar, who was taking care of my sister's kid. She was tall, thin, with short jet black hair, and these amazingly deep, dark brown eyes. I asked in my best Spanish if she would like to go out that evening, and to my surprise she said yes. I am always surprised when I muster up enough courage to ask a woman out and she agrees.

It was a full moon, and I took her for a carriage ride in Central Park. I tried to kiss her, but she wouldn't let me. One year later, on the 27th of November, 1991, we were married by the county clerk in downtown New York. They told me at immigration, if it doesn't work out this time... *don't come back*.

I settled down to waste ten solid years of my life. I am not blaming my wife for this, and I hold myself solely responsible, even though she did not help matters. Domestic life can kill you artistically. Even to this day, when I start to think about buying furniture or getting new curtains, I stop myself dead in my tracks.

My sister has a house out in Montauk, and I would spend time out there in the summer. I got a gig working at The Clam Bar, an outdoor restaurant. I would set up outside and play as folks stuffed themselves with lobsters and clams. This was the first time I played covers since The Nerves' early days. My new repertoire was cool, Hank Williams, Johnny Cash, Dylan, Ray Charles, Kris Kristofferson, even Chubby Checker. I would throw in the occasional original, but stuck mainly to the classics.

I began setting up outside, and who should be sitting right in front of me, but Axl Rose. In the fantasy world that I usually lived in, I might think this was my big break. Axl would hear me, jump up, and say that I was his new discovery. What actually happened is I damn near killed him.

I hauled in my gear, and leaned my two old speaker columns against the wall at an angle, to get optimum sound dispersion. I turned around to get my amp, when a sixth sense made me look back. A gust of wind had caught one of the speakers, and it was falling toward the back of Axl's head. I caught it, but the heavy speaker would have done serious damage had it landed.

Axl was unaware as he had his back to me, but a few of the patrons who knew who he was, hooted out that he had 'better call his lawyer.' So here was a guy who regularly stood under tons of expensive lighting equipment, and I could have beaned him good with an old Peavey speaker column. That would have been something for *Rolling Stone*. As it was, he ignored me completely and I played knowing that he was making more money while eating his cheeseburger than I would probably make in my entire life.

Still, The Clam Bar did pay me well. There were some magic moments, especially at sunset if the crowd was right. I could really get a mood going. Mainly though, it was as the owner once put it, "Paul, having you play is like having flowers in the bathroom."

In 1993, I did manage to muster up enough creativity to write and record a new record, *From Town To Town*. We cut it in one day at Sourcer Sound. It was Easter, so they gave us a cut rate. I was working with bassist Rick Wagner from The dB's, guitarist Arty Lenin from The Flashcubes, Billy Ficca from Television, and Will Rigby also from The dB's. This record was country-tinged Americana style power pop.

PAUL COLLINS WITH (L TO R): ARTIE LENIN (FLASHCUBES), BILLY FICCA (TELEVISION) AND RICK WAGNER (THE DB'S), CIRCA 1995.
photo courtesy of Bob Wagner

      This time out I did not even bother to approach record companies, I would put it out myself. Rick and I decided to form a label, Wagon Wheel Records. We had a distribution deal with Caroline Records, sold lots of CDs, but we couldn't make a dime. The music industry just isn't set up for small companies to make a profit. We did have fun though.

PAUL COLLINS, CIRCA 1996.
photo courtesy of Juan Martin "Chas"

Our most successful release was in 1994 — a CD reissue of The Beat's first album. It seemed like a runaway hit to a small label, and it helped put me back on the map.

In June of 1994, a son was born to Pilar and me, Noah Vincent Collins. He was a beautiful baby boy. In a way, that's the day I really became a man. Now I had someone other than myself to think of, someone who really needed me to come through.

After The Beat reissue, our label put out *Pop Matters Vol. 1*, a compilation of new pop bands from around the country. We decided to support it by doing something that had not been done for many years, a Dick Clark-style travelling road show. We had seven bands from all over the country, one set of equipment, and each band played for about twenty minutes. The whole show was over in less than two hours, and the ticket price was a measly five bucks.

If I thought things were bad when Steve Huff and I last toured together, now it was even worse. There were eighteen of us, and on some nights we outnumbered the crowd. Our best night was when we hit Charlotte, North Carolina, and our one paying customer felt so bad for us, he bought fifty-dollars worth of merchandise.

My second marriage was deteriorating. I felt like it was mostly my fault, and this was one of the few things my wife and I agreed on. Back then, I thought if I had been more successful, everything would have turned out better. Now I know that's not true, because we lived like kings on a shoestring. We travelled all over, trips to Spain, with summers in Mallorca. Our apartment in the East Village was beautiful, but small. That grated on my wife, who expected more from me, and I guess, from life. But she was able to spend twenty-four hours raising our son, and you can't put a price on that.

On one of our family trips to Spain, we spent some time in Segovia where my wife had family. I was walking down a beautiful old cobblestone street when an old fan, Jose Luis Garces, approached me. He couldn't believe that I was in Segovia, and asked if I would be into playing a show. I have never turned down work, so I said yes. We packed the place, the show was great, and we recorded it.

It was released as *Live In Spain* in 1997 on the Spanish label Fonomusic. It was my first live acoustic record. I toured behind it, and this turned into about five years of gigging as a solo acoustic act. I had always worked with a band, so it took me some time to get it going, but when I did - it was great. They used to say I was 'The man with two guitars' because I had so much energy, I could fill a room with just my guitar and voice.

Wagon Wheel Records didn't count on the returns of CDs that didn't sell. This could have killed us, and it did kill a whole slew of smaller labels. I remember Jeff Murphy of Shoes telling me how a tractor trailer pulled up to his house, with boxes of returns that they had to pay for. We saw the writing was on the wall, and folded the label. Once again it was a bust, and I returned to doing nothing in New York.

So these were the 1990s, and one of the worst periods of my life. I sat in my shoebox-sized apartment, looking through pictures of my glory years, that I kept in an actual shoebox. I thought grunge had obliterated all its predecessors, so perhaps the most significant event of that decade was Christmas of 1999, when my mother bought me a computer. At first I resisted it, but soon realized what an amazing work tool it was for people like me, who were off the grid. In the '90s, I felt like no one had the slightest interest in '80s power pop, other than a handful of die-hards geeks and weirdos. Now, I was able to see that there was strong interest in the era I cut my teeth on, and an audience.

That's when I decided to go back to California, to look for Jack Lee.

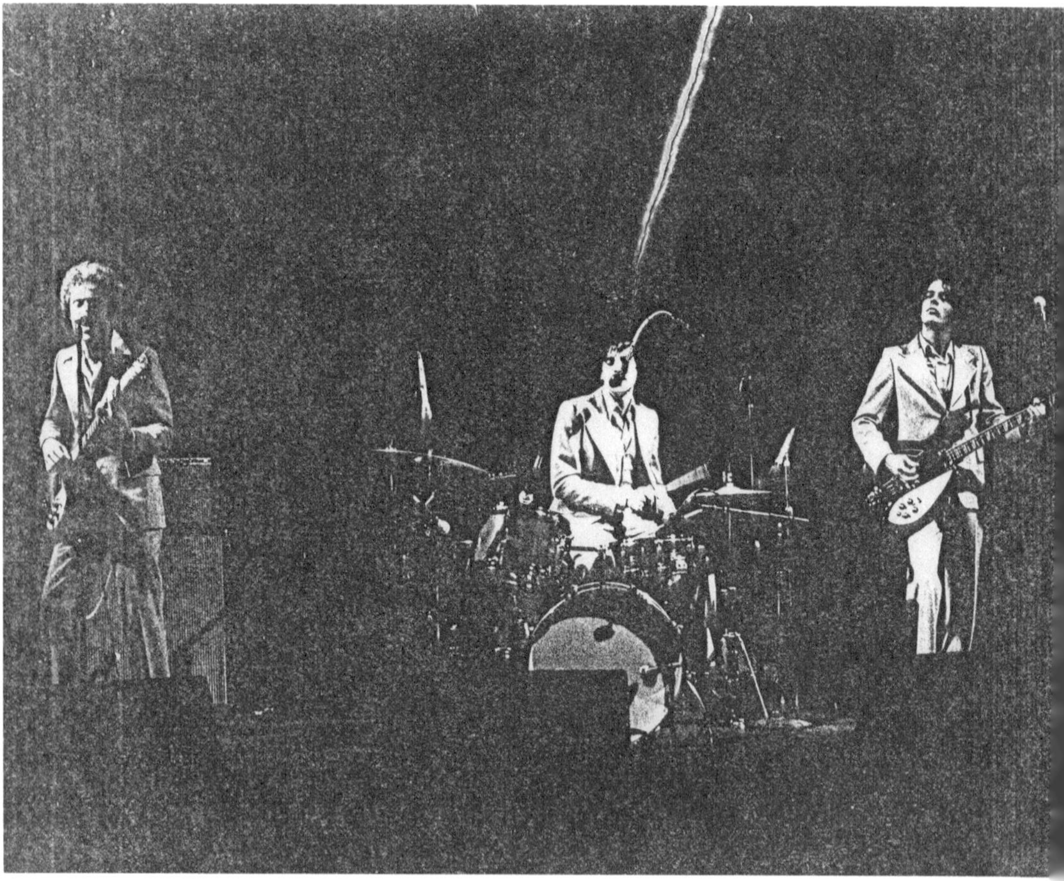

CHAPTER SEVENTEEN:

The NERVES Movie

Whatever I do at this point, it has to be a zero to 60 move.

I have not seen Jack in about 15 years. I must be out of my fuckin' mind. I have had to listen to people in bars, nightclubs, offices, banks, trains, planes, and busses, telling me about all the insane things they've done. I know I am not alone in this...

...but in a way I am.

I find Jack's number somehow, and call him out of the clear blue. He has a suspicious tone, asking me "Who's this?" but then saying "Hey Paul! It's good to hear from you! How are you?" I find out that Jack is living *The Life of Riley*. He has a lawyer, an accountant, and he is sleeping on the floor of a North Hollywood studio he intends to buy. I tell him I have been trying to write a book about my life.

> "Paul, there's nothing sweeter, than taking in a lifetime of failures, and turning it into something!"

I tell him that I think we should make a movie about The Nerves. He laughs and says:

> "I live in Hollywood, man! Everyone here has a script for a movie, even the guy at the dry cleaners."

Just like when we first met Peter, I am discouraged. I think I need Jack if I am ever going to get out of this mess. Then, a few days later, he calls me back.

> "You know Paul, I've been thinking, maybe a movie is not such a bad idea after all!"

We pick up right where we left off. What is twenty years to a couple of nuts like us? In a matter of minutes I am back under his spell. I am so desperate, I am willing to do anything to make it. With Jack at the helm, I am sure it is in the bag.

This time we are going all the way. We are done fucking around, and no more Mr. Nice Guy. This time we are going to kick the world right in the balls. We are going to make a guerrilla-style, self-produced, feature length major motion picture. Oh yeah, and we are going to involve the whole town of North Hollywood. We actually *join* The Hollywood Chamber of Commerce.

I have goosebumps going all up and down my arms. The fucking genius of it! Now all the stupid shit that had happened to us was going into the movie:

The Nerves:

"The Greatest Rock 'N' Roll Band That Never Was!"

According to Jack, the first thing I have to do is have him give me a crash course in screenwriting. He claims he used to be a script doctor for Robert Evans, one of the biggest producers in the business. I start reading Syd Field's well-known screenwriting book cover to cover. Every night, while my wife and kid are asleep, I am on the phone with Jack from midnight to six in the morning, writing the script. I'm in New York, he's in LA, so we run up huge phone bills. We get three quarters of it done, when Jack proposes that we meet up someplace and have a face to face.

I had been planning to take my wife and son to Las Vegas. Jack says, "Perfect, I'll meet you there!" We arrive, and I am shitting bricks as I walk down the plush carpeted hallway to his room. What will it be like? I feel like I am going to meet my maker. It is fitting that I am in Vegas, because I have it all riding on Jack. My whole wad is on red number 7, and if it doesn't pay off, I am ruined.

Just like I did some twenty-six years ago, Jack opens the door, and I am looking into those pale blue eyes, framed by golden curls. *It's Jack fuckin' Lee!* He has the room completely blacked-out, just like Howard Hughes, and he ushers me in. The room reeks of cigarette and marijuana smoke. I am in a daze trying to keep my balance, and not lose my cool - but I am way out of my league as usual when it comes to Jack.

He is playing U2's "Beautiful Day" for me loudly on a huge boom box. I can't really focus, my mind is racing, and I try to bring this scene down to earth, so we can talk about the movie, but nothing happens.

We go down to the pool so Jack can meet my wife, who looks at him suspiciously. Jack thinks my kid is great. As I lay on the chaise lounge, I notice that Jack keeps all his money, a roll of hundred dollar bills, in an ankle wallet. I have never seen an ankle wallet.

He is skinny as a rail, and I am doing my best to suck in my stomach. Peter Case had recently told me that "Jack looks the same, man," but he doesn't. It would be like saying Keith Richards looks the same. Jack is older, crazier, and the lines of time have taken a toll on his face. He gets a phone call and abruptly tells me he has to get back home. Before he leaves, he asks when can I come out to LA, and get to work. That is it, my big meeting with Jack. It is over and done with before I know it, but we are back in business.

When I get back to New York, I start making my plans to go to Los Angeles. My wife looks at me like:

> "So you are just going to leave us here?"

I make a lame ass excuse about how this was for our future, but I know she doesn't believe it. I don't believe it, but I had spent years believing that Jack Lee was the only guy who could take it all the way to the top. I'm not going to pass up this chance to get on that ride.

When I call Jack from LAX, he tells me that something came up, and I should take a cab to a hotel right next to the studio. Fuck, this is not starting out like I had imagined. For some reason I expected Jack to pick me up in a Cadillac, and to whisk me off to his cool digs somewhere in the Hollywood Hills.

I had lived many years in LA, but had never spent any time in North Hollywood - the white trash capital of the world. I have a pit in my stomach, sitting in the rundown hotel, waiting for him to call me. There is no one I want to see, and I am freaking out, hoping I have not made a colossal mistake.

Jack finally calls, and says the first thing I have to do is meet a team of Mexican workers coming to the studio, and oversee them cleaning the whole place out. He goes into a tirade of instructions. Every scrap of paper in the studio needs to be bagged up in hefty bags, so they can be taken to his storage space. He tells me:

> "There might be the title of a hit single written down on one of those scraps!"

I get to the 12-room, burned-out two story studio. Hollywood is full of these kinds of buildings. I have to pry open the door, and when I finally get it open wide enough to peer in, the first thing I see is one of those ½ inch thick plastic hospital mattresses on the floor. The next thing I see is that the room is filled waist-high with shopping bags of garbage. There are bottles of yellow liquid lining the walls. I see more bags, and there is a stench that can only mean one thing:

> "Oh shit! This is really fucked up; I have entered into an insane asylum!"

When any other sane person would turn and run, I decide to stay. I clean out one of the offices, get a mattress with a bed frame, and end up living here. I am at the lowest depths of my life, but I am going to get through this. Jack starts paying me about a grand a month, so I become his boy again, doing all kinds of shit. We construct an outdoor shower. Jack decides to put some rugs in, and paint the place, in that order. I tell him that we should do it the other way around, but he won't listen. We end up having to hire guys from Home Depot to come clean the paint off the rugs.

I am a wreck, and I can't get out from under Jack's spell. He has me by the short hairs, and I am powerless. I am never able to figure this one out - some deep down part of me will just do whatever Jack says. He knows it, and I guess I do too.

Part of the ordeal is Jack's extreme mood swings - going from rage to serenity in the space of an instant. He is bipolar and if he goes off his meds, all hell will break loose. One minute he is practically foaming at the mouth; the next minute he is purring like a kitten. Then he tells me something nice to make sure I will stay — *and obey*.

One late night, "Hanging On The Telephone" comes up in our conversation. I finally tell Jack how I pitched The Nerves EP to Blondie's management back in 1977. Jack says: "I don't know what you're talking about, man!" and tells me the 'official story' about Jeffrey Lee Pierce of the Gun Club giving it to Blondie on a mixtape.

> *I had never heard that story before Jack told me, but I believe it's true. I also know that what happened with me, Peter Leeds, and Richard Gottehrer, all those years ago is true, because I lived through it. I'm assuming both things happened. Maybe Blondie and Leeds first heard something on the EP other than "Hanging On The Telephone," and thought it sucked. Or, perhaps they instantly knew they wanted to record it, and wanted The Nerves to disappear so we wouldn't be any competition. Who knows? I will probably never find out.*

Then, Jack tells me that he "knew The Nerves were going to be huge," but he "just couldn't do that" so he "had to break it up." I look at him like "What the fuck are you talking about?" Jack says he thought we "were all so talented, and that we all needed to do our own thing." I don't know; it is just crazy talk. No one knows what is going to happen.

We finish the script and go into production, buying shit left and right. We even buy a bus, just like the one I wrote my first two songs in. It shows up on a flatbed truck, blocking traffic for miles.

"Where do you want me to put it?"

In a few months we rack up enormous bills. It is insane as it can only be in Hollywood.

We have castings, readings, production meetings, and photo shoots. I manage to convince Mackie, a sound company, to send us a $50,000 audio production set up, for free.

Rex "Hoss" Thompson (an aspiring director and a friend of Steve Huff's) looks every bit like a young Alfred Hitchcock. He wants to scout locations. I meet him in San Francisco, and we run all over town shooting footage of our old haunts. Our last stop is the flophouse where The Nerves used to rehearse. Now it is a million dollar home. Like I had done so many years before, I knock on the door, but this time I have a guy with a movie camera behind me. The lady living there opens the door, and gladly shows us around the place. Something about a movie camera makes people open up.

> *I feel very weird, standing in the basement, looking out the little window where the neighbors had stuck that note so many years ago. A lot has happened to me, but I'm still no closer to figuring things out. I'm getting a*

little dizzy, with 25 years of feelings flying around inside of me.

The walls have been painted, the carpet is gone but I can still feel all the hope and aspiration in this room. I start to rip apart inside; remembering everything now. I'm going back and forth in time, seeing myself as a young kid sitting here with Jack and Peter. I see how determined we were, and how we knew we were going to conquer the world. Then, like a kaleidoscope, I see all the shit that subsequently went down, and it brings me back to the future; into the here and now.

I bite my lip, turn to the director and say:

"Think you got enough light to shoot in here?"

Right then and there, I know that we are never going to make this movie.

Peter is in town, but he's not coming anywhere near this one.

Jack's daughter moves down from Sacramento, with her boyfriend. All of a sudden there are all night parties, and then the cops are showing up. I'm freaking out. I am thinking that I'm going to get arrested. *I gotta get the fuck out of here!* After two months I go back to New York with my tail so far between my legs, it was all the way up my ass. The dream has ended, and there is no other possible way to look at it. It is over, for real.

You know that look – that's the look my wife gives me. It is bad enough that I am going down in flames, but now I have company. I am certain that it is pointless to think I could make it as a rock star.

I am a broken man.

I'm still in Jack's clutches for a little while. He calls me up, and tells me we need to start doing this or that. Another member of Jack's family shows up in North Hollywood, and he wants me to make sure she's getting money out of his account. He is offering me secretarial work, and I say:

"Yeah Jack, yeah."

Jack doesn't call back. He never does stuff like that. Jack forgets what he tells you, and just moves on. To this day, he calls me periodically and says:

"You need to make 20 copies of that script; we need to send them out!"

"Yeah Jack, sure."

I hang up with Jack, and just like that, it is over and done with. I am clean. *I purge myself of him.* I come to the realization that in order to make it, *I am going to have to make it myself.*

Two weeks later... Osama Bin Laden destroys the World Trade Center.

PAUL
COLLINS

photo credit: Bob Wagner

CHAPTER EIGHTEEN:
King of Power Pop

I guess we first heard the term 'power pop' back in The Nerves. The first reaction that I remember was, "what the fuck is this shit?" We never thought of ourselves as power pop. We very simply thought of ourselves as a rock 'n' roll band. The term 'power pop' sounded kind of wimpy to us, a journalist's term to separate us from the mainstream.

The only outlets were major labels and radio. We were in their world, and they weren't going to play power pop or punk, so it worked against us. At least punk bands were being written about, but power pop never got that far.

It wasn't until the next generation when power pop stopped being a stigma. I started seeing 'Top 10 of Power Pop' articles covering Cheap Trick, Big Star, The Raspberries; bands I never considered power pop. They were a lot more successful and managed to transcend it. For some of us (20/20, Shoes, The Pop, The Nerves) – 'power pop' was the kiss of death.

I really didn't start seeing the value of associating myself with power pop until the late '90s/early 2000s, when my mom bought me a computer. In the first week, I sold Get Hip Records $2000 worth of Beat CD's! 'Power pop' was no longer a dirty word. New power pop bands were coming up. I was like "wow, kids are aligning themselves with us!" I saw the resurgence; a rekindling, and it grew from there.

***

On Tuesday, September 11th, 2001, I took my son Noah to school. When I got back to our apartment, on our small TV, I saw the second plane flying into the World Trade Center. My wife Pilar was on the bed screaming, convinced that World War III had broken out, and that we'd all be dead in a matter of minutes.

Have you ever been in a very small apartment with someone who thinks a war has broken out? "Come on honey, calm down! It's not going to happen, this is America!" Telling a woman to 'calm down' is never the right thing to say.

She told me "That's it, I am taking my kid and moving back to Spain."

We went back to the school to get Noah. It was a beautiful day, but up in the clear blue sky, you could see two columns of smoke blowing toward Brooklyn. There was utter silence; a deafening silence. You couldn't hear a single shout, or a horn blowing.

The school staff were petrified; freaking out, but they didn't want to cause a panic with the kids. Everyone knew there had been a bombing, but there wasn't an official statement yet. We waited for a while in the teacher's room. Women were talking on the phone to their husbands: stock brokers and employees who were in the twin towers. Some of those men never made it out alive. It was pandemonium, and panic be damned – we decided to take our kids and leave.

We headed to my mom's apartment, and saw the first group of survivors walking up Sixth Avenue. They were covered in white ash, looking like zombies from *The Night of The Living Dead*. We caught the last train out of Penn Station to Montauk.

Three weeks later, I packed up my family and moved back to Madrid. I went into business with my old buddy Eric Kelly, who I had known from my days on 45th Street. We had recently reconnected, and after I told him about how great Madrid was he said, "Let's go open a bar there!" We started looking for a location, found an old run down lounge that had been closed for a while, and converted it into the stylish Manhattan Martini Bar.

On the day we opened, Eric said "I don't have any more money!" The market had taken a nosedive, and his American business had disappeared overnight. His wife took his house, his BMW had no resale value, and he had been diagnosed with colon cancer. What could I say to that? He split back to New York, leaving me to run the bar on my own.

I worked that sucker for about two years, seven nights a week, three hundred and sixty-five days a year. I taught myself how to make the best cocktails in Madrid. Students, expats, and locals all came out for what became known as the best cocktail in the city. I surprised myself and thought that maybe I'd finally found my calling.

At the bar, I would deliberately play music that was not rock 'n' roll – old obscure jazz records; music I had never heard.

As my six year old nephew Orrin used to say back then, "You are so not right!"

The economy started to slide, and two years to the day, we had to close Manhattan Martini Bar. By this time, both my wife and my partner had completely abandoned me. I had thought that rock'n roll was hard, but it was easy compared to this.

My wife and I made a few unsuccessful attempts at marriage counseling, but the last visit ended with the counselor throwing us out, so we got divorced. The proceedings were in Spanish, and no one spoke English, including my lawyer. My wife did, but she wasn't speaking to me.

I went back to my little duplex apartment alone. I was not in the best of moods, but I had to put on a happy face for my son's benefit, when he would come home for lunch.

I saw my guitar there every day, just hanging on the wall, but I didn't touch it. It was a leap for me, to put the guitar on the wall, work at a bar, and throw myself into it one-hundred percent, like I do everything. To tell you the truth, it was kind of a relief. I wanted a legitimate career, where I didn't worry about where my next meal was, or if a paycheck was going to come.

Music was always such a hustle, from day one, and it never got any easier. It was always starting over and over again at ground zero.

One day, it was like my guitar asked me, "Hey you, fucker! C'mon, take me off this goddamn wall!" I started playing. In a very short amount of time, I happily realized I wasn't washed up, and I still had things to say.

I stopped trying to write hit songs, or attempting to get a record deal. I still loved playing music, and still had what it takes to do this. I started finishing songs I'd been working on for years, from back in the '90s on 9th Street in the East Village.

One night, something came back to me like a ton of bricks. I just started thinking about my high school friend Bobby. Back then, it was too much of a shock to absorb, so I just moved on, and didn't deal with it. I blocked it out of my mind, but I think Bobby's suicide was always kind of kicking around. Every once in a while it might just pop up in my subconscious.

Now, in the throes of my mid-life crisis, I finally understood why some people might want to do that - when you don't feel like you have any other way out, and the personal pain is so deep and unending. For days I was terrified at the prospect that I would even consider doing that to myself. Eventually I had to deal with it, so all these years later, I wrote a song about it – "Bobby." It talks about what happened, and it says to Bobby, "I hope you're alright now."

> *I wish I could tell you about the art of songwriting. It's a very elusive, extremely difficult thing, and I don't feel I know any more about it now than I did back then. It's a question of sitting there with a guitar, banging, and waiting for some little tidbit of inspiration to come along. That will start the ball rolling. Sometimes it's a chord progression, a vocal idea, or a song title you want.*
>
> *Unusual things will happen every once in a while. I remember being on hiatus from The Nerves, staying with my sister, and walking home from Max's Kansas City very late at night. This was back when NYC was still dangerous. I was alone, scared, and the streets were dark. A bus went by in slow motion, lit up so I could see everybody looking at me, wondering what this weirdo is doing out on the street. I felt very self-conscious, and very out of it.*
>
> *When I got to my sister's, where I was sleeping on the couch, I could see her husband's Gibson guitar sitting on a stand in the living room. It just came to me; I started seeing the chords of "I Don't Fit In," by just looking at a guitar, and not playing it. The next morning, I actually started playing it! "I Don't Fit In" was probably the only song I've ever written that way. Usually it's just a lot of trial and error.*
>
> *I say as a musician, you have to have your antennae up, and ready to receive. If I get something, I usually don't record it right away. Since I'm writing pop stuff, my logic is, if I can't remember it, it can't be that good. I just use my memory as my tape recorder, when working on tunes.*

All of a sudden, I had an album's worth of material that I really felt strongly about. So in my home, without a lot of preparation, I began work on two unpretentious small projects that really brought me out of my depression. I began writing this book, which has taken me all this time, and I started working on what would become my first collection of new songs in 13 years... *Flying High*.

Flying High *was important.*

> *I can really pinpoint the beginning of my second act right then and there. It marked the beginning of finding my way back - and rebuilding myself into what I am today. It was a considerable distance.*

I got together with Octavio Vinck, a guitar player, arranger, musicologist, and a great friend of mine. We found Carlos Guardado, the bass player from Burning, a very popular rock band in Madrid, and Ginez Martinez, a cartoonist, red wine drinker, and drummer.

We cut *Flying High* in my apartment, on a 16-track mobile ADAT recording unit owned and operated by our buddy, Astrayo Astray. We spent about 1000 Euros making it. We had no producer, just four guys who loved playing music - who would let the songs do the talking. It was released on Lucinda Records in December of 2005. It's a very simple recording, and I'm very proud of it.

***

In February of 2006, we were invited to play a punk rock festival in Rome, called the Road To Ruins. Bands like The Avengers, The Terminals, and White Flag were playing. I said to my manager Juancho - "Why do these guys want me to play a punk festival? They are going to destroy us!" I thought about not putting "That's What Life Is All About" in the set, because it's *so* Buddy Holly. When I ended up playing it for 600 kids, and they were all singing along, it blew me away. People told me after we played that 'every DJ in Italy plays that song!'

I remember Juancho saying "See that guy with the long hair, dyed bright red? That's Chips Kiesby, one of the biggest producers in Sweden! He produced The Nomads and The Hellacopters! He's a fan!" I had no idea what I might say to him, but before I knew it, I asked Chips if he would produce my next album. He said "You bet!" I couldn't believe it.

Our record label Rock Indiana spent way more money than anyone should have. Chips was expensive, and had a recording process that was elaborate and time consuming – but he made a deal with Pablo from Rock Indiana. So my Spanish band (Juancho, Octavio, Pablo Cabanes) and I went to his studio in Gothenburg, Sweden, for two weeks in the dead of winter.

Ribbon Of Gold was released in 2008, and it was part of a one-two punch that started with *Flying High*. People loved those records, and it really resurrected my career. We started touring all over, overseas, and in the United States. It just started snowballing from there.

I played South By Southwest, and it was a way for me to reintroduce myself to the American audience – most of whom probably thought I was dead. I met a ton of people, like Gentleman Jesse, who had a band that embodied late '70s Nick Lowe, Elvis Costello, and power pop – the perfect backing band for me. The first thing he did was say "We're your guys! You're going to tour, and we will be your band! We are just going to do this!" I said 'Ok, cool.'

So in 2009 we put together a tour of the USA, one of the most successful tours I've ever done. We sold-out shows, had great deals with the clubs, and made a ton of money. I saw that now there was a whole new way to tour in America, and it worked great. I told myself that this would be my future.

When we got to my home in New York, I dumped about six thousand dollars in cash on the bed, and we all started rolling around in it! We went out, bought some steaks and Jameson whiskey, and I cooked us up a kick-ass meal as we divvied up the money. When they left, all I thought about was, "when can I do this again?"

So in 2010 I started a Facebook page called 'The Beat Army.' I was on a mission to let the world know that power pop was back! I was sure if people listened to the music, they too would fall in love with it. I wanted to show people in the industry that power pop wasn't some forgotten genre from days gone by. To prove it, I wanted the page to create a number for this genre of music – where people could see that there were 3,500 likes, 6,000 likes, or whatever.

I wanted a collective of power pop fans, and bands promoting themselves. Yes, I wanted to promote myself too, but after 30 or 40 years of blowing your own horn, you kind of get burned out on it. I wanted to promote the whole thing, especially the young bands that I had met along the way.

When I began touring again, it opened my eyes up to how you could do this. You didn't need an agent. You could just get in touch with the clubs, and do handshake deals. These days, most of the clubs were straight up and honest.

I developed a network where instead of sleeping on couches and floors or expensive hotels, we were staying with people in their homes. We were sleeping in nice beds and they would be cooking us delicious dinners in their kitchens. Touring became nice and comfortable, like taking a big trip to visit family.

***

In 2010, Patrick Boissel of Alive Records, who had put out some recent Nerves compilations, wanted a new solo record from me. Patrick suggested Jim Diamond, a well-known producer in Detroit. Jim is perfect for small labels. He can make a record in 3 days that is sonically good, but cheap – and that's what you need these days.

I like working with Patrick at Alive, because he knows up front how much everything is going to cost. If a project sells what he thinks it will, he will at least break-even. That's how he stays in business. Another bonus of working with Alive is they are affiliated with Bomp! Records, who had championed The Nerves in the '70s. Bomp! was now run by Suzy Shaw, wife of the late Greg Shaw. I had met her when I was just a kid. She was always at the office taking care of business. I felt like I had come full circle.

With the *King Of Power Pop* LP, I wanted to connect all the dots, from The Nerves and The Beat, up until now. I began digging deep into the back catalogue, to find songs that were overlooked. "Don't Blame Your Troubles On Me" is a very early song from the mid-'70s, back when I was in San Francisco. I used to sing "The Letter" by the Box Tops in The Nerves. "Losing Your Cool" was from the '80s, when I was living in New York, playing the clubs as "Paul Vincent" on acoustic, with my brother Patrick playing piano. The *King Of Power Pop* was just a mishmash of all this different stuff.

I would have never called the album 'King Of Power Pop' if I had not written a new song called that. When I ran it by Patrick at Alive, he agreed, saying "In rock 'n' roll, you have to have balls." Still, I was trepadicous, but I did it anyway. One day, I was sitting around the house and the phone rang. It was Dwight Twilley! Oh shit, I had completely overlooked what his reaction might be, to calling myself 'The King Of Power Pop.' I started apologizing profusely.

Dwight magnanimously said, "Paul, you can be the King of Power Pop, and I'll be the King Of Power Poop!"

***

In 2011, I had gotten an email from someone telling me Green Day was performing "Walking Out On Love" on Broadway. I looked it up, and there were dozens of videos of Billie Joe Armstrong singing my song for the encore of his Broadway play, *American Idiot!* Then I was doing a radio show with a guy named Rich Russo, who has a syndicated program called *Anything Anything*. Rich told me he was going to the after-show cast party of American Idiot at The Bowery Electric. "Hey Paul, I can bring a guest, and I'm leaving in an hour. Do you want to go?" It was literally 10 minutes from my house, and even being the lazy old bastard that I am, I couldn't refuse.

I met Billie Joe, and he was lovely – acting like a fanboy, flattering me, hugging me, telling me how much he loved "Walking Out On Love," and saying it's one of his all-time favorites. He was buying me drinks, and I was sitting there looking at a guy from one the biggest bands on the planet, who plays stadiums, and he was treating me like an old bud. Then he turned to me, and said "C'mon on man, play 'Walking Out On Love' with us!"

Green Day played for hours in this little nightclub, like a straight-up punk band back in the day. They were getting drunk, and doing originals and covers. They played for so long that I could barely keep my eyes open, and I was about to leave.

Then they brought me up to play "Walking Out On Love" with them! The song is like a minute and a half, so it was over before you knew it. Then they said "No, let's do it again!" So we did it three times in a row! It was great.

As a songwriter, the fact that they play my song is extremely flattering.

(L TO R): PETER CASE, PAUL COLLINS, GARY MYRICK, CARMINE APPICE,
AND ROGER TAYLOR, CIRCA 1981.
courtesy of Paul Collins' Archives

CHAPTER NINETEEN:
You Can't Go Back

The possibility of The Nerves getting back together seemed like a million miles away.

This is what happened when Peter and I got back together after god-knows-how-many years, to do what became a big rock 'n' roll mess.

The way the whole thing went down was, a few years prior to the Case/Collins Tour, Alive Records had released two Nerves compilations, and The Breakaways - *Walking Out On Love (The Lost Sessions)*. Patrick of Alive Records suggested that Peter and I tour together. I said "Patrick, don't tell me! I've been trying to do this forever, so you are preaching to the choir."

At that point, Peter and I weren't very close. He was very standoffish with me. Every once in a while we would have some contact, and I'd say "Hey, it would be great if you ever wanted to do something together." *I kind of got tired of saying that.*

Then one day in 2012, and I'm not sure exactly what precipitated it, someone on Peter's team saw the logic in us touring. They thought it would be a great way to promote the Alive releases. It all sounded good on paper. If Peter and I got a chance to sing all those great songs; those great harmonies from The Nerves, The Plimsouls, and The Beat, how could we miss? It would be a hell of a great show.

Peter called me and said "Look, I will do this, but my guy has to manage it." Peter had a whole business team in place, and I was alone with a lot of DIY touring experience under my belt. Peter laid it out for me: his manager would run things, and his agent would do the bookings. We were assured of doing good shows with big guarantees every night, and we were counting on making a ton of cash – kind of our big payday.

I had no problem with that, and it sounded like music to my ears. I was sick and tired of hustling up every show, touring on a shoestring, and this would seem like a five star tour by comparison.

We never contacted Jack and asked him if he wanted to do it. That wasn't even part of the plan. Peter would never go out with Jack; they had been at odds for a very long time. Peter and Jack's history went back to long before I showed up in San Francisco. There was always an underlying tension between them that I really wasn't privy to. I just knew they could go at each other like mad dogs if things ever boiled over. Jack could be very imposing with me, but never with Peter.

This was going to be as close to a Nerves reunion tour as anyone was ever going to get.

We agreed on a basic time frame and started to work out the details. I had a working band of young guys who would love to do it, and wouldn't rake us over the coals for a paycheck. I knew the guys at Burger Records were touring monsters, and would supply the van and driver. To round out the whole package, The Summer Twins (two young ladies and their back up band) would love to be the opening act, and would supply all the gear, to boot.

We committed ourselves to a grueling travel plan, taking us from Vancouver down to San Diego, across the desert to Austin for SXSW, and then clear through to the east coast.

The first thing Peter's management did after I went over the whole setup, was meet with my contact from Burger Records. They cut a deal with him directly, and immediately tried to remove me from the thing. I was like 'what the fuck?'

We weren't getting very good offers. I told everyone that I had all these contacts, who I then got to counter with much better offers, which were accepted by Peter's agent. So I would stick my neck out to get better offers, but was still paying a percentage to Peter's agent, who didn't even get the offer.

I was respectful, but this was misconstrued as me stepping in to do someone else's job. For the most part, all I was really doing was saying things like "Hey, contact this person I know, we need a show in St. Louis." Peter's manager and the agent were like "Paul, butt out! You're just a problem, and you don't know how to do this!" So, I was banned from using any of my connections, or know-how about doing this kind of thing.

It was agreed that we would meet up in Seattle, where my longtime friend Ingrid had a mansion. We could hole-up and do the rehearsals before starting the tour on March 1, 2012 in Vancouver, at The Old Ironsides.

As I was getting ready to go, I had that funny feeling in my stomach. My son was saying "Dad, don't go, don't do this! There is something wrong, and I can feel it!" I went anyway.

The rehearsals started off badly. Peter and I didn't see eye to eye and that caused friction. We were never able to get in sync. There was also this alpha dog thing going on, and we were arguing. At that point, there was all this tension over whose songs we were going to do. Peter wanted to do covers, and I didn't.

The West Coast portion of the tour went fairly well, but then things got tough. The big shows never really materialized, and they just kept booking, booking, and booking. We probably should have just done the West Coast, called it a day, and waited for the offers to come in.

We got to South By Southwest. It was hot. I headed to the bare-bones dressing room. Someone told me, "Hey! Bill Murray is up in that vintage store over there, talking to some young chicks. He was at your show at the Continental last night, and he's a really big fan!" So I went up there:

"Hey Mr. Murray, how are you doing? I heard you were at our show!"

"Oh yeah, I love you guys!"

I told him that we were playing tonight, too. He said "Ok, I'll introduce you guys!" The kids went nuts when he brought us onstage.

All in all, we played about seven shows at South By Southwest. None of them really paid that much, but we did get to play "A Million Miles Away" with Peter Buck of R.E.M. He was totally cool, laid back, just into the music, and no star-tripping. We also got to play Alejandro Escovedo's showcase at a taco stand. I had to recede into myself when I got onstage in my leather jacket and sunglasses. I loved playing rhythm guitar, just standing on stage, looking cool.

But Peter and I weren't getting along. There wasn't a real friendship vibe so that really hurt. It sucked.

Back in the day, I had looked up to both Peter and Jack, much in the same way a little brother would. But it wasn't back in the day, and I wasn't a little kid. We were two old men and there was no real bond anymore. Peter wasn't teaching me anything and we were no longer shoulder-to-shoulder. We were just trying to prove who could be boss, and no one was going for it.

Touring in and out of SXSW was a huge mistake. Any agent in America will tell you, if you are trying to book around SXSW, good luck. There are 10,000 bands on the road that will all play for anything and anywhere, so it's really hard to get good-paying gigs coming out of Austin.

One of the last shows we did was in Oklahoma City. We found out we weren't getting our guarantee. At the end of the show, we said "Where's the hotel?" and the club said "What hotel?" It was the middle of the night, and we were running around, eight people, and no hotel. I was like "C'mon man, this is the tour we are going to get rich on?"

Then, in Kansas City, Lee from Burger Records was driving. Since I was the only one with a credit card, I was responsible for all the hotel arrangements, and checking us in. I was tired, we got to the hotel, and when I tour, hotels are really important to me. I want my time in them.

They told me to go check-in, and I said I'm going to bring my stuff up. They said 'don't worry; we will get your stuff for you.' I went in to do the check-in, and saw the drummer and bass player coming in with their own suitcases, and Peter's suitcase. I thought, okay, I've got to go back and get my stuff. I found out the van was gone. The bass player and drummer told me "Peter and Lee had to go to a pharmacy to get Peter's prescription."

"So you bring his fuckin' suitcase in, and you don't bring my fuckin' suitcase in? What is the fucking matter with you guys? *I want to go to my fuckin' hotel and take it easy!*"

I blew up at them. I just wanted my goddamn suitcase and my guitar with me. I don't like keeping my shit in the van, and then the van took off – goodbye! I mean, anything can happen to your stuff. If you have a two or three-thousand-dollar guitar on the road, *you keep it with you*. So that's what happened. When Peter got back, he asked:

"What are you yelling at the guys for?"

"I'm yelling at the guys because they bring your fuckin' suitcase in, not mine, and you're out driving around with Lee! I wanted to go to my room, take my toiletry bag out, and take a fuckin' shower! What the fuck is my suitcase doing in the van?"

"Uh, well Paul, you need to watch your shit!"

"No, I don't need to fuckin' watch my shit! Here I am checking the whole fuckin' band in, and you guys take off with my shit! *Fuck you!*"

It all fell apart in Springfield, MO. We got paid, and I was having some shots with the owner in the back. We got in the van, drove away, and I was good and toasted. I remember yelling at the top of my lungs about how we had kicked ass that night... 'that's rock 'n' roll!'

Peter had been a big drinker and I'm sure in his mind, I was drinking too much. I was also smoking, and he had quit, so I'm sure those two things annoyed the hell out of him.

So that night I was rooming with the bass player, and the next morning Peter came in and said "Okay, let's take a look at the money, I want to divvy up." So I had all the money, split it up, Peter took his share and said...

"Okay, that's it, I'm out of here! You're out of here! We're out of here, that's it... we're done!"

I go "What?"

He goes "Yeah! The rest of us are leaving in twenty minutes, so get your shit out of the van!" They had obviously made some agreement amongst themselves to continue on without me. I was a bit shocked, but I said,

"Wait a minute, I want my shit! I want my merch!" They gave me my records and said,

"*Yeah, take the fuckin' t-shirts!*"

So now I had all my stuff, and and it was obviously a lot more than one person could move. I was like 'Oh fuck. What am I going to do with all this shit?' So I collected myself, called the club owner, said I needed some help, and he came over and picked me up.

There was a rumor that they left me high and dry. Nobody leaves me high and dry. I have an American Express Gold Card, and I went out and

had a $160 dollar steak lunch with the owner of the club.

We went to the club owner's house, I boxed up all of my stuff, took it to the post office, and I mailed it to myself in New York. I bought a plane ticket, stayed in Missouri for a couple of days, and then I flew home.

So I got fired from my own tour, and the boys carried on without me. It was conveyed to me by the powers that be that I had become 'too difficult to work with.' Shortly after that, the tour ended in Connecticut, and they drove everyone back home.

For a while, it was online testosterone high school shit. It's your fault, my fault, whatever. But now Peter and I don't really have anything to do with each other, and that's probably for the best. I don't see him; I don't speak to him.

Obviously there are two sides to every story.

I know my side.

So I probably acted like an asshole, but I was definitely pushed to do it.

I would imagine there is an unwritten rule somewhere that says 'you never leave a guy out on the road.' If knives and guns were involved, then maybe, but outside of that, you don't leave anyone behind - even someone that you think is an asshole.

When I told Jack about it, he laughed his big laugh. "Oh boy, I could have told you that would happen!"

I just had to just pick up the pieces and keep working. I mean the Case/Collins Tour could have been a big blemish on my name, credibility, or whatever, but fortunately it didn't amount to much of anything.

After that, I toured with The English Beat. Dave Wakeling was a real sweetheart! He called the tour 'Two Beats Hearting As One.' I worked with countless young musicians, touring all over America and Europe. I even went to China, Japan, and Australia. At one point, I had four working bands: one in Madrid, one in Milwaukee, one in Sydney, and one in New York! I averaged about a 100 dates a year. I recorded two more albums: *Feel The Noise* with Jim Diamond in Detroit, and *Out Of My Head* – which marked the return of me playing drums on my own records again.

I carried on.

> *There's a natural order to these things. When bands like The Police, B-52's, or Devo get together, and all the people who saw them back in the day come out again, thousands of people – these are the things that make sense. I don't know what you can expect from the reunion of a band that never played for more than 150 people, tops...*

> *...except to destroy the myth.*

The Nerves achieved one great thing: we achieved a moment when three young men truly bonded together as one. We were able to put aside our differences, and not succumb to petty bullshit. What hurt me the most, when it was all over, was the separation. I felt like my arms were cut off. I couldn't understand how three people could be so close, and then there was nothing. No contact, just nothing.

My mother used to tell me, 'if you have three good friends in your life, you are lucky.' I know a lot of people, but three good friends I do not have, unless of course you count – *me, myself, and I*. Those three guys are always there; ready to go at a moment's notice. They're some good friends. Maybe that's what my mother was talking about. I know she wasn't, but sometimes you have to improvise.

When The Nerves formed, there was no home technology, the record industry was shrouded in mystery, way up high in their ivory towers. They controlled everything, and they were completely unapproachable. The records we would see in the stores seemed to be made by gods, not humans. Everything was perfect, even the artwork was air-brushed into perfection.

Our music was so far away from what was happening, we had no choice but to do it ourselves. We became 'DIY' without even knowing it, but you still had to play by the rules. You couldn't just make a record at home, or on your own. You had to go to a recording studio, and in those days, most of those studios were servicing the record companies. And they were extremely expensive.

I am glad we did what we did, and I am glad I was a part of it. We were trying to take on the whole world. We had no friends, and no support group or family, other than ourselves. We had to push so hard, all of the time, and we could never let up. In the end, we did it. We paved the way for what would become an avalanche of groups to do it themselves. They would eventually topple the grip that the major labels had on the scene, and replace it with their own independent record companies.

But there was no victory party for us, no back-slapping or toasts in our honor. The new crowd excluded us just as vehemently as the old crowd. It's a crazy way to live, sometimes I love it and sometimes I don't. But as Jack always said, "It sure beats working."

Then I'd say, "Yeah, but it's hard work not working!"

Then Peter would always say, "Will you guys please shut the fuck up?"

But we wouldn't. We would go on and on about some new scheme we were working on, happy as pigs in shit.

We were after all, having the time of our lives.

In memory of Larry Whitman,
he went out like he lived, balls to the wall.
photo courtesy of Catherine Sebastian

To Eddie Money, as Steve so aptly put it...
we wouldn't be here without you.
photo courtesy of Adriana Lopetrone, New York, 2010.

And to Bill Graham,
one of the last great American
impresarios. When he died in a helicopter crash,
half the lights in Northern California went out.

PAUL COLLINS DISCOGRAPHY: 1976-2020

-The Nerves-

Albums + EPs
- 4-track debut 7" EP (Nerves-self released), 1976.
- *Jack Lee, Paul Collins, Peter Case* compilation LP, Offence Records (France), 1986.
- *25th Anniversary* 10" compilation EP, Penniman Records (Spain), 2001.
- *One Way Ticket* compilation LP, Bomp!/Alive Records, 2008.
- *Live! The The Pirate's Cove* LP, Bomp!Alive Records, 2009.

Compilation appearances
- "Working Too Hard" *Trouser Press: The Best of America Underground*, ROIR, 1983.
- "When You Find Out" and "Hangng on the Telephone" *DIY: Come Out And Play - American Power Pop I (1975-78)*, Rhino Records, 1992.
- "Hanging On The Telephone" +9 *That's Totally Pop*, Revenge (France), 1992.
- "One Way Ticket" *Children Of Nuggets- Original Artyfacts From The Second Psychedelic Era 1976-1996*, Rhino, 2005.
- "When You Find Out" *Songs In The Key Of Paul*, MOJO (UK), 2013.

-The Breakaways-

Albums + EPs
- *Walking Out On Love (The Lost Sessions 1978)* LP Bomp!/Alive Records, 2009.

-The Beat / Paul Collins' Beat-

Albums + EPs
- s/t debut LP Columbia/CBS, 1979.
- *The Kids Are The Same* LP, Columbia/Wolfgang, 1982.
- *To Beat or Not To Beat* 5-track 12" EP, Passport Records, 1983.
- *Long Time Gone* 6-track 12" EP, Closer Records (France), 1985.
   - reissue on Frodis Records, 2016.
- *Live at the Universal* LP, Producciones Twins Records (Spain), 1986.
- *One Night* LP, Producciones Twins/Stoneage Records (Spain/France), 1987.
- *Long Time Gone/To Beat Or Not To Beat* Wounded Bird Records, 2004.
- *The Beat/The Kids Are the Same* Wounded Bird Records, 2005.
- *Ribbon Of Gold* LP, Rock Indiana/Get Hip Records (Spain/US), 2008.
- *1979 Live* LP, Burger/Lady Kinky Karrot Records (Italy/US), 2010.
- *Long Time Gone/To Beat Or Not To Beat* Lollipop Records (US), 2017.
- *Another World (Best of the Archives)* Alive/Bomp! Records (US), 2020.

-The Beat / Paul Collins' Beat-

Singles
- "Let Me Into Your Life" b/w "Walking Out On Love" CBS Records, 1979.
- "Let Me Into Your Life" b/w "U.S.A." CBS (Australia), 1979.
- "Different Kind Of Girl" b/w "Working Too Hard" CBS (Australia/Europe), 1979.
- "Don't Wait Up For Me" b/w "Walking Out On Love" CBS, 1979.
- "Rock 'n Roll Girl" b/w "You And I" CBS (Netherlands/Spain/UK), 1979.
- "On The Highway" b/w "Crying Won't Help" CBS, 1982.
- "The Kids Are The Same" b/w "It's Just A Matter of Time" CBS (Netherlands/Spain), 1982.
- "All Over The World" b/w "Always Got You On My Mind" Record Runner/Closer (Spain/France), 1984.
- "Why?" b/w "Price To Pay" Producciones Twins (Spain), 1988.
- "This Is America" *from split 7" with Radio Days* Surfin' Ki Records (Italy), 2009.
- "Baby I'm In Love With You" *+1 from split 7" with The Maxies* Radius Records, 2013.

Compilation appearances
- "Don't Wait Up For Me" *The Now Wave Sampler*, Columbia, 1979.
- "Walking Out On Love" *Waves Vol. 1*, Line/Bomp! (Germany/US), 1979.
- "There She Goes" *Caddyshack Motion Picture Soundtrack*, CBS, 1980.
- "Don't Wait Up For Me" *Lo Mejor De New Wave*, Epic (Mexico/Venezuela), 1980.
- "Dejame Entrar En Tu Vida (Let Me Into Your Life)" *New Wave*, Epic (Argentina), 1980.
- "Rock 'n Roll Girl" *Steppin' Into The 80's*, CBS (Netherlands), 1980.
- "Don't Wait Up For Me" *Rockwärts In Die 80er*, CBS (Germany), 1980.
- "Rock 'n Roll Girl" *Rock Of The 80's*, CBS (France), 1980.
- "Don't Wait Up For Me" *Breaking The Rules*, CBS, 1980.
- "Walk Out Of Love" *Best Of BOMP!*, Disc AZ/Bomp! (France), 1982.
- "Always Get You On My Mind" *Greetings From The Sunny Beach - Best Of Closer*, Closer (France), 1984.
- "Good Times" *Primera Entrega Internacional "Segundos Fuera"*, Producciones Twins (Spain), 1986.
- "All Over The World" *Repérages Couleur 3 Vol 1 1983-1986*, Evasion Disques (Switzerland), 1990.
- "Work-A-Day World" *DIY: Shake It Up! - American Power Pop II (1978-80)*, Rhino, 1993.
- "You Won't Be Happy" *Just Can't Get Enough: New Wave Hits Of The '80s, Vol. 2*, Rhino, 1994.
- "Don't Wait Up For Me" *Punky But Chic... The American New Wave*, Risky Business, 1994.
- "Working Too Hard" *Into The Anxious 80's*, Risky Business, 1995.
- "I've Always Got You On My Mind" *Yellow Pills - More Great Pop! Volume 3*, Big Deal (Japan), 1995.
- "Rock 'n Roll Girl" *On The Wave*, Contraseña (Spain), 1997.
- "Rock 'n Roll Girl" *Poptopia! Power Pop Classics Of The '70s*, Rhino, 1997.
- "Different Kind Of Girl" *Just Say New Wave*, Madacy (Canada), 2000.
- "Working Too Hard" *New Wave Hits Of The 70's & 80's*, Sony, 2002.
- "Rock 'n Roll Girl" *20 Greats From The Golden Decade Of Power Pop*, Varèse Sarabande, 2005.
- "All Over The World" *Of Hands And Hearts: Music For The Tsunami Disaster Fund*, Integrity, 2005.
- "Heartwaivers" *Felipop X Aniversario*, Felipop (Spain), 2009.
- "Untitled" *Under The Covers: Tribute to Paul Collins, Peter Case & Jack Lee Vol. 2*, Volar, 2010.
- "Hanging On The Telephone" *Cherry Blossom Clinic Live Sessions Vol. 4*, WFMU, 2010.
- "She Doesn't Want To Hang Around With You" *This Is Rock 'n' Roll Radio, Volume 4*, Kool Kat Musik, 2017.

"Rock 'n Roll Girl" *On The Wave*, Contraseña (Spain), 1997.

-Paul Collins Solo-

Albums + EPs
- s/t debut LP DRO Records, 1992.
- *From Town To Town* LP/CD Caroline/Wagon Wheel Records, 1993.
- *Live In Spain* CD Fono Music, 1997.
- *Flying High* CD Lucinda/MVS/Get Hip Records, 2006.
- *King of Power Pop* LP/CD Alive Records, 2010.
- *Feel The Noise* LP/CD Alive Records, 2014.
- *Out of My Head* LP/CD Alive Records, 2018.

Singles
- "Just Give me Love" b/w "She Says" Producciones Twins Records, 1988.
- "I Told You So" (both sides) DRO Records, 1992.
- "You're Never Gonna Find That Girl" (both sides) DRO Records, 1992.
- "It's Gonna Be A Long Time" (both sides) Caroline Records, 1993.
- "Let's Go" b/w "She Says She Loves Me" Pop The Balloon Records, 1999.
- "With A Girl Like You" b/w "You Belong With Me" Big Legal Mess Records, 2011.

Lo Mejor De New Wave compilation LP (CBS Venezuela, 1980), featuring The BEAT's "Don't Wait Up For Me."

Acknowledgments

I would like to express thanks to the following people for all their help in completing this book. First off to Todd Novak for instantly wanting to publish the book. His enthusiasm was wonderful and his contributions to it's layout and design were invaluable. Secondly to Chuck Nolan who worked with me tirelessly to get this manuscript into shape. There was a lot of work on the writing and the research involved to make this the definitive book about my career in music, both personally and professionally. I argued a lot with Chuck but he stuck to his guns and therefore, there is a lot of information in the book that I would have probably left out.

I would like to thank all the photographers for graciously giving us the permission to use their work. They are Ralph Alfonso, Randy Bachman, Richard Creamer, D. Cooper, Juan Fran "Chas", Gary Green, Bob Gruen, Gabrielle Hernandez, Patty Hefely, Kike Jimenez, Pat Johnson, Jenny Lens, Adriana Lopetrone, Dave Marx, Rob Overtoom, Catherine Sebastian, Bob Seidman, Tom Sorem, Bob Wagner, K.C. Webb, Ron Yocom, and Neil Zlozower.

The quality of a lot of these photographs are due to the expert scanning and retouching by my good friend Derek Davidson. I would like to thank my girlfriend, Barbara Baruch (*Are you really going to say that?*), for helping me to be succinct. And my sister Adrienne Collins for digging up all the old photos of when we were kids. They are great to have as a part of this collection.

Paul Collins, NYC, 2020.
photo courtesy of Bob Gruen

Chuck Nolan would like to thank:
Steve Huff, Marci Marks, Mike Ruiz, and Rex "Hoss" Thompson
- for their help with jogging Paul's memory.